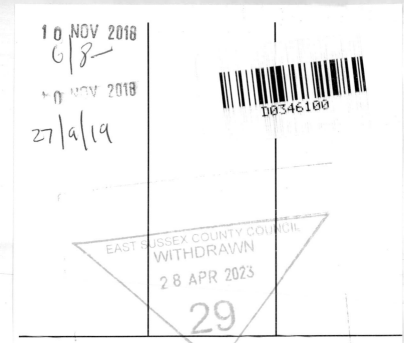

Please return or renew this item
by the last date shown. You may
return items to any East Sussex
Library. You may renew books
by telephone or the internet.

0345 60 80 195 for renewals
0345 60 80 196 for enquiries

Library and Information Services
eastsussex.gov.uk/libraries

– THE –
BREXIT
CLUB

THE INSIDE STORY OF THE LEAVE
CAMPAIGN'S SHOCK VICTORY

OWEN BENNETT

Biteback Publishing

First published in Great Britain in 2016 by
Biteback Publishing Ltd
Westminster Tower
3 Albert Embankment
London SE1 7SP
Copyright © Owen Bennett 2016

ISBN 978-1-78590-098-3

10 9 8 7 6 5 4 3 2 1

A CIP catalogue record for this book is available from the British Library.

Set in Minion by Adrian McLaughlin

Printed and bound in Great Britain by
CPI Group (UK) Ltd, Croydon CR0 4YY

MIX
Paper from
responsible sources
FSC
www.fsc.org
FSC® C020471

*For Lucia Florence, an example of
a successful European union*

INTRODUCTION

'**A**t the moment, Farage and UKIP are the only people speaking up for Brexit. All these Tory Eurosceptics, including yourself, you can't even admit that you are actually voting out. Why should we be listening to you? That's exactly why Farage and UKIP are the leading voice in this campaign.'

Many of the 200 or so people in the room, including UKIP MEP Tim Aker, applauded the man's comments.

But John Redwood, the Conservative MP on the panel and the person at whom the question was aimed, simply folded his arms and spoke softly into the microphone.

'I've been careful not to make any criticism of Mr Farage or even UKIP,' he said.

> I've been working very hard to get you all to understand that we need to get together and we need to speak in a tone and in terms that address the many people out there who don't yet agree with us, rather than constantly talking to each other about whether our doctrines and views are pure enough or not. I really would urge you to think carefully about that sound advice.

Apart from a smattering of applause, the majority of the audience were unconvinced by Redwood's plea.

They wanted a full-throated attack on Prime Minister David Cameron's plan for renegotiating the UK's relationship with Brussels.

They wanted Redwood to lambast the political establishment for its dedication to a European project that had slyly stolen sovereignty from Britain since 1973.

They wanted to be told that the Out campaign was going to win the upcoming referendum, which many had been awaiting for forty years.

They did not want to be told to 'think carefully'.

Tim Aker, who less than a month earlier had failed to win a seat in Parliament at the 2015 general election, did give the audience of Eurosceptic campaigners what they wanted.

In his grey double-breasted suit – which made him look a generation older than his thirty years – Aker decided now was the time to kill his idol.

'It saddens me that someone who's so learned about the European Union can be so half-hearted in their approach at this point in time,' he began, before raising his voice along with his rhetoric:

> I grew up in politics and so on, reading your books, John, and you were a great inspiration, but to be on a panel where *now*, after the Lisbon Treaty, after every battle that you have fought against and lost, you still say, 'We might stay in the European Union; I might vote to stay in', I find that absolutely ridiculous and disingenuous to the people listening here tonight and the people who will see it on YouTube.

He wasn't finished: 'To see that you can say, after everything, after 300,000 net immigration, after the complete reduction of our fishing waters, of everything else, for you to say, "I might just think about staying in and not commit," I think that's very disingenuous and I'm very disappointed.'

The room broke out in applause. Redwood, who had let out a loud sigh during Aker's speech, was in an unfamiliar situation: he was being accused of not being Eurosceptic enough.

It was not a claim often levelled at him.

John Redwood – the man who at the height of Conservative divisions over Europe in the mid-1990s challenged Prime Minister John Major for the leadership of the party.

John Redwood – the man who repeatedly attacked the European super-state through numerous books, such as *Just Say No!: 100 Arguments against the Euro* and *The Death of Britain?*.

John Redwood – the man who as a 23-year-old campaigned for a 'No' vote the last time there was a referendum on the UK's European membership, in 1975.

John Redwood – the archetypal Conservative Eurosceptic.

And yet, on 1 June 2015, the 63-year-old Wokingham MP was deemed to be not Eurosceptic enough by the majority of the audience at a meeting of the Bruges Group.

Formed in 1989, the group was inspired by Margaret Thatcher's speech in Belgium the previous year attacking the creeping powers of the European project.

The group holds regular events, mainly in the plush surroundings of the Royal Over-Seas League House, located a stone's throw from St James's Palace.

The Bruges Group had kept the Eurosceptic flame burning ever since its creation – through the knifing of Thatcher, the turmoil of the Tory Party in the mid-1990s, and the virtual irrelevance of the Conservatives in the noughties.

Speakers addressing meetings would often deliver their anti-EU musings from a podium that had a signed black-and-white framed photograph of Thatcher attached to the front.

The Iron Lady was always looking out at the group's members, who could derive solace from her gaze.

But that night's meeting, titled 'The EU and the Future of Britain', was proving a tough ride for Redwood – one of Thatcher's favoured sons.

Much of the evening had involved Aker talking up the brilliance of UKIP leader Nigel Farage, insisting that the only reason an EU referendum was now going to happen was because of him.

For Redwood, this was not a point worth debating – climbing the mountain to victory was what mattered now, not how the Eurosceptic supporters had reached base camp.

The surprise general election win by the Conservative Party twenty-five days earlier meant the EU referendum would now have to happen before the end of 2017.

The pledge had been included in the Tory manifesto, and the party's unexpected win meant it had not been horse-traded away in coalition agreement discussions. The Tories were ruling alone, so the referendum was on.

But before the vote, there was the small matter of Cameron's renegotiation of the terms of the UK's membership.

During his speech before the question-and-answer session, Redwood told the audience:

> I know there are some here who would rather just leave the European Union tomorrow. I have to tell you, you have not attracted enough support for that proposal and there is no majority in the House of Commons for that proposal, and that should be of interest and concern to you. The route we have chosen may take a little longer, may be more subtle than some of you wish, but it is meant well and I ask you to hear me out and to understand the journey we are embarked upon. If, as many of you think, there is no such sensible deal on offer, do you not see that it would be much

easier to persuade our fellow citizens that we must leave the
European Union because a serious-minded and intelligent
Prime Minister had done his best to try and deal with the
obvious difficulties that many British people find with our
current membership? If he is unable to deal with those issues
then it would be that much easier to persuade the necessary
number of people to vote 'no' in a referendum.

The subtlety of the argument was lost on many, including Aker.

Redwood ended up almost pleading with the audience to think
beyond how to appeal to just those in the room.

'If you spend your whole time shouting at people that they've
got to leave tomorrow, you are not going to win,' he said.

Looking on from the back of the room was Michael Heaver, the
25-year-old recently appointed by Farage to be his right-hand man.
For him, the reaction of the audience at the meeting confirmed what
he had long thought: Nigel Farage should lead the Out campaign.

Over a glass of wine in the reception area of Over-Seas House
once the meeting had ended, Heaver batted away alternative names
put to him as potential leaders – including the Tory rising star
Priti Patel.

As far as he was concerned, it was only Farage who could appeal
to the millions of undecided voters across the country.

During the meeting, Aker was asked: What happens if Farage
does become the leader of the Out campaign?

'We win. It is that simple,' was his reply.

What he didn't know was that plans were already afoot – plans
with roots stretching back long before the general election – to
make sure that didn't happen.

CHAPTER 1

'**G**entlemen, I fear we're being hijacked. Reload!'

Chris Bruni-Lowe and Raheem Kassam smiled. When Nigel Farage bellowed 'reload' it was usually because his pint glass was empty and another ale was needed quick-sharp.

But this time Farage was not issuing the order in the Marquis of Granby pub in Westminster, or any of the other taverns and clubs he had drunk in over the previous few months as part of his campaign to get elected to Westminster.

This time, Farage was in his office in UKIP's London headquarters, moments away from telling the party's National Executive Committee whether he still intended to quit as leader – as he had vowed three days earlier – or had changed his mind and would lead the party into the EU referendum.

Farage was a political gambler – a man who always liked to raise the stakes in order to make any victory taste extra sweet. In September 2013, when he first predicted UKIP would win the following year's European Parliament elections, not many people took him seriously. But his party did win – and he helped to push the Conservatives into third place in a national election for the first time in the Tories' history.

A year after that prediction, he persuaded Conservative MPs Douglas Carswell and Mark Reckless to defect to UKIP, and the pair won the subsequent by-elections under their new party colours at a relative canter.

Farage was unstoppable – or so he thought.

With the polls indicating UKIP was on course to finish third in the popular vote in the 2015 general election, Farage decided to up the ante again.

In his book *The Purple Revolution*, he vowed to quit as party leader if he did not win the seat of South Thanet in Kent. 'So over to you, dear voter. It's all down to you now,' the book ended. The plan was for the good people of South Thanet to heed their leader's call and carry him to victory on a wave of Eurosceptic populism.

The gamble did not pay off, and Farage failed to get elected to the Houses of Parliament – finishing second to Conservative candidate Craig Mackinlay.

In bright morning sunshine on 8 May, while David Cameron was celebrating his unexpected general election victory, Farage told a horde of journalists that he was honouring his promise and quitting as UKIP leader.

Three days later, in his Mayfair office, he decided to 'reload'.

The NEC had already told him he didn't have to resign. Thousands of UKIP members and supporters had emailed the party asking Farage to reconsider his resignation, and donors such as Arron Banks were desperate for him to stay on. There was, after all, a referendum to fight and, for many, Farage was the one who could lead the Eurosceptic movement to victory.

Farage didn't take much persuading, but any doubt over whether to stay on was swiftly removed after he received a phone call from Douglas Carswell – the only Ukipper who had managed to win a seat in the general election.

Farage said:

> I had the bizarrest phone call with him. Deeply unpleasant,
> really deeply unpleasant. Even if I tried I couldn't behave that

nastily. It reminded me of the sort of chap that put a pistol
in your back and said: 'If you don't go over the top I'll shoot
you.' 'You are going, you absolutely have to go, blah blah blah
… the referendum was too important and you can't have a
voice in this referendum campaign.'

Carswell does not remember making such remarks. As far as he
can recall, he praised Farage for the 'fantastic job' he had done in
making UKIP the third biggest party in vote terms in the UK and
simply agreed that he should now step down.

'I thought we needed a new leader to take us to the next level
and I think I'm right in saying I said it would be wonderful if
I could buy him lunch so we could talk about his ideas of who
should take over,' Carswell said. 'That was my recollection of it.
I can be quite outspoken and I can be quite critical but he says it's
one of the nastiest phone calls – if someone says they are leaving as
leader, why would I have an incentive to be unkind towards him?'

Farage called his close advisor, Chris Bruni-Lowe, who was with
the UKIP leader's chief of staff Raheem Kassam and party director
Steve Stanbury looking at new offices for the party in Westminster.
Farage told Bruni-Lowe: 'You won't believe what Carswell's just
said,' before going on to claim that UKIP's only MP had branded
him 'toxic' and told him if he didn't quit as leader, he would lose
the referendum for the Eurosceptics. Bruni-Lowe and Kassam hur-
ried back to UKIP's offices to discuss the turn of events.

Not long after that call, Suzanne Evans, deputy chairman of
UKIP and the person Farage had announced should take over as
interim leader while his permanent successor was found, walked
into his office.

'There was a lot of speculation [about] what was going to happen at the NEC meeting and Suzanne said: "Nigel, you can't be
involved in the referendum campaign,"' said Farage. 'I realised
then that something was going on.'

With the 'reload' order issued, the UKIP leader strode into the meeting room, told the NEC he would not be resigning, and immediately turned his mind to the EU referendum.

Farage's fear was simple: the 'posh boys' wanted to run the Out campaign – and they would lose.

Sitting in his office, smoking his Rothman cigarettes – the smoking ban did not apply in UKIP HQ, apparently – Farage would wind himself up as he contemplated Carswell and Tory MEP Daniel Hannan's desire to exclude him from what should be the greatest political fight of his life.

To the UKIP leader, Hannan was the ultimate posh boy. A multi-linguist who was born in Peru, Hannan was educated at Marlborough College in Wiltshire and then Oxford University – as was UKIP's former Rochester and Strood MP Mark Reckless.

Despite Reckless passing through the same educational establishments as Hannan, Farage never classed him as one of the 'posh boys' – even though the future UKIP MP studied that most clichéd of university courses for aspiring politicians: philosophy, politics and economics.

It was at Oxford that Hannan and Reckless formed their first anti-European group in November 1990.

'It was the period between the deposition of Thatcher and John Major putting his initials on Maastricht, so between 22 November and 6 December 1990. I and Mark Reckless and a fellow undergraduate set up the Oxford Campaign for an Independent Britain in the Queen's Lane café in Oxford,' recalled Hannan.

Despite also attending a fee-paying school – Dulwich College in south-east London – Farage did not go to university. He jumped straight into the 'real world', and at the age of eighteen became a trader in the City of London. But, like Hannan, the formative political moment of his life came when John Major signed the Maastricht Treaty – the document that created the modern-day European Union and set the wheels in motion on the euro.

It wasn't just Eurosceptics outside Parliament who were motivated to act by Maastricht, and Major faced numerous rebellions from his own backbenchers as he tried to get the treaty adopted into UK law.

In 1993, after losing a Commons vote on a technical aspect of the Treaty, Major took the bold step of calling for a vote of confidence in his own government. The gamble paid off, and Major secured the backing of Parliament by forty votes.

While both Hannan and Farage were motivated by the same aim – getting the UK out of the EU – they chose different routes to pursue their shared goal. Hannan sought to influence Conservative Party and 'establishment' thought from the inside and, after graduating from Oxford, became a leader writer for the *Daily Telegraph* and a speechwriter for then Tory leader William Hague.

Farage, after seeing an advert in the *London Evening Standard* for a meeting of the Campaign for an Independent Britain (not to be confused with Hannan's Oxford-based organisation) in 1993, helped form the United Kingdom Independence Party, and became its first ever election candidate when he stood in the 1994 Eastleigh by-election.

While Hannan spent much of his time writing about the EU, democracy and political philosophy – he has produced at least thirteen books on the subjects – Farage focused on grassroots campaigning, building up UKIP into the third party in British politics and honing his public image as a man of the people.

Hannan, who on Twitter would often respond to a particular news item with a quotation from a Shakespeare play and the hashtag #nothingescapesshakespeare, clearly saw himself as a man *for* the people more than a man *of* the people.

'It was perfectly clear on 11 May where everything stood,' Farage said, and he was determined not to let the 'posh boys' destroy everything he had worked so hard for by running a referendum campaign based on issues that appealed to privately educated university graduates – rather than the millions of people who had voted UKIP at the general election.

Luckily for Farage, he already knew the man who could help make sure he would get a platform on which to play a key role in the campaign; a man who had deep pockets, a huge sense of mischief and would be up for the challenge of taking on the establishments of not just Downing Street, but Hannan and his friends too: Arron Banks.

Based in Bristol, Banks exploded on to the political scene in October 2014 when he announced he was donating £1 million to UKIP to help fund the party's general election campaign.

The insurance tycoon, who also owned shares in a South African diamond mine, was originally going to hand over £100,000, but after Tory grandee William Hague said he had 'never heard of him', he upped the donation to a cool million.

Speaking in front of journalists and TV cameras who had been invited to his country estate just outside Bristol, Banks said he hoped Hague would 'now know who I am', thanks to the sizeable donation.

He seemed to like the attention he received that day, and the businessman quickly became a fixture on the UKIP campaign circuit.

On the night of the general election, Banks was sat in the lounge area of the Walpole Bay Hotel in Margate with a horde of journalists, watching the results come in. Farage, who was staying in the same hotel, was upstairs with his wife, Kirsten, getting some sleep ahead of a declaration which ultimately wouldn't take place until gone 9.30 the next morning.

Farage's failure to win the seat of South Thanet was a huge disappointment to Banks. He was a fan of the UKIP leader – perhaps more so personally than politically – and identified with his 'anti-establishment' rhetoric.

He was supremely disappointed with Farage's decision to quit as party leader the following day, and felt UKIP needed a fundamental shake-up if it was to have any success in the future. In an email sent to then party treasurer Andrew Reid at 11.17 p.m. on Sunday 10 May, Banks offered his services as chief executive and spelt out exactly how he would reform the party.

'I agreed to help you with the organisation in the run-up to the election but the current structure is appalling and we did well in the election despite it. There was no point because it's chaos,' he wrote, before adding: 'We all got carried away and Nigel in fairness rode it until it bucked him! He's a genius.'

Banks went on to explain how he would split the party up into different administrative and campaigning branches, and offered himself as chief executive.

'I'm happy to spend time in London and get stuck into this – I'm currently paid a million pounds a year from my insurance businesses. So you get a million-a-year CEO for free – the aim is to have it running so smoothly I just oversee it.'

It is clear from the email that he expected Farage to return as UKIP leader, saying that the defeated candidate 'needs a smooth machine behind him'.

UKIP did not take up Banks's offer, but Farage was not going to turn him away. Well aware that Hannan and Carswell would be working on establishing their own Out organisation for the referendum campaign, the UKIP leader knew Banks's money and enthusiasm could help create a powerful rival group which would put him front and centre.

'We contacted Banks and we said to him not to put the money in UKIP, but set up something else – Banks, I think, had wanted to do this anyway – to give Nigel the voice which we knew he wouldn't get,' said Bruni-Lowe.

Banks needed no second invitation, and immediately set to work on his own Out campaign – one that would frustrate, bamboozle, annoy and battle the 'posh boys' right up until referendum day.

CHAPTER 2

Matthew Elliott had a lot on his plate – and not just the one in front of him as he ate his lunch. That morning, the Conservatives had won the 2015 general election, and a promise he had made to his friend Daniel Hannan three years earlier was about to become reality.

But first, there was the small matter of his honeymoon to New Zealand. The political lobbyist had actually got married in August 2014, but the celebratory holiday had been delayed until after the May vote. The trip would only be short, but before he could start packing he knew he needed to set the wheels in motion on the Out campaign for the EU referendum.

Elliott was dining with Tory MEP David Campbell Bannerman and two media relations workers – Nick Wood and Matthew Walsh – to discuss the plan of action. There was much they didn't know. David Cameron had promised to hold the referendum before the end of 2017, so it was feasible there could be a long, drawn-out campaign. Alternatively, Cameron might want to capitalise on his own political honeymoon and go to the country sooner rather than later. But there was of course the renegotiation of the UK's relationship with the EU to consider. The Conservative Party's general election manifesto had set out some vague commitments to reducing bureaucracy and red tape, but nothing concrete enough to suggest the Prime Minister would seek fundamental reform of the EU's key treaties.

Either way, an Out campaign would need to be formed – and quickly.

The Leeds-born Elliott had already been identified three years earlier as the man to run the campaign, by Daniel Hannan. The pair had known each other for more than fifteen years, with Elliott working in the European Parliament at the same time Hannan was first elected as an MEP in 1999.

Elliott had studied government at the London School of Economics in the late 1990s and after graduating he worked for Tory MEP Timothy Kirkhope. When he was in his mid-twenties, he formed the TaxPayers' Alliance pressure group and quickly garnered a reputation as one of Westminster's most effective lobbyists. After starting another pressure group – Big Brother Watch – in 2009, Elliott was chosen to run the No to AV campaign in the 2011 referendum on the UK's voting system.

It was his success in this role – No secured 68 per cent of the vote – which made Hannan sure Elliott should be the man to run the Out campaign if the UK ever had a referendum on the EU.

Hannan said:

> In summer 2012 I approached Matthew Elliott and said: 'Would you be ready to run the campaign when it comes?' He had distinguished himself in the AV referendum, and the way he had distinguished himself was [in] his ability to withstand friendly fire. In politics, you can sustain an almost unlimited amount of ordnance from the other side: it bounces off, you barely notice. But there was a time in that AV referendum where it looked as though it was going badly. All of the anti-AV papers were blaming him and that's very, very hard to withstand, but he stuck to his numbers, he stuck

to what his focus groups were telling him and stuck to what
he knew was going to be a winning strategy.

The No to AV campaign's main tactic was to focus on the cost
of a change to the electoral system. Billboard posters showing a
battle-ready soldier with the words 'He needs bulletproof vests
NOT an alternative voting system' were plastered in key areas.

Elliott's tactics were constantly called into question by those
in Westminster, and privately even Hannan thought his strategy
was 'crazy ... I thought his arguments were stupid.'

Yet, despite all the criticism, Elliott delivered the victory.

'Every MP, every right-wing journalist thought he had the way
of winning if only Matt would do what he said. Matt politely and
patiently did his own thing and was completely vindicated. It was
an amazing achievement,' said Hannan.

The MEP approached Elliott in the garden of Eurosceptic campaigner Lord Leach's holiday home in Norfolk in 2012 and asked
him to run the Out campaign, should the situation arise.

Six months later, and the notion of an in/out referendum on the
UK's EU membership stopped being a discussion point for just
Eurosceptics on the fringe of political influence and went main-
stream. In January 2013, David Cameron stood up at Bloomberg's
London headquarters and said:

> The next Conservative manifesto in 2015 will ask for a man-
> date from the British people for a Conservative government
> to negotiate a new settlement with our European partners
> in the next parliament. It will be a relationship with the Sin-
> gle Market at its heart and when we have negotiated that
> new settlement, we will give the British people a referen-
> dum with a very simple in or out choice: to stay in the EU
> on these new terms or come out altogether. It will be an in/
> out referendum.

The referendum was now on the table, and even though there was no guarantee Cameron would win the 2015 election, Hannan and others could not run the risk of being unprepared for the battle.

Looking at the 1975 referendum, in which a business-led Yes campaign helped convince 67 per cent of voters to back the UK staying in the European Community, Hannan and Elliott realised they needed to get as many business voices as possible to back, at the very least, reforming the EU if they were to have a chance of winning.

In April 2013, Business for Britain (BfB) was launched, with Elliott as its chief executive, and the organisation signed up more than 500 businesspeople to support fundamental reform of the EU – or Britain's exit from it.

BfB quickly became the pre-eminent Eurosceptic pressure group, and much of its infrastructure and staff would go on to be part of Elliott's Out campaign.

But the battle could not be won just by business groups alone, and, over lunch on the day after the Conservatives' surprise election victory, Elliott and Campbell Bannerman discussed how to create an outlet for all those Members of Parliament – Tory or otherwise – who would back leaving the EU.

Campbell Bannerman had already produced a strategy document in February 2015, which had been circulated to Elliott, explaining how he felt any Out campaign could reach out to target voters. At the lunch, the idea of a Conservatives for Britain (CfB) group, which had already been mooted before the election, was given the green light by Elliott. The group would bring together Tory MPs and MEPs under a banner of supporting Cameron's renegotiation, but be prepared to call for an Out vote if the PM failed to reform the EU. Like Business for Britain, its line was 'Change or Go'.

Despite the agreement, there was a problem: as effective as Campbell Bannerman could be with strategy documents and the like, he was an MEP not an MP, and so didn't have the reach, influence or access to bring together Tories in Westminster.

The pair knew they needed someone on the inside to act as a point man for Tory MPs – but who? There was no shortage of candidates. Longstanding Eurosceptics such as John Redwood, Sir Bill Cash and Bernard Jenkin could all do the job, but it was felt that a fresher face was needed. That person was the little-known Wycombe MP Steve Baker.

Baker had barely registered on the radar of all but the most plugged-in of political journalists since his election as a Conservative MP in 2010. The former RAF Flight Lieutenant had seemed to be just another Eurosceptic Tory backbencher – a true believer in the anti-EU cause but not in the same league as stalwarts such as Jenkin, Cash and Redwood. After leaving the RAF in 1999, Baker retrained as a software engineer and ended up working for Lehman Brothers in 2008 – just as the global economic crash kicked in. But it was not what he saw while working for Lehmans that made him want to get into Parliament and change the country, but what he heard from David Cameron in 2007. In a speech in Prague that year, the then Leader of the Opposition spoke these words on the European Union: 'It is the last gasp of an outdated ideology, a philosophy that has no place in our new world of freedom, a world which demands that we fight this bureaucratic over-reach and lead Europe into the hope and potential of a new, post-bureaucratic age.'

Baker later claimed that it was this that inspired him to enter politics, and in Westminster in 2015 said: 'I agreed with David Cameron so strongly that at that time, when I was very upset about the handling of the Lisbon Treaty, I joined the Conservative Party and sought election. So here I am.' After successfully defending his seat in 2015 – increasing his majority by 5,000 on the way – he returned to the Commons determined to put pressure on Cameron ahead of the renegotiation.

Matthew Elliott was a fan of Baker. His speeches on radical financial reform, such as denationalising money, were attractive to Elliott, a self-described classical liberal. 'Baker's very much on the anarcho-capitalist scale. So there's a natural overlap with our philosophies,' he said. The Wycombe MP had made all the right moves in Parliament since 2010, including being one of the eighty-one Tory MPs to rebel against the government and back a motion calling for an EU referendum in 2011. Elliott was confident Baker would be an acceptable leader to the established Eurosceptics, as he 'had been working very closely with them for a number of years and meeting with them, he was well trusted by them so he had their confidence'. It was agreed that Baker and Campbell Bannerman would co-chair Conservatives for Britain. But there was one more person Elliott wanted as part of his team: Dominic Cummings.

Cummings was widely regarded as fiercely intelligent and full of self-belief, but somewhat lacking in people skills. Douglas Carswell considered him 'an absolute genius' and 'one of the most astute, intelligent and perceptive people, who has a great appreciation of intellectual rigour'.

'If people can't get on with him, sometimes that says more about them,' he added.

To Nigel Farage, Cummings was an 'interesting bloke but clearly a bit domineering – or attempts to be domineering – of every situation that he's in'.

'You can be too clever and at the same time be extremely stupid. Dominic Cummings very certainly came into that category,' said Arron Banks, while David Campbell Bannerman felt he 'didn't really take people with him. It was a sort of contempt.'

One lobby journalist who had dealings with Cummings likened him to The Joker in *The Dark Knight*: 'Some men just want to watch the world burn, and he is one of those men.'

Cummings had been around the political scene for more than fifteen years, and was best-known for serving as a special advisor to Michael Gove in the Department for Education. The Durham-born, boarding school-educated Cummings graduated from Oxford University in 1994 with a First in ancient and modern history. He then moved to Russia for three years, becoming fluent in the native tongue. After returning to England, he became involved with the anti-euro group Business for Sterling in 1999, first as director of research and then as campaign director. It was while working for Business for Sterling that he became friends with Michael Gove, who at the time was working as the leader writer for *The Times*. The pair recognised in each other a love of historical analogies, a sizeable intellect and a zeal for change.

Cummings first became officially involved in the Conservative Party in 2002, when the then leader Iain Duncan Smith appointed him as director of strategy in a bid to modernise the Tories. While Cummings was ready for the Conservatives, the Conservatives were not ready for him, and in his mere eight months in post, he riled up many of the old guard.

One notable clash came after Cummings claimed the Tories were so unpopular that the party should not take a leading role in the battle to save the pound. His comments infuriated then Conservative chairman David Davis, who was subsequently demoted by IDS as he sought to stamp his authority on the party. Lord Tebbit called for Cummings to be sacked just a month before he eventually resigned, saying the party needed to get rid of the 'squabbling children' and 'spotty youths' in Tory HQ.

A year later, Cummings penned an article for the *Telegraph* in which he said IDS was 'incompetent, would be a worse Prime Minister than Tony Blair, and must be replaced', adding: 'The party is a joke – around the country, people increasingly laugh at "the Conservative Party".'

In 2004, Cummings signed up for another campaign – this time on whether the north-east – his home part of the country – should have a regional assembly. He campaigned against the move and

helped deliver a decisive victory in the referendum: 78 per cent
against, just 22 per cent in favour. It was here that he first got to
know Bernard Jenkin, who was then the Tories' shadow Minister
for the Regions.

It was also in 2004 that he first met Matthew Elliott. The
TaxPayers' Alliance headquarters were located in the same office
block as the New Frontiers Foundation – the think tank that
emerged from Business for Sterling once it became obvious the
UK was not going to join the euro.

In 2005, Cummings's good friend Michael Gove was elected
to Parliament as MP for Surrey Heath. After serving as shadow
Housing spokesman, Gove was promoted to shadow Secretary of
State for Education, and allowed a special advisor. The call went
in to Cummings – the man who just four years earlier had publicly called the Tories 'a joke'.

When the Conservatives entered government in May 2010,
Gove tried to bring Cummings with him as his official special
advisor. Yet, so worried were the Prime Minister's team that
Cummings would be more of a liability than an asset, Downing
Street's director of communications Andy Coulson blocked the
move. After Coulson resigned to face phone-hacking charges
relating to his time as editor of *News of the World*, Gove was able
to manoeuvre Cummings into the Department for Education.

Cummings left the position in January 2014 and launched a
full-nuclear attack on the government and Whitehall shortly after
departing. He described David Cameron as a 'sphinx without a
riddle', the PM's chief of staff Ed Llewellyn as 'a classic third-
rate suck-up-kick-down sycophant presiding over a shambolic
court' and Deputy Prime Minister Nick Clegg as 'self-obsessed,
sanctimonious and so dishonest he finds the words truth and lies
have ceased to have any objective meaning'. (For his part, Clegg
responded by calling him 'some loopy individual who used to be
a backroom advisor'.)

Cummings then set up his own company, North Wood (it 'tries to solve problems – management, political, communication', according to Cummings's blog), and one of its first pieces of work was for Business for Britain in June 2014, on what swing voters think about arguments over the EU.

'The official OUT campaign does *not* need to focus on immigration. The main thing it needs to say on immigration is "if you are happy with the status quo on immigration, then vote to stay IN"', was one of Cummings's conclusions.

When Elliott had originally suggested Cummings as Out campaign leader to Daniel Hannan, the MEP replied: 'Matt, you're in charge. You know what you're doing, you've already shown you know what you're doing. If you think he is the best guy to deliver – maybe not to deliver elegantly but to deliver a victory – do it.'

Little did either of them realise that Cummings's lack of elegance would bring their Out campaign to the verge of collapse at a crucial moment.

CHAPTER 3

On the morning of 8 May, Richard Tice was panicking. David Cameron had won the election and the re-elected Prime Minister was already being fêted by friends and former naysayers alike. With this much adoration, Cameron would win the referendum at a canter, Tice feared.

While the Tories' victory had been confirmed in the early hours, the result of the South Thanet vote had still not been announced when the sun came up. A nervous Tice fired off a quick email to a friend he had made in the run-up to the election: 'Arron, hope all well. How is it looking for Nigel? Either way should talk re referendum as likely to be sooner rather than later,' he wrote.

Just under forty-five minutes later, Banks replied: 'Doubtful for Nigel – would love to catch up. I would say there is zero chance of a fair referendum.'

Farage did not win, of course, and UKIP returned just one MP. To Tice, this was a disaster. Farage and a cohort of Ukippers in the Commons would fight tooth and nail to ensure Cameron carried out a fair referendum. Without them in Parliament, the chance of an establishment stitch-up was likely. The fifty-year-old property developer was frustrated. Not just with the result of the general election, but with himself for not trusting his instincts months earlier. And he was also frustrated with Matthew Elliott.

Seven months earlier, in October 2014, Tice and Elliott sat down for dinner in the Osteria dell'Angolo restaurant in Marsham Street, Westminster. It was the first time the pair had met, and Tice, as a signatory to Business for Britain, wanted some clarification on the organisation's plans for the referendum. He was left disappointed.

'I wanted to understand when Business for Britain was going to make the case to leave, to which the answer was it wasn't, because that wasn't its job,' recalled Tice.

> Then I said: 'When are you going to make the move across?', to which the answer was, 'I need to wait until he's [Cameron] come back, we've got to go through the journey, basically, when he comes back from the summit.' That didn't work for me, I felt that was too late. If he was going to run a No campaign – if – you couldn't wait that long. I went away quite troubled. I just felt there was a mismatch. I was expecting him to say that he would back Leave much earlier, and move across to being involved in a No campaign.

Although disheartened, Tice tried to salvage something positive from the meeting.

> What Elliott did say was he's a campaigner, he's not a policy thinker, and he didn't have a credible answer to 'What does it look like after Brexit?' We went away and at [anti-EU think tank] Global Britain we produced a paper that was released in March 2015 in which we which analysed the various options: Norway, Switzerland, Canada and WTO [World Trade Organization] plus.

While working on this paper, Tice set up another meeting with Elliott to press home his view that the Out campaign needed to start work as soon as Cameron arrived back in Downing Street after the general election.

Over lunch on 16 February 2015, again at Osteria dell'Angolo, Tice quizzed Elliott over why Business for Britain was not calling for the UK to leave the EU, why it was still backing reform, and why it wouldn't declare for Out now. Elliott again explained the position was 'Change or Go' and the Prime Minister needed to be allowed to go through the renegotiation process. Tice was again frustrated, and this time laid out his campaign blueprint:

> My idea was the day after the general election I wanted to issue a press release saying the Leave campaign, or then, as it was going to be, the No campaign, was forming; that it had pledges already of X million pounds; that it was carrying out a search for a chief executive; it was under way – bang. I put this idea to Matthew in February 2015, three months before the election, saying this is what we've got to do. And he said: 'No, far too early, wrong strategy.' He's supposed to be the serious campaigner and there was only so much time I could focus on it at the time so I didn't realise he was saying that because he wasn't ready.

Looking back, Tice is convinced Elliott poured cold water on his idea out of personal ambition. 'It was pure vested interest,' he said.

> He didn't like that idea because he didn't want there to be a search for a chief executive. He wasn't ready to move from Business for Britain then, and Business for Britain wasn't ready to switch to Out, and therefore he didn't want anyone else going round basically setting up a Leave campaign.

Whatever the reason, it was clear Tice was getting nowhere with

Elliott. But his new friend Arron Banks was a man he could do business with.

A mutual friend had introduced Banks to Tice and the pair had immediately hit it off. Whereas Banks was a recent convert to Eurosceptic campaigning, Tice had been involved in various anti-EU groups since the late 1990s – including Business for Sterling, the campaign which employed Dominic Cummings from 1999 to 2002. Tice had the experience and contacts, Banks had the money and showmanship.

Almost twenty-four hours after the country discovered Farage had not been victorious in South Thanet, Tice penned another email to Banks:

> The Tories are going to use their majority to push for an early referendum in my view and they will think the Out campaign is weakened now.
>
> We need to prove them wrong quickly. My idea is to accumulate some pledges from people over next two weeks to get us over £1m pledged / raised and let press know that the Out campaign is forming, raising money and identifying possible campaign CEO and leaders. I am good for £100k.
>
> I am convinced we can win referendum.

Banks was keen, but was mulling over getting more involved with UKIP. On 15 May – four days after Farage's unresignation – he met with the UKIP leader in the party's headquarters in Mayfair to discuss how to move forward.

'Banks said: "Nigel, you're my hero. Politicians are a joke, we need to give you something that will give you a voice,"' remembered Farage's advisor Chris Bruni-Lowe.

With the plan to help give Farage a prominent role in the referendum agreed, Banks began working with Tice on building a fledgling Out campaign. Working on the assumption the question on the ballot paper would be a replica of the 1975 vote – 'Do you think the United Kingdom should stay in the European Community (the Common Market)?' – an advertising agency was hired to begin coming up with campaign slogans.

Tice recalled:

> The original slogan was 'When you're in the know, you'll vote No – Be in the Know'. Very clever because it was created by a very bright agency, a couple of young ladies who didn't vote in the general election because they didn't know, they knew even less about the EU referendum, so we thought it was really clever.

With the advertising agency working on the brand, Banks and Tice started hitting up business contacts to drum up support. They both felt that having non-political voices at the top of the campaign would ensure their message got through to a public generally turned off by Westminster figures. But wherever they turned, Banks and Tice time and again found themselves hearing the same words: 'In private, I back you; in public, I won't.'

Tice admits he was 'overly optimistic' to think he and Banks would be able to secure such a range of well-known figures. 'It's quite hard for non-politicians to put their heads above the parapet. People like Arron and I are quite unusual,' he said.

Banks tapped up Farage for a contact list of people who over the years had shown sympathy for leaving the EU, but was equally as frustrated as his business partner:

> Nigel gave a huge list of people he'd been cultivating for years. At the very beginning, it became clear that UKIP were not as friendless as people thought. There are a hell of a lot of people that have a lot of secret sympathy with them who weren't about to put their head above the parapet.

> We used to have dinners with all sorts of weird people – earls, dukes and industrialists and all sorts of people. This idea that Nigel is a lone voice was slightly silly. There are a hell of a lot of people who liked him and supported him and wished him well but weren't prepared to put their heads above the parapet.

Despite trying to use Farage's contacts to drum up support, both Tice and Banks publicly sought to play down any notion that the campaign would be built purely around the UKIP leader.

Tice said:

> He's a well-known politician but we had a very clear view that we wanted a much broader debate from lots of different people. If you want to talk about borders and controls, bring in a highly experienced borders and controls guy. You want to talk about military and defence, bring in a general.

A month later, in an interview with the *Telegraph*, Banks rammed home the point:

> Nigel is a great communicator but I don't believe UKIP is the right vehicle to take this forward. It is not a political campaign. This is too important to leave to politicians. They can endorse it and support it but they will not be involved in the campaign.
>
> Nigel is not the right person to lead the campaign. He does not reach out to everybody.

The notion that UKIP's highest-profile donor would launch an EU referendum campaign and not let Farage play a key role in it did not hold much water in Westminster. Many journalists had seen first-hand how close Banks and the UKIP leader had grown during the general election campaign, and there had been no hint of a falling out between the pair.

But, as of that moment – regardless of whether The Know was a thinly veiled front for UKIP – they were the only ones who were publicly prepared to take the battle to Cameron.

CHAPTER 4

I t wasn't the highest-profile speech Nigel Farage had ever given, and it certainly wasn't the largest audience he had ever faced, but his address to the party faithful in Eastbourne on 6 June 2015 had suddenly become one of the most important.

It had been twenty-six days since he had 'unresigned' as UKIP leader – an act that provoked a civil war as senior party figures questioned not just his judgement but that of those advising him.

Carswell was one of the angriest. After the phone call ahead of Farage's unresignation, Carswell believed the UKIP leader would hold true to his word and step down.

Later that day, he had a meeting with two UKIP officials over how to spend the so-called Short money – the public cash available to political parties who have seats in Westminster. Parties get £16,956.86 for every seat won at the most recent election, plus £33.86 for every 200 votes gained across the country. UKIP were entitled to £650,000, but Carswell, who had long campaigned for reducing the cost of politics, did not think that a party with just one MP could justify taking all the cash. A heated row broke out between UKIP's only MP and those at the top of the party over who controlled the fund, how much they would claim and what it would be spent on.

The problem was, UKIP really needed the money. After the

election, the party was forced to leave its Mayfair headquarters as, while the office space was provided free of charge by its treasurer Andrew Reid, the business rents alone meant it was too expensive to stay. UKIP press officers were forced to work from the nearest Caffè Nero, their own homes, or just 'somewhere round here with Wi-Fi', said one party source. The plan was to use some of the public money to fund an office move, but Carswell was refusing to sanction the cash being handed over to those at the top of the party.

The source added:

> We were in real financial trouble, we'd lost our offices. That's why there was the trouble with Douglas, who had been put on the spot and it wasn't his fault, but he didn't have the wit or the flexibility. Carswell knew there was financial trouble and it put him in a very strong position. So he played badly, they played badly, it fell apart. Up until that point it was alright.

The day after that fractious meeting over the Short money, Farage decided he needed to speak to his only MP face to face to try to resolve the issue, but, despite getting together, no agreement was reached. On Thursday 14 May, MEP Patrick O'Flynn – the former political editor of the *Daily Express* who was now the party's economic spokesman – claimed Farage's senior advisors had turned him into a 'snarling, thin-skinned, aggressive' man.

In an interview with *The Times*, O'Flynn said UKIP was now 'open to the charge that this looks like an absolutist monarchy or a personality cult'. In a subsequent interview with Sky News later that day, he denied he was taking part in any sort of 'coup' against Farage, whom he labelled his 'political hero', but added: 'A couple of people in his inner circle – for want of a better term – they are wrong 'uns.'

O'Flynn didn't mention them by name, but it was clear who he was talking about: Farage's chief of staff Raheem Kassam and party secretary Matthew Richardson. Both were seen as the architects of the 'shock and awe' style of campaigning that had led to Farage using HIV sufferers as examples of benefit tourism in a televised leaders debate ahead of the general election. The pair were also blamed for cutting Farage off from many others in his party, encouraging his drinking and, ultimately, responsible for his defeat in Thanet South.

Kassam was due to leave his job as Farage's chief of staff after the election anyway, but the attack from O'Flynn ensured he left with a bang instead of a whimper. Speaking on Sky News from New York, where he had travelled for a post-election holiday, Kassam gave it to O'Flynn with both barrels:

> You cannot go to a newspaper and air internal party griev-
> ances as an elected representative of the party. It's wholly
> unprofessional and I think Patrick should absolutely con-
> sider his position. I have no problem with him as a bloke,
> he's a nice chap, he has some good ideas, but unfortunately,
> over the past twenty-four hours, he has shown himself to
> be utterly unprofessional and undeserving of holding that
> title and holding a spokesman role for the UK Independ-
> ence Party.

Arron Banks also weighed in, accusing O'Flynn of working with Carswell in a bid to freeze Farage out of the EU referendum campaign. 'It's all related to Carswell. They want to be the voice of the "No" campaign in the referendum,' he said, adding: 'People like Hannan and Carswell are paper Eurosceptic tigers. Nigel is a big beast in the jungle.'

Later the same day, Farage faced an uncomfortable appearance on the BBC's *Question Time*. The first question was simple:

'Is there a place in today's politics for snarling, thin-skinned and aggressive leaders?' Farage batted the question away, putting O'Flynn's comments down to someone 'letting off steam' after an intense general election campaign. On the Short money issue, he offered an olive branch to Carswell: 'I'm going to recommend that we don't accept any of it. Given we've had an argument over this, I don't want UKIP to look like other parties, grubbing around after public money.'

Peace offerings were not offered to Patrick O'Flynn or UKIP deputy chairman Suzanne Evans. On Tuesday 19 May, Farage accepted O'Flynn's resignation as the party's economic spokesman. The same day, Evans's contract as the party's policy chief was not renewed. The two people who had sat alongside Farage when UKIP unveiled their general election manifesto in April were now gone. Farage was the undisputed king of UKIP again.

His control over the party may have been restored, but the row over Short money, coupled with the telephone call on the morning of Farage's 'unresignation', meant the relationship between Carswell and Farage was hitting new low after new low. It fell even further on Saturday 16 May, when the UKIP leader read an article in his copy of that day's *Times* newspaper headlined 'Farage needs to take a break from UKIP'.

'There's an article in *The Times* under the byline of Douglas Carswell and a sentence in there I've never forgotten,' Farage said.

> There are two things he says. The first thing he says is: 'We must not challenge the Prime Minister. We must allow Dave to go and do his stuff.' What?! And there is the phrase I shall never forget, where Mr Carswell says: 'We must not make immigration synonymous with EU membership.' I thought: 'Fucking hell. I spent ten years trying to do that!' I've spent ten years when Jo Public thought the EU was over there and immigration is over here and I've always known if you put

the two together... and here he is saying we must not do this
in this campaign.

The article further fuelled Farage's suspicions that Carswell was
working under orders from Daniel Hannan – indeed, he believed
Hannan had written the piece. From where Farage was looking,
conspirators inside and outside his party were plotting to stop
him from taking an active role in the referendum.

'I knew within a fortnight of the general election exactly what
was happening, exactly what they were trying to do. I sussed it
out that morning. It was wrong, it got even worse thereafter,' said
Farage.

Knowing a rival Out campaign would be formed which would
have no room for him, it didn't take much for Farage to work out
who would be running it: Matthew Elliott. So Farage arranged
to meet him.

Six days later, on Friday 22 May, Farage and Elliott shook
hands in the tea room of Claridge's, the five-star hotel in London's
Mayfair. Farage was not expecting to learn anything he didn't
already know from Elliott, but he wanted his suspicions confirmed. To the former metals trader, Elliott was just another posh
boy in the image of Hannan – another member of the Westminster
establishment who did not understand life outside SW1. 'They are
creatures of the political class,' said Farage.

Elliott, for his part, was no big fan of Farage either. The two first
shared a platform in June 2013, when they were booked to appear
on a cruise organised by the Midlands Industrial Council (MIC),
a group of wealthy businesspeople, which has poured money into
Eurosceptic pressure groups and the Conservative Party. Aboard
the luxury *Queen Elizabeth* cruise liner, Farage and Elliott took
part in a debate on the future of the EU and the UK's place within
it. It was there that Elliott experienced Farage's take-no-prisoners
style of debating first-hand.

Elliott recalled:

> I remember speaking after Nigel, and I basically gave the BfB
> [Business for Britain] pitch of 'Change or Go', making it very
> clear the sort of changes I wanted – it wasn't just a twiddle
> round the edges, it was fundamental changes. He really laid
> into me in quite a vicious way on the platform, it was slightly
> a grandstanding way.

As a fellow Eurosceptic, the lobbyist expected to be wooed by
Farage, not barracked, and said:

> I was precisely the sort of person you should be trying to
> win over, or, if you disagree, you disagree politely. From that
> point he probably got the idea that what BfB was about was
> a bit of a takeover plot by Tory Eurosceptics to take away his
> rightful platform as head of the Brexit campaign.

Over coffee, Farage pressed Elliott on what his plans were now
the Conservatives had won the election, and when BfB would
commit to an Out vote. If Elliott, Hannan and all the other posh
boys wanted to run the show, why didn't they just get on with it?

'I was always quite open with him,' remembered Elliott. 'I
wouldn't be cagey with him, so I would say: "Look, we haven't
got a rationale to change to leave yet because the government
hasn't resolved the negotiation."'

Farage knew that was the case, but he wanted to hear it for
himself. It gave him all the ammunition he needed to seize the
initiative and begin his own campaign.

On 6 June, Farage took to the stage at UKIP's south-east conference in Eastbourne. Pacing around the Congress Theatre stage,
he wasted no time in attacking those who did not want either him
or his party to play a leading role in the campaign.

We're being told by a predominantly rather snobby bunch of Tories that UKIP should back off [audience boos], we should leave it to the real experts [more boos, cries of 'Rubbish!'], we should leave it to the kind of people who, even when they did rebel against the Maastricht Treaty, at the end of the day did not have the courage to face up to John Major and vote against him in that confidence vote.

We are being told to stand aside for these guys. There's not a cat's chance in hell that I'm going to do that, or we're going to do that.

Having been briefed on the Bruges Group meeting from earlier in the week by Michael Heaver, Farage turned his attention to John Redwood.

We even have people like John Redwood, now I'm told he's very clever – I don't know. We have John Redwood, last Monday debating at the Bruges Group with Tim Aker, saying that we must not give the Prime Minister a shopping list, that we must not give him a series of demands, we must pat David on the back, we must encourage him with his renegotiation.

Now, that strategy is flawed, folks, because unless we challenge this renegotiation, we're allowing him, we're allowing Cameron to set the terms of the agenda and set the terms of the debate.

So, frankly, what I'm seeing from many of these so-called Tory Eurosceptics is they are people I suspect – I know some of them will be principled and I know some of them will stand with us when this referendum comes – but my suspicion is quite a lot of them will be prepared to put their own careers before the interest of the independence of this country and I don't trust very many of them.

He concluded by talking up what UKIP could bring to the campaign:

> I am not for one moment suggesting that UKIP should be and has to be the only single and dominant voice in the No campaign. I'm not saying that, I'm looking forward to seeing a big umbrella group of businessmen, celebrities, whoever they may be who form the official No campaign, and we will form a significant part under their leadership of that campaign. But the reality is we are the only Eurosceptic organisation in Britain that has got 50,000 members, 300 branches and thousands of activists who are ready.

Farage's speech, unsurprisingly, went down well with the UKIP faithful watching on, and he got the customary standing ovation.

Yet, while the sound of applause was still echoing around the theatre, the 'so-called Tory Eurosceptics' were about to reveal themselves to their friends, enemies and rivals alike.

CHAPTER 5

t is usually London's restaurants that play host to informal sum-
mits of MPs as they plot and scheme. Tony Blair and Gordon
Brown famously reached agreement over which of them would
stand for the Labour leadership in 1994 while dining at the Granita
restaurant in Islington. The Gay Hussar in Soho is adorned with
caricatures of its famous political customers, while Shepherd's in
Marsham Street is one of the favoured places for a 'good bit of
grub' by Nigel Farage.

On 17 May 2015, it was not a restaurant but the kitchen of Tory
MP Bernard Jenkin that played host to one of the most important meetings of the referendum campaign. Jenkin was one of
Parliament's best-known Eurosceptics, and could even lay claim
to that most revered of titles – a Maastricht rebel. Although he
had technically abstained on a 1993 Labour amendment to the Bill
which led to the government's defeat, Prime Minister John Major's
thin majority meant not voting was a serious act of rebellion –
a courageous move for a 33-year-old who had only been elected
to Parliament the year before.

Seated at Jenkin's kitchen table were Steve Baker, Dominic
Cummings, Matthew Elliott and Owen Paterson, the Tory MP
for North Shropshire. All five agreed that David Cameron was
not going to achieve any substantial change to the terms of the

UK's EU membership – it would be a 'patsy renegotiation', said Jenkin. They knew Cameron would want to get talks with his European neighbours started immediately, but they had differing views as to when the referendum would actually be called. Jenkin was fearful it would be a quick process, with a snap vote called in early 2016. Paterson, who had observed Cameron at close quarters, having served four years in his Cabinet, believed the Prime Minister might wait until the latter half of 2017:

> I was pretty sure he would go for autumn 2017, when the UK had the presidency of the European Union and he would do great events at places like Holyrood and Greenwich. He could present himself as a hugely important person UK-wise and a hugely important person EU-wise. It was quite a good message. I thought that was what he would probably do.

The first order of business was to decide how to move forward in Parliament. The government would need to put legislation through the Commons setting out the terms of the referendum and how the campaign would be conducted. If this Bill wasn't scrutinised properly, Cameron could fix it so the full weight of the British government was pumping out pro-EU propaganda right up to polling day. The Eurosceptic Tory response to this would need to be coordinated. Baker's Conservatives for Britain organisation was the perfect vehicle. He would bring together as many Tory MPs as possible on a mailing list, where he could keep fellow Eurosceptics up to date with information and plans. The group would go public at the beginning of June, under the auspice of wishing Cameron well at the European summit in Brussels later that month. The group adopted the same position as Business for Britain – Change or Go – but Jenkin, Baker and Paterson did not believe Cameron would achieve a deal that would convince them to stay.

Paterson took on responsibility for sussing out the Eurosceptic position of the new intake of Tory MPs. There were seventy-four new faces on the Tory side of the green benches, and if Conservatives for Britain could get to them early, especially with the line that they were supporting the Prime Minister in his renegotiation, it would provide the movement with a sizeable parliamentary army.

Some of the 2015 intake needed no convincing. Tom Pursglove, at twenty-six years old the youngest Tory MP, was a staunch Eurosceptic. Prior to being elected Corby MP, he had run an EU referendum of his own in Northamptonshire in 2014, along with MPs Peter Bone and Philip Hollobone (81 per cent voted Yes to leave, out of 14,431 votes).

Craig Mackinlay, who had destroyed Farage's dream of finally winning a seat in the Commons in South Thanet, was also a confirmed Outer. Prior to joining the Tories in 2005, he had been a member of UKIP, even briefly acting as leader in 1997, so his anti-EU credentials were firmly established.

Others, such as new Braintree MP James Cleverly, were instinctive Outers but wanted to be seen to give Cameron a chance to succeed with his renegotiation. Cleverly realised it would be easier to convince the public to back leaving the EU if they felt all had been done to reform it, and it wanted to show support for 'The Boss', as he called Cameron.

Cummings, meanwhile, was tasked with helping Matthew Elliott establish the campaign. At this stage, Cummings was clear that he would help set up the campaign, but did not want to lead it and would bow out once it was up and running. Cummings was also asked to propose a structure for the various groups to operate within. The Labour Eurosceptic movement – which would get slightly smaller in the coming months – was already mobilising, and the Democratic Unionist Party, now the joint fourth largest party in the Commons, would also have a role to play.

There was of course the issue of UKIP. Having Farage involved in the group in an official capacity was completely out of the question. 'At the front of our mind was always the fact that Farage himself could not even win Thanet; if he couldn't win Thanet then UKIP couldn't win the referendum. If it was a UKIP-fronted campaign, it would fail,' said Jenkin. But the five men also knew that if this campaign was to work, it would need to be able to work with some of the more Westminster-friendly members of Farage's party.

Elliott would continue in his role as chief executive of Business for Britain, sticking to the line of 'Change or Go', but would begin to prepare the ground for a move to become an Out campaign.

With dinner eaten, wine drunk and the roles dished out, the group left Jenkin's house to set in motion the beginnings of the Out campaign.

The five reconvened for breakfast at Sapori's, an Italian café on Horseferry Road in Westminster, three days later. Over cappuccinos and croissants, they exchanged progress updates. Cummings had been busy, and had turned around his paper setting out how to organise the campaign in a matter of days. One of the key proposals was to establish a cross-party exploratory committee to coordinate Eurosceptic activity across the divide. It was agreed the meetings would take place every Wednesday afternoon in Paterson's office after Prime Minister's Questions, chaired by Bernard Jenkin, and Labour, UKIP and even Green peer Jenny Jones would be invited to attend. Jenkin would be the group's chairman.

Cummings also put forward another key aspect of the plan: he would not run the campaign. Paterson remembers: 'It was also intended that, according to the original Cummings paper, Dom Cummings would stand down; it was never intended that he would run the campaign. He always made it clear he would set it up, then he would fade away.'

Paterson, too, had been busy, and had arranged the first of his receptions for new Tory MPs to take place on the evening of Wednesday 27 May – the same day as the first Conservative-only Queen's Speech since 1996. About fifty MPs turned up and, while drinking wine and eating nibbles, were gently probed for their EU views.

Baker's charm offensive of the parliamentary party was also gaining ground and, after sounding out key figures such as John Redwood, he set out the aims of CfB in a document marked 'Confidential'. The group was for those Tories who 'consider the UK's present relationship with the EU to be untenable' and 'support the Party's policy of renegotiation and referendum'. As well as exploring 'what objectives the negotiations must achieve', the group would also 'discuss how to prepare for a possible "out" campaign, to be activated if it is apparent that negotiations will not achieve the objectives'.

According to the document, meetings would be held ten times a year, alternating between the European Parliament and Westminster. Baker noted that 'speakers are anticipated from the spectrum of politics, business, diplomacy and trade economics'.

There was also a list of 'key issues', ranging from asking Parliamentary Questions about the 'EU aspects of the work of every department' to 'selection of messengers and media'.

The group's 'immediate priorities' were simple: 'establishing membership; implementing our programme; establishing a briefing operation'.

Within days, MPs were signed up to the group's mailing list, including Cabinet ministers – who were assured that their names would be kept out of the public domain.

Early meetings of CfB were held in Baker's office every Tuesday at 4 p.m. and, as the group grew in size, the weekly get-togethers were moved to one of the committee rooms in Parliament.

The first kite from the group was flown by David Campbell Bannerman on Sunday 31 May with an article in the *Sunday Telegraph*. Headlined 'Cameron's EU reform must not be a "sham"', it set out three red lines for the PM's renegotiation: immigration controls, full parliamentary democracy and a drastic cut in the UK's contribution to the EU budget (he used the gross and net figures in the article). The MEP was well aware he was setting 'expectations impossibly high'.

'We had the ability to set the agenda and say, look, unless you get X, Y and Z back you've failed in your renegotiation, so we set the bar very high,' said Campbell Bannerman.

Throughout the following week, Baker worked on signing up more and more Tories to CfB, and by the following Saturday it had secured the backing of fifty MPs.

As Nigel Farage was lapping up the applause in Eastbourne for attacking the 'so-called Tory Eurosceptics', Baker was putting the finishing touches to an article for the next day's *Sunday Telegraph* in which he would publicly reveal the sleeper cell he had created in the Conservative Party.

Under the headline 'Conservatives will stand up for Britain if the EU lets us down', Baker set out the group's aims:

> Conservatives for Britain has been formed among Tory parliamentarians to discuss the criteria by which to judge the government's EU renegotiation. We are willing to consider how to prepare for an 'out' campaign if, lamentably, the European Union establishment will not allow the UK a new relationship of trade and cooperation.

There was praise for Cameron in the article, describing the PM as 'spectacularly successful in Europe' and adding that 'no other Prime Minister has secured a cut in the European Union budget', but it was clear this group was preparing for Out.

'Unless senior EU officials awake to the possibility that one of the EU's largest members is serious about a fundamental change in our relationship, our recommendation to British voters seems likely to be exit,' wrote Baker.

One thing the article did not mention was how CfB would seek to influence the government on the terms of the referendum. It wouldn't be long before Cameron found out.

CHAPTER 6

t is always polite for politicians to say they are 'astonished' when invited by the Prime Minister to join the Cabinet, but in John Whittingdale's case, it was true.

It had been ten years since the Maldon MP had been part of the Conservative Party's top team, serving as shadow Culture, Media and Sport Secretary under Michael Howard's leadership from 2004 to 2005. He then spent a decade as the chairman of the Culture Select Committee, and on Monday 11 May 2015 was fully expecting to carry on serving David Cameron from the back benches.

Yet on that morning he received a surprising phone call from Downing Street, offering not just a position in the government but a seat at the Cabinet table. With Sajid Javid becoming Business Secretary, there was a vacancy at the top of the Department for Culture, Media and Sport, and Whittingdale was asked to fill it. 'I was thrilled about it, particularly this job, which is a job I had always wanted to do,' he said.

There was just one matter that the Maastricht rebel needed to raise with the Prime Minister, though: that of the EU referendum. He recounted:

> I said: 'There is just one thing we need to clarify. I am not in Better Off Out but you'll know my voting record and my

speeches and everything I've ever said and, unless there is a fundamental change, I think it will be very hard for me to campaign to stay in the European Union.' The Prime Minister said words to the effect of: 'I know that, I understand that, give me a chance and see what I can deliver.' I said: 'Of course, if you can deliver then I will be the first on board.'

It wasn't just new government ministers who were pressing the Prime Minister over Europe. At one of the first Cabinet meetings after the election, Work and Pensions Secretary Iain Duncan Smith quizzed David Cameron over whether he would allow ministers to campaign with their conscience when it came to a referendum. 'I don't want to talk about that, I hope it won't ever arise. I hope I come back with a deal which everybody can support and therefore it's not an issue,' the Prime Minister replied, according to one Cabinet minister.

Pressure on Cameron was also coming from outside the Cabinet – particularly from the new Tory MP for Uxbridge and South Ruislip, Boris Johnson. In August 2014, Johnson had set out his own expectations of the renegotiation in a speech at Bloomberg's London headquarters – the same venue in which Cameron had promised a referendum nineteen months earlier. Based on a report by Dr Gerard Lyons, the then London Mayor's Chief Economic Advisor in City Hall, Johnson set out what he believed Cameron should be trying to secure from Brussels – and it was a long list: migration controls, cuts in the Common Agriculture Policy, a system to allow national parliaments to veto EU legislation and directives, ending the supremacy of the European Court of Justice over Home and Justice affairs, and even potentially opting out of the Social Chapter, which guaranteed employment rights for workers.

He said:

> I think we can get there, but if we can't, then we have noth-
> ing to be afraid of in going for an alternative future, a Britain
> open not just to the rest of Europe but to the world, where
> we have historic ties and markets with vast potential for all
> the goods and services that originate in London – and will
> continue to do so under any circumstances.

Johnson may have set his own reform targets high, but he was interested in renegotiation, not just going along with the pretence of a deal before opting for Out, as many other Eurosceptics were doing.

In what was his second 'maiden' speech in the Commons on 1 June (he had previously been an MP from 2001 to 2008), Johnson made it clear how he expected Cameron to behave:

> I congratulate the Prime Minister on the élan and success
> with which he has begun his pan-European schmooze-
> athon in the chancelleries of Europe. I believe his efforts
> will be crowned with success, but I would remind him of
> something that I think all of us would want to remind him,
> our negotiators, the Foreign Secretary and everybody else:
> if you are going to go into a difficult international negotia-
> tion, you have to be prepared to walk away if you do not get
> the result you want.
>
> If we do not get a deal that is in the interests of this country
> or of Europe, we should be prepared to strike out and forge
> an alternative future that could be just as glorious and just
> as prosperous, with a free-trading arrangement.

A week later, and the issue of whether ministers would be allowed to break from collective responsibility when the referendum arrived – as Harold Wilson had allowed in 1975 – spilled into the media. In a rare misstep in his media relations, Cameron tied himself up in knots over the issue while at a G7 summit in Schloss Elmau in Germany. It was the day after Steve Baker announced Conservatives for Britain in the press, and rumours were that some Cabinet ministers had signed up to the mailing list. (Whittingdale was indeed on the list, and had been assured his membership wouldn't be made public, although, as he put it, 'I wouldn't have been that concerned if that had been known, as anybody who looked at my track record wouldn't have exactly been shocked that I was a member.')

Cameron was asked by the press if he had 'absolutely closed his mind to allowing ministers a free vote'.

He replied: 'I've been very clear. If you want to be part of the government, you have to take the view that we are engaged in an exercise of renegotiation, to have a referendum and that will lead to a successful outcome.'

When asked if that meant anyone in government who opposed the position would have to resign, the Prime Minister said: 'Everyone in government has signed up to the programme set out in the Conservative manifesto.' He added:

> If I can get a position where Britain would be better off in a reformed Europe then obviously that is not something the government is neutral about. It's not a sort of 'on the one hand, on the other hand' approach. If I can secure what I want to secure, I will have secured what I think is the right outcome for Britain.
>
> I am carrying out a renegotiation in the national interest to get a result that I believe will be in the national interest. I'm confident I can get that.

The next day, Cameron woke up to newspaper front pages he was not expecting. The *Telegraph* splashed on 'Cabinet told: Vote for Europe or resign'; *The Guardian* led with 'PM: I will sack ministers who call for EU exit'; while the *Daily Mail* had 'PM: Back me or I will sack you' emblazoned across its front page.

The Prime Minister had not meant to be anywhere near as definitive as he had been. Well aware that such a position could trigger Cabinet resignations, he quickly rowed back. At a post-summit press conference, Cameron claimed his comments had been 'misinterpreted'.

He said:

> I was clearly referring to the process of renegotiation. But the point is this. I have always said what I want is an outcome for Britain that keeps us in a reformed EU. But I have also said we don't know the outcome of these negotiations, which is why I have always said I rule nothing out.

The Prime Minister then turned on the journalists in the room: 'If you're not certain about something I said yesterday, then ask and we'll happily make it clear,' he said. The hacks were not happy with being accused of misrepresenting Cameron. 'Extraordinary suggestion from PM that no-one in gov realised there was "mis-interpretation" issue until he woke up & saw newspaper coverage,' tweeted the Press Association's James Tapsfield. 'Many of the Cameron government's problems occur when journalists write down what he says and put it in their newspapers...' was the *Sunday Times* political editor Tim Shipman's take on the matter.

The slip-up, or 'misrepresentation', was a public example of what was going on behind closed doors in Downing Street. Cameron was undecided about suspending collective responsibility for the referendum, but Chancellor George Osborne was counselling against the move. According to Iain Duncan Smith:

> What he was thinking was if he didn't let them campaign, that would have locked Michael Gove in because he wouldn't

have resigned, that was his thinking. I think Cameron veered at the beginning to the idea that you should run it as collective responsibility but it became clear to him as the year went on that this was going to be almost impossible.

The battle over whether Cabinet ministers could campaign for Out would continue for the rest of the year and, by the time it was over, Cameron would be lining up against both friends and rivals.

CHAPTER 7

Discussing the future of the country underneath a painting of Charles I certainly focuses the mind. There can be few more stark reminders of what happens when the London establishment loses touch with the people than a picture of the last English king to be beheaded.

That was precisely the reason Owen Paterson had the portrait hanging on his office wall. For Paterson, the EU referendum would be a 21st-century re-run of that civil war, which ended with the monarch's death in Whitehall – although of course not even the most ardent Eurosceptic wanted to see David Cameron's head in a basket.

It was beneath the gaze of Charles I that the plotters of 2015 would meet each Wednesday afternoon after Prime Minister's Questions. Sitting at the long table in Paterson's office, representatives from the Conservatives, Labour, UKIP, the Greens and the DUP would update each other on their activities and plot their next moves.

One of the key points of the group was that it should not be Tory-dominated, meaning just three Conservatives took part: Bernard Jenkin, who would chair the meeting; Steve Baker, responsible for relaying the latest Conservatives for Britain activities; and Paterson himself.

With so many Tory Eurosceptics wanting to play a key role,

and so few places available on the steering committee, some
Conservative MPs' noses were put out of joint. Douglas Carswell,
UKIP's representative on the group, said: 'I think there was tension in the Conservative Party where perhaps in order to make
sure it wasn't a Conservative-dominated thing there had to be a
limited number of Conservatives there, and I think perhaps that
probably caused a bit of tension.'

John Baron, the Tory MP for Basildon and Billericay whose 2013
amendment to the Queen's Speech 'expressed regret' at the lack of
a referendum pledge, welcomed the structure – even though he
wasn't at the 'top table':

> It allowed that certain individuals could focus on certain
> key issues without competing for top slot, in the nicest pos-
> sible way. I think that worked very well. It addressed a key
> concern that on the Eurosceptic side of things there had
> sometimes – sometimes – been a jockeying for position
> which muffled the message. It allowed … the campaign to
> focus on the issues we thought important, whether it was
> focusing on the rear-guard action on things like purdah,
> financing, the wording of the referendum.

On the Labour side, the Eurosceptic stalwart MPs Kate Hoey,
Kelvin Hopkins and Graham Stringer were regular attendees,
as were Labour donor John Mills and, later, Brendan Chilton –
the man who would help administer the Labour Leave group. In
an ironic twist, Paterson's office was directly underneath Alan
Johnson's – the man running the Labour In campaign.

'It was always quite amusing because we'd go up in the lift
and we'd very regularly bump into Alan Johnson and the Labour
Remain committee. It was quite funny because we'd all sort of
stand either side of the lift and say, "Good afternoon,"' remembered Chilton.

Matthew Elliott and Dominic Cummings would also drop in to keep an eye on progress, and also to provide updates of their own. According to the pragmatic Elliott:

> The idea behind that group was basically twofold: a) the referendum legislation was going through, so let's make sure it's as fair a referendum as possible, and b) let's start thinking about the sort of campaign we need. You know, a bit like an exploratory committee for a potential race – you're not committing yourself to running, but you're sort of finding out. Testing the water. So that was the idea behind that.

Despite bringing together groups of politicians who would normally waste no time in tearing strips off each other, it was 'all very collegiate and inclusive', remembered Carswell.

'Oh, we got on fine together. Initially, I mean – this has always been the case with the EU as an issue,' said Mills.

After a month of meeting, the group – now known as the Exploratory Committee (ExCom) – revealed itself with a mission statement, signed by the seven Tory, Labour and UKIP MPs, on Thursday 18 June 2015. The statement was much more aggressive than the article by Baker announcing Conservatives for Britain. Whereas the Wycombe MP had showered Cameron with praise before setting out his hope for reforms, the ExCom statement was blunt:

> There is little if any indication that the government is even asking for significant reform or fundamental change. In particular, there is no sign of any proposals either to end the supremacy of EU law over UK law on over wider matters, or to resolve the question of what should be the relationship between the Eurozone and non-Eurozone states.

The statement went on:

> There are therefore many issues that need urgent attention,
> including –
>
> - Legal issues arising from the Referendum Bill (e.g. rules
>   for 'purdah', the impartiality of EU and government
>   institutions and broadcasters, funding limits, designation
>   of IN and OUT campaigns, etc.).
> - How an OUT campaign might best be formed and run
>   to inform the public about the issues.
>
> We are therefore forming a cross-party group to consider these
> questions. This is not the 'OUT' campaign, but we are seeking
> urgently to provide resources for crucial thinking and to
> promote cooperation amongst those who might contribute
> to an OUT campaign.

The day after the announcement, Cummings took to his blog to
dampen down reports that he was running the committee, despite
the fact that he had been involved in its creation.

> Contrary to some media reports, I am not 'running' anything.
> Contra *The Times*, I am not 'overseeing' ExCom. (ExCom
> is a set of meetings, it is not an organisation, and I do not
> chair it.) I go to their meetings, listen, and give advice. I am
> talking to people about whether they would be interested in
> leaving their job to work for a NO campaign and how they
> think it should work. It is extremely hard to create political
> organisations that can take decisions fast and effectively so
> getting the foundations right is vital. Also, building a national
> network of small businesses to make the case for NO in their
> community, so essential to winning a referendum, will take
> time so people need to start now.

I will not be 'running the NO campaign'. I am helping
people get something started because I want to see the
arguments put to the public in as sensible a way as possible.
Soon I will return to my studies.

With CfB and now ExCom in the public domain, some Conservative MPs began to worry. Were Baker, Jenkin and Paterson really
supporting the Prime Minister? Or was this actually all a front for
a No campaign? Many MPs had signed up to CfB because they
genuinely did want to show support to Cameron, and were going
to make their decision on whether to back staying in the EU based
on the deal he returned with.

Jenkin remembers:

We had a lot of conversations with colleagues who said:
'Well, why are you starting the No campaign now? Surely
you've got to wait?' We explained to them that if we waited
until the final deal was completed, then tried to start the No
campaign, there wouldn't be much of a campaign because
there wouldn't be enough time.

A week after ExCom was announced, it became a lot clearer what
David Cameron would be asking for in his renegotiation. On
Thursday 25 June, the Prime Minister travelled to Brussels for a
two-day summit with other EU leaders. Top of the agenda was the
growing migration crisis in the Mediterranean and, as was becoming tradition, the parlous state of the Greek economy. That evening,
Cameron was given five minutes by European Council President
Donald Tusk to make a brief statement to other leaders setting
out his hopes for reform of the UK's relationship with the EU.
However, a more detailed account of his thinking found its way
into *The Guardian*, which printed a leaked copy of a diplomatic
note recounting a meeting between Cameron and other EU leaders.

According to the note, Cameron told his European counterparts his 'firm aim' was 'to keep the UK in the EU'. There were
four key areas of reform: exempting the UK from 'ever closer
union' and introducing a red and yellow card system for blocking
EU proposals; cutting red tape on the EU service sector; ensur-
ing those countries outside the single currency would not be
bound by new rules introduced in the single market; and introducing restrictions on EU citizens claiming benefits. Crucially, it
appeared the notion of an 'emergency brake' on migrants' access
to benefits was dropped. The brake was one of Cameron's flagship
proposals, and would have allowed the UK to suspend in-work
benefits to EU migrants if immigration was deemed to be at a
level that was affecting public services.

The note also revealed Cameron's tactic to win the referendum, which was likely to be held in 2016: 'He believes that people
will ultimately vote for the status quo if the alternatives can be
made to appear risky.' This line was deliberately reminiscent of
the campaign used by those calling for the Scots to reject independence from the UK in the 2014 referendum – a style dubbed
'Project Fear'.

With the demands out in the open, there was pressure from CfB
and BfB to declare they were for Out immediately. Elliott resisted:

> A lot of Tory MPs wouldn't have been able to join because
> they still needed the cover of it being 'Change or Go', and
> to be fair a lot of them wanted to see the change the PM
> wanted. But obviously we needed a critical mass to be able
> to get the changes to the legislation and get the momen-
> tum going.

One person not being shy about getting the No campaign going
was Cummings, who on 7 July posted an open invitation for
recruits to join the organisation he was helping to create.

After a quote from Bismarck ('Better to be a hammer than an anvil … If revolution there is to be, better to undertake it than undergo it'), the blog kicked off with a line that could have come straight out of the mouth of Nigel Farage. 'Some Tory MPs have said "we must wait for the prime minister to return from his renegotiation before we talk about a NO campaign, we cannot prejudge it, party unity demands…" No, no, no.'

After warning Conservative MPs to 'focus on the interests of Britain, Europe, and the wider world – *not* party interests, including "party unity"', Cummings listed all the vacancies he was hoping to fill: researchers, programmers, web designers, experts in advertising and marketing, and spokespeople ('fancy yourself a cross between Bill Clinton and Milla Jovovich, get in touch').

Along with the long list of the kinds of people Cummings *did* want, there was one group who need not email in: 'We are not yet in a position to deal with grassroots volunteers but we should be by September.'

Recognising his own reputation as a man who is not always easy to deal with, Cummings offered this reassurance: 'Finally, you don't have to worry about working for me because I am NOT "running the NO campaign" whatever you read. I don't have the brains, skills, or personality. I am helping establish some foundations and a core team and helping people focus on essentials.'

He added: 'Once things are moving, I will be returning to my studies, helping in minor ways only.'

It was not just unemployed Clinton/Jovovich crossbreeds who were attracted by Cummings's blog. Following the EU summit in Brussels, Boris Johnson had found himself disheartened by Cameron's ambitions – but also sympathetic with the Prime Minister for having to negotiate with such a rigid entity. He came across a post written by Cummings on 23 June, in which he brainstormed a radical strategy for getting the UK a better deal with the EU: a double referendum.

Referring to staying in the EU as Yes and leaving the EU as No, Cummings wrote:

> One can see why NO might argue for a second vote. It ena-
> bles NO to make a NO vote seem much less risky. 'If you
> vote YES, you won't get another vote for another 40 years
> – if ever. You should vote NO to Cameron's rubbish deal.
> If you vote NO, you will force a new government to negoti-
> ate a new deal and give you a new vote. *A NO vote is much*
> *safer than a YES vote.'*

He added:

> This approach might allow NO to avoid its biggest prob-
> lem – the idea that a NO vote is a vote to leave in one jump
> and is therefore a leap in the dark. It would allow NO to
> portray YES as the truly risky option. This approach would
> enable NO to build a coalition between a) those who think
> we should just leave (about a third) and b) those who dis-
> like the EU but are worried about leaving (about a third) and
> who may be persuaded that 'Cameron's deal is bad and we
> should try to get a better one but the only way to force this is
> to vote NO'.

After reading the post, Johnson confided in friends that this plan of action could be the only way to get serious reform. A friend of the Mayor told the *Sunday Times*: 'I don't think in his heart Boris wants us to walk away. But he's interested in us saying no because [the renegotiation] won't be what we want. That would mean a second vote. He thinks the only way to deal with these people is to play hardball.'

With the kite flown, Johnson expanded on the idea in an inter-view with *The Times* on 11 July. He described himself as 'very interested' in the second referendum plan and added that he would be prepared to vote Out: 'No one goes into a negotiation without being willing to leave. I love our friends and partners in Brussels, I understand quite deeply the way they do things, they are not remotely interested in you unless you tell them no.'

Johnson's mind was spinning over how he would campaign in the referendum, and it would not stop for a long while.

CHAPTER 8

Most people don't spend their 77th birthday contemplating fundamental reform to the way the country is run – but John Mills is not like 'most people'. The son of a colonel – also believed to be a spy who, according to family legend, foiled a revolutionary attempt in Cuba by Fidel Castro – Mills studied politics, philosophy and economics at Oxford University.

It was while at university that his entrepreneurial spirit came to the fore. The young Mills began selling cleaning products door-to-door before hiring a plane to fly fellow students to Canada for summer work. 'Nowadays everyone flies all over the place. In 1958 it was a bit more of an adventure,' he told the *Telegraph* in 2013.

He quit a graduate course at Unilever to form his own business, initially selling, then manufacturing, household products. It went bust in 1984, but Mills started all over again with John Mills Limited (JML) in 1986 and this time used in-store video demonstrations to market his products to customers. It was a success, and almost thirty years on JML had an annual turnover of £100 million, sold 15 million products a year and even ran a TV shopping channel.

But it was not his innovative marketing of mops, pans and ironing board covers that had made Mills a big player in Westminster. In 2013, he donated shares worth £1.6 million to Labour – the party he had represented as a councillor in Camden from 1971 to 2006 – which led to journalists taking more of interest in the businessman. At a time when Labour was overtly pro-European, his anti-EU stance marked him out from his comrades.

Despite being of an age when most people are content with observing politics instead of actively taking part, Mills was determined to play a role in the referendum. For him, this would be a chance to exorcise the demons of 1975, when as a younger man he had been a vigorous campaigner for the UK to vote No in the country's first referendum on European membership. Recalling the campaign forty years later for a BBC radio series, he said: 'The disparity in resources between the No and Yes was enormous – something like ten to one, and I don't think that was a very fair way for this referendum to be fought.'

Bearing the scars of that fight, Mills vowed that, should a vote ever arise again, he and other Eurosceptics would be fully prepared.

Just twenty-three days after David Cameron's Bloomberg speech, Mills registered 'Labour for Britain' with Companies House. A month later, the businessman registered another company, 'Labour for a Referendum' – a group that backed David Cameron's commitment to hold an in/out vote on the UK's EU membership. It attracted the support of about thirty MPs, but the majority of them endorsed the campaign on democratic grounds, not because they wished to leave the EU.

Mills said:

> My personal position has never been violently against the EU, I just always thought that Britain never really got the right deal out of the EU. And, you know, if Cameron came back with what he said he would get at Bloomberg and elsewhere I might well have had a different view.

The man tasked with being Labour for a Referendum's campaign director was Brendan Chilton, a borough councillor in Ashford,

Kent, who would go on to contest the parliamentary seat of the same name in the 2015 general election. Having previously worked for Mills, and being of a similar Eurosceptic mindset, he was the businessman's obvious choice to run the campaign.

Mills didn't see the Eurosceptic battle purely through the prism of the Labour movement. He was first and foremost a pragmatist, and as well as setting up Labour for a Referendum in 2013, he also joined with Matthew Elliott to become co-chairman of Business for Britain.

Leading into the 2015 election, Mills was facing the situation that a Conservative victory – something that from a domestic perspective he was opposed to – would be the catalyst for the referendum he had waited forty years to see. On 8 May 2015, Mills's 77th birthday and the day after the general election, his brain was already whirring with how to move forward. As a Eurosceptic Labour Party member, there were several problems ahead. First, would the party now, finally, back the referendum, or would it continue its policy of opposing a vote? If the party did oppose the vote, could it club together enough Europhile Tories to block the legislation going through Parliament? Alternatively, if the party now decided to back a referendum, would it put forward a negotiating stance of its own for when David Cameron went to Brussels to seek reform? Or would it just support the government's proposals? All of this was being considered in the immediate aftermath of Ed Miliband's resignation, even before the candidates for the new leader had made themselves known.

Chilton and Mills immediately began pondering what to do next, and realised they needed to get their act together quickly. Chilton recalled:

> Once it became clear it was Tory government we needed
> to make sure straight away there was a Labour presence in
> the Leave outlet, because UKIP voters were going to vote

> to leave, 60 per cent of the Tories were going to vote to leave,
> so the swing vote was the Labour vote. The people who can
> deliver the Labour vote are Labour people.

Matthew Elliott and Dominic Cummings took no persuading. They both realised it was crucial to have voices from across the political spectrum in the campaign in order to appeal to as wide a range of people as possible. But, more importantly, they also knew that when it came to designating an official Out campaign, the Electoral Commission would take into account the breadth of support each group could command. Cummings had already envisaged Labour MPs being part of the exploratory group he had come up with in his initial briefing paper.

Unlike the Tories, who were having to manage numerous egos and decide which of the party's many Eurosceptics would sit at the top table, there was an element of self-selection with Labour. By the beginning of June, the handful of Labour Eurosceptic MPs in Parliament who could be relied on to do any heavy lifting had been filtered down to just three: Kate Hoey, Kelvin Hopkins and Graham Stringer. Islington North MP Jeremy Corbyn, who had voted against European membership in 1975, against the Maastricht Treaty in 1993 and against the Lisbon Treaty in 2009, was busy trying to secure enough nominations to get onto the ballot for Labour's leadership election. John McDonnell, another Eurosceptic in the Tony Benn tradition of viewing the EU as a business club, was running Corbyn's leadership campaign. Even Gisela Stuart, the Labour MP who, after being asked to help create the European Constitution in the early noughties, was so dismayed by the process that she became a vehement Eurosceptic, did not want to be involved. 'I've been spending the last ten years trying to give up Europe,' she said.

After getting wind that the overwhelmingly pro-EU Labour Party was organising its own In campaign – to be headed up by former Home Secretary Alan Johnson – Mills and Chilton knew they needed to hit back in kind. 'Otherwise you'd get all this "You're with the Tories" and all this,' said Chilton. 'We'd look like a front group.'

The Labour Eurosceptics initially organised themselves as 'Labour for Britain' – adopting the name of the company which had remained dormant since 2013 – fitting in with the Business for Britain and Conservatives for Britain brand. 'Labour for Britain … were semi-autonomous, we were working with everyone but we wanted to keep a distinct identity,' said Chilton.

The group announced itself on 17 June with a joint statement from Hoey, Hopkins and Stringer: 'We believe that the debate about our country's future in the EU has been dormant within the Labour Party for too long. We need to have a full dialogue within our membership and with our natural supporters.'

In an interview with the *New Statesman*, the County Antrim-born Hoey did display some reservations over the group's name. 'I don't like the word "Britain" because that excludes Northern Ireland,' she said. 'I like "UK". But if you look at "Labour FUK" it doesn't exactly do very well, so we have to stick with "Britain".'

The Labour Eurosceptic group may have been small in number but, when the referendum finally arrived, it would have something the official Labour In group lacked – passion right at the very top.

CHAPTER 9

'**W**e do not want the government to suffer defeat ... it is almost certain the government will be defeated ... Please take action now.'

These lines were part of a 235-word email sent out by Steve Baker to members of Conservatives for Britain on Wednesday 10 June 2015 ahead of a vote on the EU Referendum Bill.

But far from asking colleagues to support the government, the email was instructing Tory MPs to put pressure on the top brass to change key aspects of the Bill – aspects which, if they went unchecked, could cause serious damage to the Out side's chances of victory.

The previous day, Foreign Secretary Philip Hammond – who a year before had claimed the Conservatives were 'lighting a fire' under the EU with their referendum pledge – had taken to the Despatch Box in the Commons to set out details of the Bill.

The referendum question would be 'Should the United Kingdom remain a member of the European Union?'; the rules governing who can vote in a general election would apply – eighteen-year-olds and over, UK citizens only – but the franchise would also be extended to Gibraltar. Additionally, the Bill would suspend Section 125 of the Political Parties, Elections and Referendums Act 2000 – the piece of legislation which stops the government from campaigning in favour of one side or the other twenty-eight days ahead of a vote. With this period – known as purdah – lifted, David Cameron would have the full machinery of government at his fingertips right up to election day. Treasury reports on the financial impact of leaving the EU, Home Office reports on how it would make the UK less safe, Business Department reports on how Britain would be a less attractive country for companies to invest in – these could all be pumped out right up until voters went to the ballot box.

With the eyes of Tory Eurosceptics bearing down on him from the green leather benches, Hammond set out the government's reasons for this change to the law:

> If left unaltered, section 125 would stop the government 'publishing' material that deals with 'any issue raised by' the referendum question. In the context of this referendum, that is unworkable and inappropriate. It is unworkable because the restriction is so broad that preventing publication in relation to any issue raised by the referendum could prevent ministers from conducting the ordinary day-to-day business of the UK's dealings with the European Union, and inappropriate because the referendum will take place as a result of a clear manifesto commitment and a mandate won at the general election.

Tory MP Peter Bone was the first out of the traps to grill the Foreign Secretary on this change: 'Is that not what a lot of people are concerned about – that the government will use the apparatus of state to push a case, rather than letting the two sides have equal and fair access?'

Hammond, who knew full well that these questions would be coming, tried to offer assurances:

> Clearly, it will be for the 'yes' and the 'no' campaigns to lead the debate in the weeks preceding the poll. The campaigns

will be designated by the Electoral Commission, and will receive a number of benefits, including a public grant and eligibility to make a referendum broadcast and to send a free mailshot to voters. I can assure the House that the government have no intention of undermining those campaigns, and they do not propose to spend large sums of public money during the purdah period.

He added: 'The government will exercise proper restraint to ensure a balanced debate during the campaign.'

Hammond's assurances were failing to persuade many in the Chamber. Douglas Carswell called for purdah to be re-established so that the referendum would be 'considered free and fair', while Kate Hoey stated that 'any common-sense view would be that it cannot be right to change the purdah restrictions'.

Even former Attorney General Dominic Grieve, who revealed he would almost certainly be backing a 'Yes' vote, said there must be a 'level playing field' and any change to purdah 'could convey an impression that the government will come in and try to load the dice'.

Owen Paterson's speech was the most damning. After pointing out that under the purdah rules 'we have fought a number of general election campaigns during which cars continued to be made, cows continued to be milked and the world did not stop', he said:

> What really worries me is that this extraordinary, incredibly important event in our history could be seen as illegitimate, and that whatever system of government for this country emerges after the referendum might not be seen as valid. I appeal to the Foreign Secretary to go back, talk to the Prime Minister and remove this arbitrary suspension of the process of purdah that has been thrashed out over twenty years.

After six hours of debate, MPs voted to move the Bill along to the next stage of the process – and two days of debate were set aside in the Commons the following week.

The next day, Baker sent his email round to CfB members – now numbering more than 100 – setting out tactics to get the government to perform a U-turn over purdah: 'Irrespective of your voting intentions, please ask your whip to take steps. This may mean the government accepting the amendments or pledging to introduce amendments at report stage.'

The government was starting to get worried. With a working majority of just twelve, it would only take a handful of Eurosceptics to get behind an amendment bringing back purdah to ensure defeat. That calculation, of course, depended on the Labour Party – who were now backing the referendum – voting with the rebels. Veteran Eurosceptic Bill Cash tabled an amendment to the Bill which would not only have blocked the suspension of purdah but would also have forced a sixteen-week referendum campaign – four times the length stipulated in the Referendum Act. By putting forward such an extension, it was hoped the government would compromise and meet the rebels halfway by agreeing to the standard four-week time period. But ministers would not budge.

Inside No. 10, Cameron was speculating on the outcome. Would it really be the case that five weeks into the first Tory-only government since 1997 there would be a defeat over Europe – the very issue that had so dogged John Major's premiership? At meetings of the Cabinet's European sub-committee, chaired by Cameron himself, debates were held over whether a defeat was imminent. Oliver Letwin, one of the PM's most trusted lieutenants, was grilled on how Labour would act as the PM and his team war-gamed different scenarios. One of the members of the sub-committee, Work and Pensions Secretary Iain Duncan Smith, was baffled by the government's actions. His view was that the government was 'picking a fight' it was set to lose, and would eventually be forced into a climb-down. 'The Prime Minister was quite insistent throughout that they couldn't govern unless they did this. He was very insistent,' said Duncan Smith.

With no movement on purdah and a vote in Parliament looming, it was agreed to make a small compromise on the date of the referendum: it would not be held on 5 May 2016, the same day as local elections, the London mayoral contest and votes in Scotland and Wales. This was seen to benefit Brexit campaigners, as London and Scotland in particular were seen to be pro-EU strongholds, and timing the referendum to coincide with votes on the same day as the referendum could have led to an increased turnout for the In camp.

Europe Minister David Lidington was tasked with negotiating with the rebels, and in the week running up to the vote he held meetings with Baker to try to find a way to avert an embarrassing defeat for the government. Hammond himself even held a meeting with Baker, Paterson and Jenkin to try to reassure them that the government would not abuse its position if purdah was abolished, but he could not persuade the Tory MPs to call off their rebellion.

With no deal done, Lidington decided to bypass the rebel leaders and write to all Tory MPs setting out why they did not need to back the Cash amendment. On the morning of the vote he fired off an email:

> Working out a system that will reassure colleagues and voters that the referendum is a fair fight, yet will preserve the government's ability to act in the national interest is not straightforward. It is important that it is legally clear and robust.
> Therefore, we will work with colleagues over the next few months to understand their specific areas of concern and bring forward at report stage in the Autumn government amendments that command the widest possible support

within the House and put beyond any doubt that the campaign
will be conducted throughout in a manner that all sides will
see as fair.

The first order of parliamentary business on 10 June was Treasury
Questions, and almost as soon as Chancellor George Osborne got
to his feet, he was grilled over purdah.

Discussing a Bank of England report into the likely impact of
Brexit, Conservative MP for North Wiltshire James Gray asked:
'Does the Chancellor of the Exchequer not agree that it is vital
that such documents, which may well affect the outcome of the
referendum, are not published in the so-called purdah period of
six to eight weeks before the referendum?'

Osborne rehashed the Downing Street line that without suspending purdah the government would be unworkable, before
adding:

> We will come forward with reassurances that enable the
> proper business of government to continue and allow
> the government to make the case for the outcome that is
> achieved and the vote that we recommend, but that ensure
> that there is not an unfair referendum and that the govern-
> ment do not, for example, engage in mass communication
> with the electorate.

By the time the EU Referendum Bill debate kicked off, both sides
were nicely warmed up for the scrap. Appearing on BBC Radio 4's
World at One that afternoon, John Redwood remarked: 'It would
not be the end of the world if the government were defeated,'
while Bernard Jenkin had already told the BBC: 'I think [minis-
ters have] realised they've opened a bit of a Pandora's Box, they
will be looking for a way to resolve this. But the bottom line is
they should restore purdah in this Referendum Bill.'

Away from the broadcast studios and in the Commons itself, the language was equally as strong.

'Even people on the Yes side should not want their victory to be tainted by the perception of a fix,' said Nadhim Zahawi, Tory MP for Stratford-on-Avon.

Former Defence Secretary Liam Fox told the Commons: 'The fear is that the government at all levels – central and local – could use taxpayers' money to support one side of the debate, potentially changing its course. The precedent that that would set in this country would be extremely unfortunate.' He then added: 'I have not once, in twenty-three years in the House of Commons, voted against my party on a whipped vote. I urge my Right Hon. Friend the Minister for Europe not to force those of us who are in that position to take an alternative course tonight.'

Yet, for all the plotting and griping of the CfB MPs, the actual power to defeat the government did not lie exclusively in their hands, but also in the hands of their Labour rivals across the Commons floor. During Prime Minister's Questions a week earlier, Labour's interim leader Harriet Harman had grilled Cameron over his purdah plans, asking: 'Why are they changing the law to exempt the government from the rules which are there to ensure the government do not inappropriately use public funds or the government machine in the short campaign. Will he think again on this?'

With questioning such as that, the signs looked good for the Tory rebels that Labour would back their amendment and the government would be defeated. But what they didn't realise was how the suspension of purdah was causing just as many splits in the opposition as in their own party. Harman was opposed to Cameron's plan, arguing that the referendum needed to be fair – and that suspending purdah would prevent that. Shadow Europe Minister Pat McFadden was reluctant to do anything that would align Labour with the Tory rebels – many of whom were on the right of the party – and also believed suspending purdah would be necessary for Cameron's government to make the case for In. Shadow Foreign Secretary Hilary Benn, who had quietly supported holding a referendum for years, was in favour of getting the Referendum Bill through Parliament as quickly as possible in order to crack on with the actual campaign. With Harman wanting to join the rebels, McFadden wanting to see purdah lifted and Benn wanting to get on with it, the compromise position of abstaining on the vote was reached at the eleventh hour – shattering Tory rebel hopes of beating the government on purdah.

Speaking from the Despatch Box, McFadden explained why Labour had tabled its own amendment, calling on the government to clarify just what it would seek to do in the run-up to the referendum if purdah was suspended.

Jenkin was baffled, and asked McFadden: 'Why has his party decided not to support Amendment 11, which would reinstate purdah, until he has received those assurances? Why is he letting the government off the hook – or is it part of a Euro-stitch-up to rig the referendum?'

He later added:

> I am deeply disappointed that the Labour Party has abandoned all its principles, but we know that it is split on the matter. On Second Reading, it was in favour of scrapping purdah. At Prime Minister's Questions, it was against scrapping purdah. Last night, Labour Members were going to vote for Amendment 11, but today they are no longer going to do so. I think that they are in a bit of a muddle, and I suspect that quite a few pro-EU Labour Members would like to help to rig the referendum in favour of the Yes campaign.

Even with the backing of the Scottish National Party and a handful of Labour Eurosceptics, there was no chance the government would be defeated. Just twenty-seven Tory MPs rebelled and

backed Cash's amendment – meaning the government won easily: 288 to 97.

That day's battle may have been lost, but the rebels knew they
would have another chance to take on the government when the
Bill came back before Parliament in the autumn. While the margin of their defeat had been great, a rebellion of twenty-seven
just six weeks into a new government was not a good look for
any Prime Minister, and the summer would be spent negotiating
with Lidington, Hammond and Cameron about a compromise
agreement.

But Iain Duncan Smith, who abided by collective responsibility
and backed Cameron despite his own personal misgivings, knew
the government had narrowly got away with it. He warned the
Prime Minister: 'Labour will wake up to the fact that they have
a major defeat of the government on their hands here over this
and they won't mind that at all. What they will discover is if they
put a motion down, then the Conservatives will vote with them.'
Little did he realise that it was his own welfare reforms that would
trigger such an act.

CHAPTER 10

Nigel Farage's view on the purdah battle was simple: 'With this vote on purdah tonight, Tory Eurosceptics have shown themselves to be gutless, spineless and useless,' he tweeted (or rather, he asked someone to tweet on his behalf – Farage did not have a smartphone). A rebellion of just twenty-seven from a party which kept claiming it was full of Eurosceptics left him deeply unimpressed.

It had been nearly three weeks since Farage had met with Matthew Elliott for coffee at Claridge's, and the UKIP leader had been busy. After repeatedly being told by Westminster politicians that he was toxic, divisive and would lose the referendum for the Out side, Farage decided to find out once and for all if that was true. He commissioned a huge opinion poll, surveying 10,000 people, to get a measure of not just his own popularity but that of other figures across the divide as well.

Farage recalls:

> What was clear from that polling was that in June 2015 the most trusted person in the country on whether to Brexit or not to Brexit was David Cameron. His popularity was about 38 per cent at that time. I was second, and Boris [Johnson]

and Theresa [May] were third and fourth. That's where we
were. Nobody else even troubled the scorer.

'The key was: Did I put off the undecideds? No. But even more
crucially: What was the issue that could switch how the undecided
voted? And I think that poll was 36 per cent of them said immigration. Nothing came near.'

The poll confirmed three things for Farage. First, he was not
toxic. 'Yes, I'm hated by the establishment and the Remainers in
an extraordinary way. Just extraordinary,' said Farage. 'But at least
they know what I'm talking about.' Secondly, immigration was
the key issue that could win this referendum for Out – no matter
what the 'posh boys' said. Finally, Cameron could not be allowed
to have a free hand to go and make a deal with Brussels.

> It was absolutely critical not to do what Business for Britain
> wanted to do and what Mr Carswell and Mr Hannan wanted
> to do and say: 'Jolly good, David, off you go.' No, no, no, no. As
> Chris [Bruni-Lowe] said to me: 'If he goes unchallenged and
> brings back a deal, we've lost.' He had just fluked a general elec-
> tion, he was very high in terms of people's rating. Challenging
> the Prime Minister became a really important part of all of this.

While the polling was being carried out, Farage and Chris Bruni-
Lowe climbed aboard the *Queen Elizabeth* cruise ship for the
third annual Midlands Industrial Council jaunt on Saturday
13 June 2015. The three-day trip – leaving from Southampton and
travelling to Guernsey and back – brought together politicians,
campaigners, entertainers and businessmen from the political right. Tory backbenchers including Graham Brady, Daniel
Kawczynski and the recent Cabinet minister Eric Pickles rubbed
shoulders with Lord Ashcroft, General Sir David Richards and
comedian Jim Davidson. Also on board was Matthew Elliott, who

had returned from his honeymoon earlier that week. He was due to address his fellow shipmates on how Business for Britain was maintaining its 'Change or Go' stance ahead of David Cameron's first post-election European summit in Brussels later that month.

As the boat set sail, and with such a concentration of pro-Brexit figures, it didn't take much persuading for Farage to give an impromptu speech. Wearing his Union Jack shoes, the UKIP leader extolled not just the virtues of Brexit, but why the campaign needed to begin immediately. Not everyone on board the boat agreed with Farage, though.

'Daniel Kawczynski, who then voted to Brexit, said: "No, I'm a fanatical stayer-in-er, Nigel, your politics is awful." He kept inter-rupting, saying: "Brexit will make us poorer. I'm Polish, I'll get sent back," and all that stuff. It was a major argument,' remembered Bruni-Lowe.

Farage and his right-hand man were also having great fun working the decks and 'tapping up' people to back Banks's campaign. 'Elliott was freaking out,' said Bruni-Lowe.

Bruni-Lowe and Elliott, who had known each other for more than five years, managed a few private conversations while the boat was sailing across the English Channel. They had a long Eurosceptic history, and the original 'For Britain' company – which was envisaged as the overarching body that would oversee all denominations, such as Business for Britain – was actually created by the pair in 2013. On a flight to America, Elliott and Bruni-Lowe had talked at length about how best to manage a successful Out campaign, and took inspiration from Barack Obama's 'For Obama' brand which had helped him win re-election to the White House in 2012. When Bruni-Lowe and Elliott returned to England, they registered 'For Britain' with Companies House on 20 February 2013. With this shared background, Bruni-Lowe tried to offer Elliott some advice: 'I told him to get Nigel in a room and say, "Nigel, we want to use you and UKIP, we're going to figure out how we can use you in a way that doesn't piss off people but we want to desperately use you."'

Elliott recalls the conversation differently, and was left with the impression that UKIP was already preparing how to exploit a referendum defeat for electoral gain: 'I remember him insisting that the referendum wasn't winnable, blah blah blah, couldn't be done. So my working assumption was basically that UKIP are working out how best to position themselves for after the referendum and do an SNP re-run.'

Bruni-Lowe's response to Elliott's claim was simple: 'That's complete rubbish!'

The *Queen Elizabeth* docked at Guernsey's St Peter Port on Monday 15 June, and Farage and Bruni-Lowe decide to venture further into the island instead of listening to a presentation from the TaxPayers' Alliance. While they were sinking ales in a pub, Elliott showed up, and again the trio began discussing the referendum. Farage repeated his view that immigration was the key, but Elliott remained unconvinced. Peace did not break out in Guernsey.

* * *

The next day, Elliott was back in London trying to hide his bemusement as he looked at Andy Wigmore's business card. He was not expecting the Brexit campaigner opposite him with the big smile to also be a trade commissioner for Belize. At the same time as Elliott was looking at Wigmore's business card, Dominic Cummings was introducing himself to Arron Banks and Richard Tice. Despite having met only a few months before, Banks and Tice were becoming quite the double act. Banks was mischievous and relished courting controversy, whereas Tice was more restrained and focused.

The group were in 55 Tufton Street, the home of Business for Britain, the TaxPayers' Alliance, the Global Warming Policy

Foundation, the European Foundation and Civitas – all right-wing think tanks, all sharing office space under one roof. For Arron Banks – the multi-millionaire who liked to portray himself as anti-establishment – this was very much enemy territory.

They took their seats in the building's front boardroom. It was Tuesday 16 June, the day of the first vote on purdah in the Commons. Sitting around the table, Banks, Tice and the permanently cheerful Wigmore set out not just the work they were already carrying out – branding, research, advertising plans – but also their future plans, which involved spending millions upon millions of pounds. Their operation would be big, in-your-face and impossible to ignore.

The trio were hoping that by demonstrating that they had fired the starting gun on an Out operation, Elliott and Cummings might be motivated to join them in actively campaigning. Despite the many differences between the two groups, Banks, Tice and Wigmore recognised that the very well-connected Elliott and Cummings knew how Westminster worked, had the ear of influential journalists and senior politicians, and would therefore be able to add another dimension to their plans.

But, much to their frustration, Cummings and Elliott stuck to their 'Change or Go' guns. The Prime Minister had to be supported in his renegotiation attempt, and then a decision would be made on whether to campaign to leave.

Banks had been prepared for this – he hadn't really expected anything different. In the hours before the meeting, Chris Bruni-Lowe had called the businessman up to find out what exactly he was hoping to get out of the meeting. For Banks, the meeting had never been about merging, but just an opportunity to get into Elliott's head. Bruni-Lowe and Nigel Farage, however, were both worried that Elliott and Cummings might persuade Banks to pull his operation and adopt their timetable.

'Nigel and I were saying: "Elliott's such a smarmy bastard he may win over Banks,"' said Bruni-Lowe.

I rang Banks on the day and said: 'Don't get won over by Elliott.' He said: 'No, no, no, I'm going to go there and shit him
up basically. I'm going to go there and frighten him and basically say I'm going to outspend you and spend my whole life
terrorising you, effectively.'

The opportunity for Banks to cause carnage came when Cummings
asked the businessman to trust his judgement over how to run
the campaign.

Banks let rip:

> To say it wasn't a meeting of minds would be an under-
> statement. I pointed out to him that I built six businesses
> from scratch and was considerably richer than he was,
> like a Harry Enfield character. His reply was along the
> lines of that he was a genius. I said: 'Well, if you're such
> a genius, why are you a second-rate spad working for
> government?'

With his goal achieved, Banks called Bruni-Lowe to tell him how
the meeting had gone. 'He rang me afterwards and said: "Elliott
was bright red, his fists were on the desk. I've shit him up mas-
sively,"' said Bruni-Lowe.

Elliott and Cummings might have been dragging their feet, but
Farage was still itching to get the campaign going. On Wednesday
17 June – the day after not only the purdah vote but also the first
meeting between Elliott, Cummings, Banks, Tice and Wigmore,
the UKIP leader also tried to fire the starting gun.

At the launch of a pamphlet by UKIP's International Trade
spokesman William Dartmouth in Westminster, Farage attempted
to smoke out other Eurosceptics, claiming there was 'a little bit of
paralysis' in the Out campaign.

Additionally, in what was a change in tone from his Eastbourne speech twelve days earlier, Farage even admitted his own short-comings.

As he put it:

> I'm not for one moment making a bid to say, 'Farage must
> be in charge of everything.' I think it would be better if it
> was someone from outside the world of politics, who had
> no political baggage. When that structure gets set up and
> the official 'No' campaign gets put in place, we will put our
> shoulder to the wheel and make it clear we will work with
> anybody to achieve this goal.

He added: 'As far as my role is concerned, look, not everybody
likes me, I accept that.'

Less than twenty-four hours later, and UKIP's deputy chairman
Suzanne Evans essentially repeated his remarks on the BBC's *Daily
Politics* show in a discussion about who should lead the main Out
campaign, saying:

> Nigel is a very divisive figure in terms of the way he is per-
> ceived. He is not divisive as a person. The way he is perceived
> is having strong views that divide people. In that sense he
> is right [not to take a leading role]. I think it will be some-
> body else that fronts it.

Evans's comments seemed innocent enough, but to Farage and his
allies in UKIP they were regarded as deeply unhelpful. Four hours
later, party director Steve Stanbury sent out a directive essentially
sacking her as a UKIP spokesman – her second dismissal in the
space of a month after having been axed as the party's policy director:

> I have just spoken to Nigel and in light of Suzanne Evans's
> comments on TDP I am issuing this directive.

1. From this moment onwards no one employed by the UKIP press office is to have any further contact with SE.
2. No bids are to be accepted for SE and she is not to be offered as an official UKIP spokesman.
3. No one is to brief SE or advise her on any issue.

Evans was baffled by the email, which was leaked to the BBC, but things took an even stranger turn the next day, when she was 'unsacked'.

'Suzanne Evans has not been sacked as a UKIP spokesman. The email seen by the BBC was issued without proper authority,' read a statement issued by the UKIP press office. The fiasco took place over the same days that the cross-party exploratory committee, the group chaired by Bernard Jenkin every Wednesday, was announced, providing an unfortunate juxtaposition for UKIP: while the party claiming it had the infrastructure and organisation to win the referendum was sacking and unsacking people apparently at random, the politicians in Westminster were getting themselves organised into a functional fighting force. Add into the mix that UKIP's entire press operation was at the moment being run from a Caffè Nero and Bruni-Lowe's flat in Maunsel Street, and the party was hardly screaming out 'professionalism'.

UKIP might have been tearing itself apart, but Banks's 'The Know' operation was going from strength to strength. Advertising campaigns had been drawn up, slogans were created and, most important of all, significant money was lined up to fund it: £20 million, according to the Bristol-based businessman's interview with the *Telegraph* on Sunday 21 June.

Three days after revealing his campaign to the public via the *Telegraph* interview, Banks and Tice invited their Tory and BfB opponents to a special presentation. A boardroom was booked at the Corinthia Hotel on the Embankment, and Tice and Banks brought along the ad agency they had hired to set out their project in glorious technicolour. Owen Paterson and Bernard Jenkin were in attendance, as were Elliott and Cummings, to see how the businessmen envisaged running an Out campaign. Both Tice and Banks were confident the watching MPs and lobbyists would be impressed.

'We had stuff on the side of buses, beer mats, all this stuff. We made this presentation, of course then it was still "In the Know", but it was great – great slogan, with a globe, it was very global, very constructive, forward-looking,' said Tice.

Banks felt his group had stolen a march on Elliott and Cummings – who seemed to him to be doing not much more than giving the Prime Minister a free pass to frame the referendum debate in his own terms. 'We hired an ad agency and we were looking at it from a business point of view. It was clear they hadn't even started,' he said.

While Banks and Tice felt they had presented a winning strategy, those watching were not as enthusiastic. Elliott described the presentation as 'slightly sort of amateur hour', and said:

> I remember the ad agency outlining how they would be doing their campaign, they were saying: 'All these TV ads, they will look great.' I said: 'You do realise you can't do TV ads in the UK?' Similarly they said: 'These are our ideas for ads, they are going to work really well.' Well, what market research has gone into this? What voters is this going to attract?

To Bernard Jenkin, it was 'quite clear they were on a completely different page to us', mainly because they 'didn't understand how toxic to 70 per cent of voters the Farage tone and UKIP tone was'.

Tice was left bemused by the response from Elliott's group: 'We made that presentation and all they were interested in talking about was "Are you going to run for designation?" That's all they wanted to know. Frankly, at that time, we didn't really know much about designation.'

Tice may not have been thinking about designation, but all the other key players involved in setting up an Out campaign certainly were.

In the run-up to the referendum, the Electoral Commission would designate one organisation as the lead campaign group for each side of the argument. As well as the prestige of being the 'official' campaign group, the designated organisation would be entitled to a range of other benefits: a spending limit of £7 million (compared to just £700,000 for any non-lead campaigns); one free distribution of information to voters; referendum campaign broadcasts; and a grant of up to £600,000. It was a sizeable prize, and one which the many Out groups would spend as much time and energy on winning as they did on fighting the referendum itself.

It was at the mention of the word 'designation' that the penny started to drop for Tice about what was really going on – Elliott had no intention of merging his group with The Know. As a businessman used to pooling resources and assets, Tice was shocked. 'It never occurred to us it would be anything else [than a merger]. We're kicking on, they were scrabbling around looking for sixty grand, we had plenty of pledges, we knew we had a quarter of a million.'

Tice added: 'The inference from the politicians who left that room was: "There, there, dear boy, leave it to us. You really don't understand." The patronising exit of the politicians from that meeting was quite a shock.'

Banks felt the response was 'very much "leave the politics to us grown-ups, you don't know what you're doing – you're a businessman"'.

The next day, David Cameron was giving his own presentation in Brussels, which was followed by the leak of the diplomatic note to *The Guardian* outlining his renegotiation plans. With Cameron's seemingly paltry demands now out in the public domain, Farage fully expected Elliott to switch BfB from 'Change or Go' to just 'Go'.

On Monday 13 July, less than three weeks after the Corinthia presentation, Bruni-Lowe and Farage found themselves once again sitting in 55 Tufton Street opposite Elliott and Cummings. Ahead of the meeting, the UKIP duo were feeling confident that BfB was now ready to join the Brexit battle. Once again, they were disappointed.

'Elliott text and said, "We need to meet you urgently,"' remembers Bruni-Lowe. 'Nigel said, "Alright, something's going down." We got there and Elliott said nothing. He just sat there staring at us and saying absolutely nothing. Nigel and I were like, "This guy's fucking weird."'

Farage tried to convince the duo to work with Banks – 'He will make your life a nightmare if you don't,' warned Bruni-Lowe – but Elliott and Cummings would not be bounced, on any issue. They would wait for the renegotiation, they would not make immigration the sole focus of the campaign and Farage would not be a spokesman. Not even the results of the 10,000-strong poll would change their minds; Elliott described the polling as 'bullshit'.

'We came away thinking, what the fuck was that meeting? It was a two-hour meeting about nothing. And that's when Nigel thought, "He's a prick, don't bother, he's a waste of time." We then rang Banks and said, "You've got to go for it, they're doing nothing,"' said Bruni-Lowe.

By the end of July, Farage had had enough. It had been more than a month since Cameron's summit in Brussels, and as far as he could see there was simply no movement from the Tory Eurosceptics. He started to seriously wonder whether they even wanted to win the referendum. During a holiday in Belize with Banks after the 13 July meeting in Tufton Street, Farage spelt out exactly how much money, time and effort would be needed if the campaign was going to be successful. This was effectively

Banks's last chance to back out. 'He said, "In for a penny in for a pound, we've got this referendum, I want to have a real go,"' recalled Farage. The pair looked over some of the 'In the Know' advertising that had already been produced, but Farage felt it was nowhere near up to the standard required. 'I'm sure the marketing teams did well out of it, but it didn't quite tick the box,' said the UKIP leader later.

While the pair were in Central America, Bruni-Lowe decided they needed to 'steal the clothes from Elliott' and launch an Out campaign as soon as possible, focused on immigration. He arranged a press conference in the Emmanuel Centre in Westminster for 30 July.

Banks met with Elliott once more ahead of Farage's big launch – a lunch at the private member's club 5 Hertford Street on Wednesday 22 July – where once again the pair failed to see eye to eye. Tice remembers Banks being a bit upset after the meeting: 'Matthew said to Arron, "I'll take your money but I have total control."'

Elliott claims Banks has 'a different interpretation of the meeting than I do', and all he was actually doing was setting out how the organisation would be run.

> I saw various emails afterwards where it was 'the arrogant Elliott came along and blah blah and demanded he and Dom have sole right to rule the roost over the campaign blah blah with no accountability', whereas in fact what I felt I was saying to him was that basically in any campaign you've got to have a situation where the people running the campaign – the chief exec, campaign director – have control over the day-to-day decision-making. Yes, they can be accountable to a board but basically it shouldn't be the case where somehow the chairman of the board is involved in the day-to-day decision-making.

In any case, Elliott was just going through the motions by attending the meeting: 'That lunch was actually more so I could say to other people that I've been to see him,' he said.

Eight days later, Farage formally announced his intention to tour the country promoting Brexit. Standing in front of a projected image with the slogan 'Say No – Believe in Britain' at a press conference in the Emmanuel Centre in Westminster, he let rip at the inertia of the No to the EU campaign.

After saying there was 'no doubt at all the Yes side are in the lead' – and name-checking the pro-EU boo boys of Richard Branson, Ken Clarke, Tony Blair and even Barack Obama – Farage said:

> Given all of this, what of the No side? Well, they've gone to ground. Those who in some cases have been calling for twenty years for a fundamental change in Britain's relationship with the European Union have decided to stand aside, to wait and see, not to snipe at the Prime Minister and to wish him well with his renegotiations.

He added: 'Quite why these Eurosceptics in the Tory Party have decided to say and do nothing, I don't know.'

Reflecting the result of his mass polling, Farage claimed that 'the overwhelming, major point that the British public want to see renegotiated is of course the question of open borders'.

And then came the kicker – the announcement Elliott, Cummings, Hannan and Carswell were dreading:

> In the absence of anybody else, UKIP is going to take the lead in this country and we are going to launch in September a major ground campaign. We are going to launch in the first week of September the biggest public outreach programme this party has ever attempted.

> I want to make this clear: I will, and we will, share platforms,
> work and campaign with anybody out there in the Eurosceptic
> movement. You'll hear no negativity from us once they've got
> off their backsides and decided to join this fight.

Farage followed it up by stating that the ground campaign was not 'some dramatic bid by me or others in this room to think that UKIP will get the official designation for the No campaign … We won't, and we won't be applying. What we will do is play our part in this campaign.'

It didn't matter whether UKIP would applying as an independent entity to get the designation – it would be almost impossible for a political party on its own to meet the Electoral Commission criteria – but what was more concerning to those in Tufton Street was whether Farage and UKIP would formally throw their lot in with Banks's The Know campaign – and who else they would be able to persuade to join them.

CHAPTER 11

Harriet Harman was bruised. All summer, her decision to order Labour MPs to abstain on the Second Reading of government's Welfare Bill had been used as a stick to beat her with. It even hung over the Labour leadership contest, with party members using hustings to demand to know why three of the four candidates – Andy Burnham, Yvette Cooper and Liz Kendall – had not voted against a Bill which would cut tax credits and reduce the welfare cap. For Harman, one of the lessons from Labour's general election defeat was that the public wanted to see a much tighter control on welfare payments. Refusing to vote against the proposals would, Harman felt, show the electorate the party was listening. The decision provoked uproar on Labour benches, and forty-eight Labour MPs, including the fourth leadership candidate, Jeremy Corbyn, defied the whip and voted against the government on 20 July 2015.

Within a month, Harman had told *The Guardian* she 'probably would' oppose it if she had the chance again, but the damage was done. Burnham, who started out as the favourite to win that summer's Labour leadership contest, went on to claim that his decision to stick by collective responsibility and abstain was the 'turning point' in his campaign.

'If I had resigned, I might have won the contest there and then,' he told *The Independent* on 2 September.

As it was, by the time the Third Reading of the EU Referendum Bill came around on 7 September, Harman was desperate to get a win under her belt – and the purdah row would give it to her.

In the run-up to the vote, David Cameron and his team were in desperate negotiations with the Tory Eurosceptic rebels to try to avoid a defeat. On Wednesday 2 September, Europe Minister David Lidington spent the day negotiating with Tory rebels and Labour over what changes could be made to the Bill. There had already been one retreat, with Cameron agreeing to change the referendum question from 'Should the United Kingdom remain a member of the European Union?' to the form recommended by the Electoral Commission: 'Should the United Kingdom remain a member of the European Union or leave the European Union?' Polling showed the alteration favoured the Out/Leave side. Another compromise then came when Cameron agreed there would be a period of purdah, albeit a watered-down version. This was a huge change from his position in June. Yet, while this new version of purdah would stop the government using taxpayers' money to pump out pro-EU propaganda, it wouldn't completely bar ministers from speaking out in favour of the UK's membership in certain areas. This was soon dubbed the 'skimmed' version of purdah, not the 'full-fat' provision normally used before votes.

Despite having had the whole summer to come to an agreement, the government left it to the eleventh hour – only tabling the new amendments to the Bill fifteen minutes before the deadline. Speaking to the *Telegraph*, Steve Baker said:

> The exceptionally late tabling of these amendments has created a wholly unnecessary period of high political drama. We would have liked to see these amendments hours, days, or weeks ago but their tabling at 16.15 – just fifteen minutes before the deadline – left us with little option but to work in the dark.

On Monday 7 September, having had the weekend to go through the amendments with a fine-tooth comb, the Conservatives for Britain high guard – Baker, Owen Paterson and Bernard Jenkin – gathered in a meeting room on the first floor of Portcullis House. They had already won some concessions, but as far as they were concerned the government was still trying to pull a fast one. 'I am absolutely clear – we want purdah,' said Paterson after the meeting. Baker, along with 1922 chairman Graham Brady, went off to meet Lidington to inform him the rebellion was still on.

As the Tory rebels were pressing Lidington to give more ground, the Labour leadership were also working on defeating the government. One of Harman's closest advisors, Ayesha Hazarika, was determined to see the reputation of her boss restored after the Welfare Bill debacle, and pushed for Labour to team up with the Eurosceptics to defeat the government. But instead of supporting a Tory rebel amendment, Labour would table its own change to the Bill, calling for the reintroduction of full-fat purdah. Labour would beat the government on its own terms.

At just before 6.30 p.m., after holding meetings with the rebels right up to the wire, Lidington took to the Despatch Box in the Commons. He set out the main concession: no pro-Remain government spending in the last twenty-eight days of the campaign. 'There should be no question of the government undertaking any paid advertising or promotion, such as billboards, door drops, leafleting, or newspaper or digital advertising during that period,' he said.

Jenkin was on his feet almost immediately. 'What is the exact meaning of what the Minister is saying?' he asked, before setting out the full-fat version of purdah. 'Do the government accept that position?' Jenkin asked.

Lidington was hardly allowed to give his answer, explaining exactly what definition of purdah the government was looking for, before pro-Brexit Tory backbencher Cheryl Gillan intervened.

'Why are the government changing the playing field and insisting on modifications to something that has worked well and that they have used in the past?' she asked.

The interventions kept on coming: Sir Bill Cash, Sir Edward Leigh, Peter Bone, Philip Davies, Steve Baker and others all took to their feet to grill the Minister for Europe – who politely and with great patience took all their interventions.

After nearly forty-five minutes of arguing with his own back-benchers about what the government could and could not do during skimmed purdah, Lidington offered up another compromise. One of the amendments tabled by Jenkin required the government to give four months' notice before the date of a referendum. This would stop Cameron from being able to call a snap vote amid any honeymoon period after securing a deal with Brussels.

Lidington announced:

> Having thought long and hard about the matter and discussed it with colleagues, I have concluded that, largely in the interests of trying to secure as great a consensus as possible, we will accept Amendment (a). As I have said, I think that a firm time limit of that type has drawbacks, but, in the interests of bridge-building – and paying due respect to the recommendation of a cross-party Select Committee – I am prepared to accept the amendment on the government's behalf.

It was another huge victory for the rebels. The question change, an assurance the government wouldn't produce pro-EU propaganda twenty-eight days ahead of a vote and a snap election ruled out – all achieved by Conservatives for Britain.

But the MPs wanted more. After thanking Lidington for accepting the four-month rule, Jenkin urged his colleagues to vote down the government's purdah amendment, and back Labour's instead. 'While I think the government have conceded the principle that there should be purdah, they have not accepted the fact of how it will apply,' he said, after claiming he was 'very reluctantly' calling for his own party's defeat.

At 9.18 p.m. – after almost three hours of debate – the vote was called on the government's skimmed purdah amendment. Boris Johnson, who had been lurking behind the Speaker's Chair during the end of the debate, joined a tie-less David Cameron in the Aye lobby, while an equally tie-less Jeremy Corbyn filed into the No lobby with his Labour colleagues.

After the MPs had voted, they took their places on the green leather benches, the smell of beer emanating from some of them who had chosen to socialise in Strangers' Bar instead of attend the debate. At 9.32 p.m., Speaker John Bercow called the noisy Commons to order, and the four MPs acting as tellers – Labour MPs Tom Blenkinsop and Nic Dakin for the Noes, Tory MPs George Hollingbery and Margot James for Ayes – approached the bench to reveal whether the government had been defeated.

Reading from a piece of paper, Dakin said: 'The Ayes to the right: 285. The Noes to left: 312.' Defeat. The rebels had won by twenty-seven votes. A muted cheer went up from the MPs. They had defeated their own Prime Minister, but didn't want to appear too ungracious in the process. While skimmed purdah was dead, Labour's full-fat amendment still needed to be voted on. Pat McFadden formally moved the amendment for Labour, but when Bercow asked for objections from the government – someone needed to shout 'no' to trigger a proper vote – there was silence. Lidington, seated just along from Foreign Secretary Philip Hammond, stayed quiet. There was no point contesting the inevitable – and why allow Labour MPs to have the glory of cheering yet another lost vote by the government? With no challenge, the amendment passed. MPs on Labour's front bench looked round

at each other, not quite believing the government had given in
so easily.

Harman had her victory, Tory Eurosceptics had their purdah,
and Cameron had changed the referendum question, lost the ability to call a snap election and would no longer be able to use the
machinery of government to push for a Remain vote.

Conservatives for Britain had achieved everything it had set
out to do.

CHAPTER 12

'The people united will never be defeated! The people united will never be defeated!' The chant kept on going, round and round, the volume occasionally dipping before being flung up again like a plastic bag in the wind.

Many of the people repeating the slogan were wearing bright-red T-shirts with the words 'Jeremy Corbyn' emblazoned on the front in white letters. They were facing the Queen Elizabeth II Conference Centre in Westminster, making themselves heard as Labour Party MPs and members entered the building.

To the right of the centre's entrance stood a group of young people wearing cloth flat caps in homage to the man who was about to be announced as Labour's new leader. It was Saturday 12 September, and after a gruelling three months of speeches, rallies and hustings, the leadership contest was over.

Inside the building, waiting for the announcement, were John Mills and Brendan Chilton. Like the leadership contenders, the pair had had a busy summer. Mills had been working with Elliott on getting what would become Vote Leave ready to go as soon as the terms of the Prime Minister's negotiation became clear. Chilton had also been liaising with Elliott, and while drawing up plans for how Labour for Britain would operate within the For Britain family, he met Dominic Cummings for the first time.

Chilton recalls:

> It was in a meeting in Matthew's flat during the summer when
> we were coming up with the broad ideas for the campaign.
> It was a very comfortable meeting and we had some lunch
> and some light drinks and we were just discussing the general
> themes, what needed to be achieved by when, who was going
> to be responsible for what, all this kind of stuff. Dominic
> arrived a little bit late, I think he'd been at another meeting,
> and just sat at the end of the table and didn't say anything. For
> a second I thought, who the hell are you? And we all chatted
> and got on and as I say I don't recall him saying an awful lot
> at that meeting, just 'Hi, I'm Dominic' and that was it.

Despite Cummings's apparent lack of enthusiasm, Chilton was in
a positive mood with regards to the campaign. The Conservatives
for Britain MPs had worked their magic in Parliament and won
a slew of concessions, and it seemed as if the cross-party activity
was bearing real fruit. But there was another reason Chilton was
upbeat. The man about to be announced as Labour leader was a
confirmed Eurosceptic, who had spent more than thirty years
making the left-wing case for the UK to leave the European club.
He hadn't shied away from expressing his views during the campaign, either. At a leadership hustings in Warrington on 25 July,
Corbyn was the only Labour leader to say he was prepared to vote
Out in the referendum:

> No, I wouldn't rule it out... Because Cameron quite clearly
> follows an agenda which is about trading away workers'
> rights, is about trading away environmental protection, is
> about trading away much of what is in the Social Chapter.
> The EU also knowingly, deliberately, maintains a number
> of tax havens and tax evasion posts around the Continent

– Luxembourg, Monaco and a number of others – and has this strange relationship with Switzerland which allows a lot of European companies to outsource their profits to Switzerland, where tax rates are very low. I think we should be making demands: universal workers' rights, universal environmental protection, end the race to the bottom on corporate taxation, end the race to the bottom in working wage protection. And I think we should be making those demands and negotiating on those demands rather than saying blanketly we're going to support whatever Cameron comes out with in one, two years' time, whenever he finally decides to hold this referendum.

Not since Bryan Gould stood against John Smith in 1992 had such a critic of the European Union been on the Labour leadership ballot.

In the conference centre, Mills and Chilton waited for confirmation that Corbyn had won the contest. He had been leading in all the opinion polls since the beginning of August, and the only question to be settled was just how big his victory would be.

The returning officer ran through the votes for each candidate to polite applause, but when he reached Corbyn's total, cheers broke out before he could finish the whole number. He only got as far as 'Two hundred and fifty-one thousand...' before being drowned out. As Corbyn's supporters inside the room chanted, 'Jez, we did! Jez, we did!' Chilton and Mills flashed big grins at each other. 'For the first time in about thirty years we've got a Brexit leader of the Labour Party,' Chilton said to Mills as the pair escaped the celebrations and left the centre. After turning right out of the doors and then right again, they arrived at the Westminster Arms pub, where they sat down and ordered two cups of tea to celebrate. 'We were elated,' said Chilton. 'We thought it was marvellous.'

Chilton was hopeful there would now be a genuine discussion within the party as to what its EU position would be. Even if the party remained neutral – in order to balance the Eurosceptic views of its leader and a handful of backbenchers with the majority of Europhile members – it would be a tremendous achievement for the Leavers. During the leadership contest, Corbyn had even suggested a special Labour conference should take place once Cameron had completed his renegotiation in order to fully debate the party's referendum position.

The elation lasted two days. On Monday 14 September, shadow Foreign Secretary Hilary Benn took to the airwaves to declare Labour would still be calling for a Remain vote. 'We will be campaigning, and are campaigning now, for Britain to remain part of the EU', he told BBC Radio 4's *Today* programme, 'under all circumstances.'

Benn added: 'Jeremy has made it very clear we are going to stay to fight together for a better Europe.'

The night before, as Corbyn invited Benn to join his shadow Cabinet as shadow Foreign Secretary, the Leeds Central MP had set out the areas of difference he had with the new leader, including over the EU. According to a Labour source, Corbyn assured him that wouldn't be a problem.

Hours after Benn's comments on Radio 4, Kelvin Hopkins was attending a fringe meeting at the TUC's annual conference in Brighton. Hopkins, who had nominated Corbyn for leader, addressed an anti-EU meeting in a hotel on the seafront, and would be rushing back to London as soon as the event finished. When told about Benn's Radio 4 interview, Hopkins said, 'I'm surprised at Hilary Benn's comments. I just wonder if that's been cleared with the new leader of the Labour Party, because obviously there's going to be a battle between the Euro-enthusiasts and those who take a more sceptical position.'

He added:

Was his script approved? I don't know if it was – or was he speaking for himself? I think there's a lot of people even in the Parliamentary Labour Party who would be uncomfortable about that. They don't want to take that kind of hard line. I will be asking when I get back to Parliament who allowed Hilary to go and say that.

After the meeting, he went further, saying Benn 'has taken advantage of this situation', and adding:

I'm going to write to him [Corbyn] and say I think the best position he can take is we're not going to have a firm line, we're going to leave it to individual unions, working members and MPs to take their own view – do a Harold Wilson, if you like. That's the only position he can take because I think otherwise it's going to be electorally very damaging.

Any notion that Benn had been speaking out of turn was well and truly dismissed two days later. On Wednesday 16 September, while the Labour for Britain group were holding their regular post-PMQs get-together, Corbyn was also having a meeting discussing the EU.

Hilary Benn, shadow Chancellor John McDonnell, shadow Business Secretary Angela Eagle and a number of advisors gathered together to solidify the party's EU referendum position. Corbyn arrived last, buzzing after his first PMQs. One person in the room recalls the Labour leader was acting in a 'pretty arrogant' manner, believing his tactic of reading out emails from the public had bamboozled the Prime Minister. Corbyn sat down, put his arm across the back of a chair and listened to the discussion. McDonnell was clear – the Prime Minister should not get a free hand in the negotiations. The main concern centred on the protections for workers provided by the EU, and McDonnell was fearful

Cameron would be willing to trade some of these away in order to pander to Eurosceptics on the Tory right. Others in the room knew this wouldn't happen. Not only had they had assurances through back-channels that this was not part of the negotiating strategy, from a purely political standpoint it made no sense. If Cameron wanted to win the referendum, weakening the rights of millions of workers was hardly the way to convince people to back his deal. It was then suggested by McDonnell that the party should take no position, but this too was dismissed – with Benn particularly vocal about the need for the Labour Party to campaign for Remain.

Corbyn seemed to take very little persuading, and it was agreed that a briefing note should be sent to MPs as soon as possible to put to bed any rumours that Labour would not be supporting Remain. Distributed on Friday 18 September, and headed up 'From the Offices of Jeremy Corbyn, Leader of the Opposition and Hilary Benn, Shadow Foreign Secretary', the note began:

> Labour will be campaigning in the referendum for the UK to stay in the European Union. We will make the case that membership of the European Union helps Britain to create jobs, secure growth, encourage investment and enhances our security and influence in the world.
>
> We will, of course, oppose any attempt by the Tory government to undermine workers' rights. But Labour is clear that the answer to any damaging changes that David Cameron brings back from his renegotiation is not to leave the European Union but to pledge to reverse any changes by campaigning to stay in and get a Labour government elected in 2020.
>
> Labour wants to see change in Europe and we will make the case through the EPLP, our relationships with sister social democratic parties and by engaging with other EU countries.

The note was unequivocal. The only small crumb of comfort for Labour's Eurosceptic MPs was that they would not be whipped to vote for Remain – not that it would have made the slightest difference to how they cast their ballot anyway. Besides, it was a private vote, so the party would have no way of knowing which box was crossed when an MP got into the polling booth. Theoretically, Corbyn himself could stay true to his Eurosceptic beliefs and vote Leave and no one would ever know.

With the issue put to bed, the debate on the EU referendum at Labour's annual conference later that month was a formality. Hilary Benn, Alan Johnson, Pat McFadden and MEP Glenis Willmott all took to the stage in Brighton on Monday 28 September to spell out why the UK should remain in the EU. The resolution to campaign to stay in the EU was passed without the smallest hint of dissent from conference delegates.

'We did feel slightly disappointed in Jeremy, because it was as though he had gone back on a lifetime's work. In every other school he had stayed on the Bennite wing of the party apart from this issue,' said Chilton.

Labour-supporting Eurosceptics may have been feeling let down by Corbyn in the early days of his leadership, but by the time the campaign was in full swing, they would be positively delighted that the friend of the late Tony Benn was in charge of the party.

CHAPTER 13

T hroughout the summer, UKIP set about finalising the details of Farage's 'Say No to the EU' tour. Venues were booked in Kent, Belfast, Essex, Gateshead, Swansea, Chester, London, Leeds, Bolton, Redruth and Wolverhampton.

Although a complete technophobe himself, Farage wanted to harness the power of social media, and made sure the tour was broadcast on the internet – after all, it was through his European Parliament speeches being viewed on YouTube that he had picked up a swathe of supporters. 'Let's do it properly, let's live stream, let's do the stuff no one's ever done in politics before, let's ramp up social media, let's go for it,' he said.

Banks was also on manoeuvres, and completed the hiring of US referendum expert Gerry Gunster as an advisor. He had originally asked the company owned by David Cameron's election guru Lynton Crosby to run his Out campaign – a service for which he was prepared to pay £2 million. Banks claimed Crosby Textor 'thought about it for about five days' before declining. As well as hiring from outside, Banks also moved people across from other businesses in his portfolio. Liz Bilney, who was chief executive at one of Banks's insurance companies, was asked to do the same job at The Know. A call centre was created in Bristol, where up to sixty staff were employed to cold-call the most Eurosceptic areas of the country to establish a list of who to target with advertising, and also who they needed to get out to vote on referendum day itself.

Banks also kept up the psychological warfare on Elliott and Cummings. He offered Cummings £250,000 to quit Elliott's organisation and be campaign director at The Know. Cummings declined, but Banks felt it 'confused him for a bit'. The business-man then tried to make Elliott panic by reminding him just how much money he had at his disposal. Calling him from his Bristol country house, Banks told Elliott: 'We've raised £10 million, we've got commitment for another £10 million, we don't care what you do, we just want to run our campaign, but we think it would be better to merge the two together.' Elliott declined the offer, but Banks felt the call 'did seriously spook him'.

While Banks was enjoying playing with the minds of his campaign rivals, Tice was working on bringing the campaigns together. While on holiday in Tuscany on 9 August, and after a few measures of limoncello, he sat down at his laptop and spent two hours drafting an email formally proposing the campaigns should merge.

Addressed to 'Matthew and Dominic', the email began: 'The Out campaign needs to be the biggest ever in order to tap into such a wide target audience, from so many different walks of life, with different messaging to capture different groups. There are many differences to what has been done before by you and others.'

After talking up the role technology would play in the referen-dum ('Our Facebook page numbers are currently going through the roof,' he wrote), Tice warned that the donors putting up the money for the Out campaign 'want to be much more involved to ensure success'.

He went on: 'We can and must destroy the opposition but this needs: 1) an awesome alliance of skills and 2) putting self-interest aside for the sake of the country.'

Tice then set out his blueprint: Elliott and Cummings would be responsible for 'corporate and political activities/research', while Andy Wigmore would be head of media and given the title 'communications director of The Know.eu'. Liz Bilney – or 'AN Other' – would be CEO and there would be an 'executive board of big donors (8–12) who would meet once or twice monthly in person / video con / conf call to approve progress'. Banks was suggested as chair of this board – possibly in conjunction with John Mills.

Tice signed off with: 'Are you around week of 17th to meet and discuss? If we could agree in August it could be a reality in September.'

Reflecting on his proposal, Tice said: 'Matthew and Dominic should do the politicians, the Westminster bubble, SW1 and we would run the ground campaign and social media. Quite straightforward, play to your strengths, bang.'

On Wednesday 19 August, Tice, Banks, Elliott and Cummings met to discuss the email at the Taj Hotel near St James's Park. It may have been a different venue from their other meetings, but the result was the same: no merger. Tice was now reaching the same conclusion that Farage and Banks had already come to: as long as Cummings and Elliott were in charge of the rival Out campaign, there would be no joining of forces.

On 1 September, all the marketing, advertising and brand-building that had been taking place since May was turned on its head when the referendum question was changed. After pressure from the Electoral Commission and Eurosceptic MPs, Downing Street had agreed to alter the question from 'Should the United Kingdom remain a member of the European Union?' – which would have given yes/no options – to 'Should the United Kingdom remain a member of the European Union or leave the European Union?' – with remain/leave being the choices on the ballot paper. As a result of the change, The Know became Leave.EU on 23 September.

Farage kicked off his 'Say No to the EU' tour in the Winter

Gardens at Margate on Monday 7 September. He was back at the same venue where four months earlier he – along with the rest of the country – had discovered he had failed to become an MP at the seventh attempt. 'It would have been nice, of course, if I could have been stood here this evening speaking to you as an MP,' Farage told the audience, 'but that wasn't to happen.'

It was a nice line, but it did not entirely reflect Farage's real feelings about that election defeat. 'I began to view it as a blessing,' he said later. 'Can you imagine if I hadn't attended 70 per cent of votes in the House of Commons because I was travelling round the country? It would have been very difficult.'

The tour moved on to Belfast, and then to Essex, and it was there, in the town of Grays, on 17 September, that Farage learned Labour leader Jeremy Corbyn had confirmed his party would be campaigning to remain in the EU regardless of Cameron's renegotiation.

'The man of principle appears to have been bullied within a few days of winning the Labour leadership,' said Farage on the day. He added: 'It's an abject surrender. It might do him a lot more harm than he realises.'

With the tour ticking over nicely, the party's civil war seemingly over and even new offices being lined up in Westminster, thoughts turned to the annual conference scheduled to be held in Doncaster at the end of the month. With the date of the referendum still unknown – and it therefore being entirely possible that it could be called within a year – it was conceivable that this could be the last mass gathering of UKIP foot soldiers ahead of the most important vote in the party's history. For Farage, there was just one problem – what should his speech focus on? It would of course be about the referendum, and contain morale-boosting sentiments to inspire and motivate the UKIP membership, but that wouldn't be enough. It needed to have something that would move the campaign on a notch, and further highlight that while

Farage was actively campaigning, Matthew Elliott and Dominic Cummings were dragging their feet.

'The UKIP conference was coming up and Nigel and I were saying we've got literally nothing to say. What's the story?' his advisor Chris Bruni-Lowe remembers.

Salvation came in the form of Dominic Cummings. Ever since he had posted a blog on 23 June floating the idea of a second referendum, it had been publicly mulled over by many sitting on the EU fence – including Boris Johnson.

Farage felt the plan was ludicrous. His strategy was to get a high turnout in as many places as possible, and talk of a second referendum could provoke apathy. Farage wanted people to think this would be the only chance they would get to take Britain out of the EU, as that would drive up turnout. Shooting down the two-referendum strategy would be the first focal point of the speech.

The second was for UKIP to finally endorse Banks's Leave.EU campaign. Not only that, a range of other Eurosceptic outfits, from the Bruges Group to the Democracy Movement, would also break cover and back Leave.EU. The combination of UKIP's 40,000-strong activist base and the backing of Eurosceptic groups that drew support from across the political spectrum – the Bruges Group was chaired by former Tory MP and Maastricht rebel Barry Legg – would seriously strengthen the chances of Banks's organisation winning the official designation.

With the decision made, Farage decided to tell hardly anyone of his plans: not even the most trusted of UKIP's MEPs knew. UKIP may be an unconventional political party in many respects, but when it came to leaking to the media, it was right up there with the Tories and Labour. 'I've learnt. I can keep my own secrets,' said Farage.

The conference was booked in for 25–26 September at the Doncaster Racecourse, the same venue where, a year earlier, Farage had unveiled Tory defector Mark Reckless. Douglas Carswell was due to speak on the second day of the conference, but arrived in the South Yorkshire town to hear his leader's speech at noon on the opening day.

Also in attendance was Robert Oxley, a former TaxPayers' Alliance spokesman who had followed Elliott across to Business for Britain. He had been invited to the conference by UKIP, as had Elliott, who – despite being invited to address delegates from the stage – declined to make an appearance.

Farage says now: 'God, what a torturous process that was, toing and froing for a fortnight with Elliott and with Business for Britain. They refused. Why? Because they weren't even committed to leaving the European Union and they weren't challenging Dave on the renegotiation, so I thought "Let's move this along."'

Gawain Towler, UKIP's head of press, remembered being put under pressure from Elliott and Hannan – two people he had known since the late '90s through working in the European Parliament – to persuade Farage not to set the Leave campaign going at the conference:

> At that point I was having Hannan, I was having Matt, I was having others, saying, 'Gawain, Gawain, Gawain, what are you doing? Why are you forcing us to make a decision?' I will tell you why we're forcing you to make a bloody decision, because on the front page of your website you say you don't know. We have to start fighting this. Our attitude was that we're going to have to bounce the buggers because if they waited until a time of Cameron's choosing, we would lose. We knew that would be an interesting decision and we knew that Arron was going to say and do things that we wouldn't necessarily approve of.

UKIP activists were in good spirits. Farage's unresignation was in the past, the infighting at the top of the party seemed to have died down and the disappointment at not having an electoral breakthrough in the general election was replaced with a fervent desire to get cracking on the referendum campaign. Farage even met for the first time the woman who had got a picture of his face tattooed on her arm, which he duly signed. Farage told Breitbart London: 'I'm stunned, and somewhat flattered, that anyone would defile their body for me.'

Moments before his keynote speech, Farage met with Carswell – the party's only MP since Reckless had lost his seat in May – and had a brief conversation. However, the UKIP leader did not reveal what he was planning to announce.

Farage took to the stage, located inside the racecourse's main stand, to rapturous applause. After spending fifteen minutes talking about his unresignation, Cameron's renegotiation and Corbyn's about-turn on the EU, he moved on to the second referendum.

He started by attacking the 'soft Eurosceptic posh Tories who think they should lead the referendum campaign', then went on:

> There are some, as I would call them, 'soft Eurosceptics' who have suggested our best policy is to stand still and let Dave do his negotiation and see what he comes back with, and then to make our minds up.
>
> There are even some soft Eurosceptics who think we should be pushing for a two-referendum strategy, that we should vote to Leave in order to renegotiate a better deal. My message to those people is: you are fundamentally wrong.

Farage then went on to make his big reveal. After praising Banks and his colleagues for 'putting their hands in their pockets', embracing social media and having 'absolutely no personal political ambitions of their own at all', he set out UKIP's endorsement:

> There has been speculation about which group will get the official designation for the 'leave the EU' campaign. But as

I see it at the moment there is only one group that has set up an umbrella and is absolutely clear what it stands for. UKIP will now stand hand in hand with Leave.EU. We will work together as a united force of all the Eurosceptic groups that want to leave the EU. We are together, we are united and I believe that the tide has turned.

Watching from the back of the room, Carswell was taken aback. 'At no point had anyone discussed this with me,' he said. 'I'm thinking: "That's nice to know!"'

This was a serious problem for Carswell. He had hoped to make the party adopt a neutral position until the Electoral Commission ruled on who would be the official campaign, and then fall in behind whichever group received the designation. For him, that had to be Elliott's group.

Worse still, Banks had already been briefing journalists that Carswell could be kicked out of the party if he didn't switch his backing from Business for Britain to Leave.EU.

'Whoever UKIP decide to endorse, it will be hard for the Electoral Commission to say no to that and Carswell will either have to leave or do the same,' he told *The Guardian*. 'If it comes to the crunch, the whip will be removed from him or something else will happen.'

Minutes after Farage's speech finished, Carswell was giving an interview to Lucy Fisher of *The Times* in a corridor on the second floor of the racecourse stand when Banks brushed past him. Carswell took his opportunity to confront him: 'Who do you think you are, trying to encourage the party to deselect me if I don't support you?' Banks snapped back: 'Why are you attacking me?' before storming off. Within minutes, the conference was awash with talk of the confrontation between UKIP's only MP and its biggest donor.

In a press briefing later that afternoon, Farage dismissed Carswell's support for Business for Britain as being a result of his 'residual loyalty to his old friends in the Conservative Party'. He said Banks had no 'official position' within UKIP, and so the talk of deselecting the Clacton MP was nonsense. 'If Banks has no official position in UKIP, why is he standing behind you in this press conference?' asked Buzzfeed's Jim Waterson. When asked why he wasn't giving his support to Elliott and the Business for Britain campaign, Farage was blunt. After describing them as running a 'talking shop in Tufton Street', he said:

> The fact is Mr Elliott's group do not advocate leaving the European Union. They might do one day. It's a bit like John Redwood, who has been a Eurosceptic for twenty five years, who says we must wait to see what Dave comes back with. Our view is that is absolutely hopeless and allows the Prime Minister to set his agenda. It is wholly unacceptable.

After the press conference, Banks decided to get the last word in with regards to his row with Carswell. Speaking to the author and Waterson once Farage and the rest of the press pack had made their way downstairs, Banks let rip: 'He is borderline autistic with mental illness wrapped in.' Standing next to him, his advisor Andy Wigmore urged Banks to say the comments were off the record, but Banks refused. Waterson and the author sprinted down to the press room to file the copy, knowing Banks's comments would cause huge controversy. Yet, before either journalist could hit publish, Banks appeared in the press room, walked over to reporters from Sky and ITV, and repeated the insult without the slightest provocation. He was clearly not backing away.

By 5.30 p.m., the comments were out on Twitter and published on the Huffington Post and Buzzfeed sites. Farage was furious. Just five hours earlier he had been talking up Banks, telling his party and the country that Banks was someone he could do business with. Now, he had made a comment that would potentially overshadow the whole conference. The parallel with UKIP's 2013 conference – in which then MEP Godfrey Bloom branded a roomful of women 'sluts' and then hit reporter Michael Crick with a copy of the event's programme – were stark.

The UKIP leader summoned Banks into a room and tore into him. 'Nigel gave me a forty-minute lecture about how you shouldn't insult people personally in politics – he gave me an absolute bollocking,' said Banks. The businessman did try to point out that earlier that day Farage had lambasted Labour leader Jeremy Corbyn as 'a vegetarian teetotaller who rides a bicycle, has got a beard and comes from north London'.

'What about not making personal comments?' said Banks.

'Not the same, not the same,' replied Farage.

'Jeremy Corbyn's not in my party,' Farage said later, remembering the exchange. 'What I said about him was absolutely factually right. Whether what he said about Carswell was factually right is, I would suggest, a matter of conjecture.'

At just after 6 p.m., an apology was issued by Banks: 'Douglas Carswell was appallingly rude and provocative towards me today, which does not justify my comments, for which I apologise.'

Carswell was understandably shocked, but stuck to his upbeat persona. 'I feel there's a tremendous place for me in UKIP,' he said when asked if the day's events would lead to him quitting the party. 'I have never had such fun as I have had [in UKIP].'

The Carswell/Banks row may have grabbed the headlines, but another article posted online that day did just as much damage to the relations between UKIP and Business for Britain. Michael White, *The Guardian*'s former political editor who now acted as an associate editor for the paper, was at the conference, on sketch-writing duties. At 5.46 p.m. – the same moment Banks was getting a 'bollocking' from Farage – he posted his take on the day's events online. It was the article's third paragraph which caused fury in the UKIP ranks: 'In the conference corridors UKIP's

Eurosceptic rivals in Business for Britain were quietly badmouth-
ing Toxic Nigel as the kind of overambitious, political egomaniac
who had weakened the Brexit movement in the past and might
do so again.'

It was that phrase again: 'Toxic Nigel'. The phrase Farage had spent
vast sums of money trying to prove wrong with extensive polling.
The phrase nearly four million votes at a general election couldn't
nullify. The phrase that, if repeated often enough, might convince donors and high-profile Eurosceptics not to back Leave.EU
due to its association with the UKIP leader.

Gawain Towler was particularly angry, and pointed the finger
squarely at Robert Oxley. He was, thanks to Elliott's no-show, the
only person from Business for Britain at the conference.

'Lie. Total lie,' said Oxley later. '[That accusation] always
annoyed me as I've never spoken to Michael White about UKIP.'

Towler was not convinced, and later said: 'Sorry, Michael White
doesn't make shit up. There they were, invited to our conference,
drinking our free wine, doing this, that and the other, going to
journalists, telling them we were toxic.'

Bruni-Lowe was equally shocked by the article. 'That was the
moment when we turned nuclear on the other side,' he said.

On the second day of the conference, Carswell was set to deliver
a speech on electoral reform. Although he had sent advance cop-
ies of his address to the UKIP top brass, there was a genuine fear
he might use his platform to attack Banks. UKIP press officers
watched nervously as Carswell spoke for about twenty minutes
from the podium, but the fears proved unwarranted as the Clacton
MP stuck rigidly to his script.

He ended with a rallying call for togetherness:

> We must put our country first. This isn't a case of who's going
> to win democratic elections; this is about whether we remain
> a self-governing democracy at all.

We must be prepared to work with anyone: left or right,
politician or undecided, all backgrounds, all faiths, all colours,
all people. There are good, honourable, patriotic members
of all parties: we must work with them all.

It's not enough to win by offering opposition to Brussels;
our challenge is to show how Britain can prosper outside
the EU. It's an enormous honour to have joined UKIP a year
ago. I made many friends and have been incredibly warmly
welcomed.

Together we have got an enormous referendum battle
ahead; let everything that we do be about winning it, let's do it.

Carswell's focus had always been on winning the referendum.
Everyone in the room, including Farage, believed that was why he
had joined UKIP from the Tories in 2014. While they were right
about Carswell's ultimate goal, none of them knew the real reason
he had defected to the party. It was all part of a plan concocted by
the Tory 'posh boys' so hated by Farage in an art gallery on the
banks of the Thames, with roots stretching back to before David
Cameron ever agreed to hold a referendum.

CHAPTER 14

Among the Constables, Turners and Blakes hanging in the Tate Britain art gallery next to the River Thames in London is a painting by William Holman Hunt titled 'The Awakening Conscience'.

It depicts a young woman lifting herself up from the lap of a gentleman, and gazing, with a hopeful expression on her face, out of a window to a sunlit garden. She seems much more excited by the possibilities in the outside world than by the man and the paraphernalia in the shadowy room.

It was fitting that a group of people who saw leaving the EU in the same way should choose the home of this painting to plot the UK's escape.

Sitting in one of the poky corners the museum offered, drinking a cup of tea, was Daniel Hannan. He was waiting for his Conservative colleague and friend of twenty-five years Douglas Carswell to arrive from Parliament – located a ten-minute walk away, up Millbank.

The pair had first met in 1993 in London. Both were decidedly Eurosceptic, but Hannan was more radical in his approach to the European project. Over lunch in Westminster that year, he explained to Carswell – who was four months his senior – why the UK should not seek to reform the EU, but quit it altogether.

Carswell's conversion took less than an hour. With this new-found purpose, Carswell immediately set about trying to find a way to make Britain's exit from the EU a reality. He was living in London at the time, completing his Master's degree at King's College, when he heard of a new party that had been formed – the United Kingdom Independence Party. Carswell considered signing up, but calculated that it would be easier to try to bend the will of an existing party than to help build up a new one. He joined the Conservatives.

It wasn't until 2001 that Carswell got his chance to enter Parliament for the first time. As a thirty-year-old first-time candidate, the Tories gave him an unwinnable seat to contest so he could earn his campaigning stripes. Carswell gave it his all, and achieved a swing to the Tories of 4.7 per cent from his Labour rival. Unfortunately for him, his Labour rival just happened to be the then Prime Minister, Tony Blair, who romped home with a majority of 17,713.

Leading up to the 2005 general election, Carswell was working in the Conservative Policy Unit – overseen by the up-and-coming David Cameron – when he was selected to fight the Labour-held seat of Harwich in north Essex. This time, he did beat his Labour rival, winning by 920 votes.

Carswell was in the Westminster Parliament, Hannan was in the European Parliament, and together the pair began chipping away at the UK's relationship with the EU. The first chink in the wall rather fell into their laps. As part of his leadership bid, Cameron vowed to take the Conservative MEPs out of the European People's Party/European Democrats grouping if elected. Pledging to cut the Tories' formal links with avowed federalists across the Continent earned Cameron the support of Carswell and Hannan.

Following boundary changes in 2010, Carswell won the new constituency of Clacton, which covered much of his old seat. Having spent five years as one of the most outspoken anti-EU

Members of Parliament, Carswell saw his thumping majority of 12,068 as proof that he had tapped into the growing Euroscepticism in the country. With the Conservatives now in power – albeit in coalition with the decidedly pro-European Liberal Democrats – Carswell sensed this was the time to ramp up his Eurosceptic activity. Within weeks he was calling for a referendum on the Lisbon Treaty, and by the following October he was one of the key backbenchers drumming up support among his colleagues when it came to backing a motion calling for a referendum on whether the UK should quit the EU entirely. Despite eighty-one Tories rebelling against the government, there was no sign that Cameron would give in and grant the UK the vote Carswell so desperately wanted.

And so it was, in 2012, that Carswell, Hannan and fellow Tory Eurosceptic Mark Reckless began meeting in secret at the Tate Britain, to discuss how to force Cameron's hand. The Tate Britain was chosen as they rightly believed no journalist, or party whip for that matter, would suspect any political plotters would convene in an art gallery.

The trio would meet regularly to discuss a plan of action. One option was to continue with a barrage of amendments and motions in the Commons and try to bring the matter to a head that way. However, the October 2011 motion had already been watered down from an in/out referendum to an in/out/renegotiate plan in order to gain support from Tories who were nervous about backing too stark a proposal. But the Tate plotters knew amendments and motions wouldn't work. To really bring the issue of an EU referendum to a head, they needed to do something more dramatic – something that would be noticed by the public as well by those in SW1. The plotters decided there was only one course open to them: trigger a wave of by-elections.

'We would leave the Conservative Party, but I and others were contemplating, "Do we re-stand as independents?" We were talking about how that would work. We started going to look at the small print of how by-elections are called,' said Carswell.

The Tate plotters believed that a staggered series of by-elections would consistently ramp up the pressure on Cameron to a point where, just for sheer party management reasons, he would have to pledge a referendum.

'I was quite prepared to sacrifice my career in politics and lose a by-election if necessary if it pushed this forward. I made the calculation, even if I lose, if you've got that happening on your back benches, he'll realise these guys mean it,' said Carswell.

But it was not just the leader of the Conservatives the Tate plotters had in their sights. It was the leader of UKIP too.

Throughout 2012, UKIP's poll ratings were slowly increasing. By the end of the year, an Opinium poll for *The Observer* had them on 15 per cent, an increase from 9 per cent twelve months earlier. Yet, far from the success of an avowedly anti-EU party giving the Tate plotters cause for celebration, it provoked concern. While support for UKIP was rising, support for leaving the EU was falling. It was labelled 'The Farage Paradox'.

Carswell said: 'The better that UKIP did, paradoxically the less support there was for leaving the EU. We could see this very clearly and we're worrying about this in 2012.'

The Tate plotters were in a conundrum. They had a plan to force Cameron into giving them their long-desired EU referendum, but faced the real risk that it would be lost by the very people – or perhaps the very person – most associated with leaving the EU.

In January 2013, Cameron delivered his Bloomberg speech, promising an EU referendum if the Tories won a majority at the next election. The Tate plotters were delighted.

'I listened to Bloomberg and I'm over the moon. I'm thinking, "Thank goodness, I'm not going to have to do what we were contemplating,"' said Carswell. The Tate plotters were feeling confident. Hannan had already approached Matthew Elliott to ask him to run the No campaign and within six weeks of the Bloomberg speech, For Britain – the company always planned to turn into the official No campaign – was registered with Companies House.

With the referendum pledge made, the Tate plotters waited for the country's Eurosceptic voters to switch from UKIP to the Tories. As the only party that could practically offer a route out of the EU, the Farage Paradox would be solved by support melting away from UKIP and towards the Conservatives. Yet, as 2013 turned into 2014, UKIP was going from strength to strength. The party was increasing in the polls despite a series of gaffes that would have scuppered most organisations seeking public office. UKIP MEP Godfrey Bloom calling for foreign aid to stop being sent to 'Bongo-Bongo Land'; Gerard Batten, another MEP, suggesting all Muslims should sign a document promising to renounce religious violence; UKIP councillor David Silvester claiming the UK was experiencing flooding because gay marriage had been legalised; and, of course, Bloom – again – describing a roomful of women as 'sluts' at a conference fringe meeting and then hitting a journalist on the head with an agenda. Yet, while none of these gaffes seemed to be damaging UKIP's poll ratings, support for leaving the EU was still in the minority.

Panic among the plotters increased when UKIP swept to victory in the European elections, a victory which meant even more airtime for Farage, and a danger that Euroscepticism would forever be associated in the public's mind with the UKIP leader.

Farage was not going away. UKIP was not going away. Neither could be subdued. They had to be detoxified – from the inside. Which meant someone would have to infiltrate UKIP and neutralise both the party and its leader.

'Douglas and I had discussed various options about this and we were both focused on winning the referendum, that's all we were thinking about,' said Hannan. 'And he took the view that he could hold his seat under pretty much any colours and that the thing he could do was prevent UKIP losing us the referendum.'

He added:

> He took the view that the contribution he could make to our national life was to win us the referendum by getting in and neutralising what was already becoming a visibly negative UKIP campaign.
>
> We needed to have that kind of relationship where we were working in collaboration with each other but working in different parties to keep the thing together. We could see the poll coming. There was this assumption that, well, the referendum will never happen. Well, I never believed that and neither did he. He played an absolutely pivotal role.

It wasn't just Carswell who was prepared to make the leap. Hannan's old friend from university, the man who had created the Oxford Campaign for an Independent Britain in a café twenty-four years earlier, Mark Reckless, decided he too would risk his political career by joining UKIP.

Carswell had already made contact with Farage the previous summer, planting the seeds of a possible defection in his mind. In his book *The Purple Revolution*, Farage talks of how he put the Tory MP in contact with UKIP peer Lord Pearson and party treasurer Stuart Wheeler 'to try to woo Douglas'. Little did Farage know that Carswell was actually wooing him.

One thing Farage did get right in his book was the catalyst for Carswell making the jump across to UKIP in the summer of 2014. The Clacton MP, who had been so delighted with Cameron's Bloomberg speech, began to suspect the Prime Minister was 'backsliding' on serious reform. Instead, Carswell feared, he would try to get some minor changes and then use the referendum to put the issue to bed for a generation.

Carswell said: 'Cameron wasn't thinking about changing the relationship with the EU, this was about stuffing the Eurosceptics on the back benches and he was going to use the hardcore UKIP strident advocates of leaving the EU to help him do it.'

After a meeting of the Conservatives' backbench 1922 Committee on 11 June, in which Cameron had failed to reassure Carswell that he was serious about reform, the soon-to-be Ukipper pressed the button on defecting. A by-election would increase the pressure on Cameron to hold to his Bloomberg speech and deliver a fair referendum; joining UKIP would enable the process of detoxifying Farage to begin.

After seeking assurances from the UKIP leader that the party had the money to fight a by-election campaign, Carswell agreed to switch. In *The Purple Revolution*, Farage describes himself as being 'on cloud nine' after a midday meeting with Carswell on 24 July, when the final decision was made. Contemplating the win, Farage said: 'We would be able to draw blood off that lot, the Camerons, the Cleggs, the Milibands – the fools who know nothing of real life.'

On 28 August – without a word being leaked and with hardly anyone in UKIP being told what was coming – Carswell walked into a press conference in Whitehall and announced to the gathered media: 'I am today leaving the Conservative Party and joining UKIP.' Members of the party in the room – including deputy leader Paul Nuttall – erupted into cheers. The press were stunned. They had been promised a major announcement, but no one suspected it would be of this magnitude.

The by-election was set for 9 October, and Carswell won it with ease – banking 21,113 votes to the Tories' 8,709. The easy bit – defecting to a new party, winning a by-election – was done. Now Carswell had to complete part two of his plan: detoxifying UKIP. He used his very first act as a UKIP MP – his victory speech – to begin the process. 'I thought, "Everyone's going to be listening, I've got about thirty seconds,"' he remembers.

'To my new party, I offer these thoughts,' Carswell said.

> Humility when we win, modesty when we are proved right.
> If we speak with passion let it always be tempered by com-
> passion.
>   We must be a party for all Britain, and all Britons, first and
> second generation as much as every other. Our strength must
> lie in our breadth. If we stay true to that, there is nothing we
> cannot achieve.

Journalists watching on immediately picked up on the change in
tone, but did not accord it any wider significance.

Carswell's mission to detoxify UKIP continued the very next
day, when he was confronted with comments Farage had given in
an interview with *Newsweek Europe*, released to the press over-
night. When asked what sort of people should be allowed to
migrate to the UK, Farage had responded: 'People who do not
have HIV, to be frank. That's a good start. And people with a skill.'

It was particularly ironic that the first controversy Carswell was
confronted with as a UKIP MP was on the issue of HIV, as his
father had actually pioneered diagnosing HIV/Aids while working as a doctor in Uganda in the 1980s.

Carswell's response to the row was just to smile and repeatedly
call for an Australian-style points-based system when it came to
immigration controls.

It was not just Carswell who had made the jump. Reckless
too defected – making his announcement to great cheers at
UKIP's party conference on Saturday 27 September. He won his
by-election in Rochester and Strood by a much narrower margin, finishing just 2,920 votes ahead of Conservative candidate
Kelly Tolhurst.

Both men had now infiltrated UKIP – they were behind enemy
lines. Was their plan working? Carswell looked at the polls. Of

the fifteen opinion polls carried out before his by-election win, ten had Remain in the lead, four had Leave, and there was one tie. Of the fifteen after his victory, five had Remain in front, nine had Leave winning and, again, one tie. It was working. 'We think we've answered the Farage Paradox. The Tate strategy has won. Little do we know that over the following six months that's not entirely the case because there's a small problem of shock-and-awful tactics,' remembered Carswell.

'Shock and awful' was the name given to the increasingly blunt style Farage had adopted when talking about immigration in the 2015 general election campaign. The high point – or low point, depending on which side of the argument you are on – came in the seven-way leaders' debate five weeks before the election. The second question of the night was: 'How will your party ensure long-term funding of the NHS, while keeping it as a public service accessible to all?'

Farage decided to focus his answer on health tourism, and said:

> OK, here's a fact, and I'm sure you will be mortified that I dare to talk about it. There are 7,000 diagnoses in this country every year for people who are HIV-positive, which is not a good place for any of them to be, I know. But 60 per cent of them are not British nationals.
>
> You can come to Britain from anywhere in the world and get diagnosed with HIV and get the retroviral drugs that cost up to £25,000 per year per patient.

Carswell later described the comments as 'awful', and said they proved to him that UKIP's toxicity had been taken to a 'whole new level' in the general election campaign. When they were later compounded by the damage caused by Farage's 'unresignation' and the Short money row, the Clacton MP realised his detoxification strategy was a failure.

'Angry, nativist UKIP risked being so toxic that if it ran the referendum it would do to the Eurosceptic cause what kryptonite did to Superman. That could not be allowed to happen,' he said. The Tate Plot had failed in its crucial second goal. But there was one small change to the plan that Carswell would make which could still blunt the impact of Farage on the election.

'I thought, "This is it, UKIP shouldn't be a strand in the Vote Leave brand. So it's about not trying to detoxify UKIP, but trying to make sure that Vote Leave is not toxified by UKIP." And that is where we got somewhere,' he said. As UKIP's sole MP, Carswell was able to claim that the parliamentary branch of the party was 100 per cent behind Vote Leave. When it came to applying for designation, he would be the proof of cross-party working.

Farage would not be part of Vote Leave. That was decided even before Vote Leave properly existed. There was no chance whatsoever of a merger between Carswell, Elliott and Hannan's group and any campaign involving Farage. All the talks were for nothing – from day one.

'There were never any merger talks,' said Elliott.

> On our side there was never any inkling that we wanted to merge with The Know, or Leave.EU, or what have you. In order for us to win over the swing voters, we believed that basically a UKIP-based campaign would be able to get up to 35 per cent, perhaps even 40 per cent on a good day in a referendum, but it wouldn't be able to get beyond that, wouldn't be able to, you know, appeal to those swing voters who frankly didn't find Nigel Farage appealing, or didn't want to feel they were voting UKIP by voting Leave.

He added: 'We were always adamant it had to be non-UKIP-based in order to appeal to those swing voters.'

Without knowing it, Farage had held open the door for a man

whose main objective was to systematically change the way UKIP operated, and undermine its leader in the process. He was there to 'neutralise', as Hannan put it. When that goal was thwarted, Carswell instead focused his efforts on making sure Farage did not play a role in the referendum campaign. Farage was right. The EU referendum campaign was being hijacked by the 'posh boys'. They were indeed out to get him.

The Tate Plot will go down as one of the most ruthless examples of political infiltration in UK history. But it did not succeed in silencing Farage.

CHAPTER 15

'**F**or fuck's sake, who's the enemy here?' thought Gawain Towler. The UKIP press chief had been reading his copy of that morning's *Times* newspaper, and was now in a bad mood. It was 1 October 2015, and former Tory Chancellor Lord Lawson had been announced as the new chairman of Conservatives for Britain. But that wasn't what had annoyed Towler; it was the op-ed Lawson had written to go alongside the announcement that had provoked his anger:

> A number of my colleagues in the Conservative Party are waiting to see what the Prime Minister negotiates before deciding which way they will vote or whether they will campaign for 'in' or 'out'. We cannot afford to wait that long. If we leave the playing field vacant, less moderate, xenophobic voices will dominate the debate and we will fail as soon as the government, the major political parties, the CBI and trade unions declare that they are backing the 'in' campaign.

Lawson hadn't mentioned Nigel Farage, but it didn't take Sherlock Holmes to realise who he was referring to. Lawson doubled down on the claim on Radio 4 that morning and, when asked who were the 'xenophobic voices' he was referring to, he replied: 'There'll be plenty, you know as well as I do.'

Lawson went on to deny that he or any other of the members of CfB were xenophobic, and said: 'None of us are anti-European. Indeed, I am speaking to you from my home in France.' The revelation that Lawson would be leading the Conservative attempt to regain the UK's independence from Europe from a house in France provoked some mild amusement on Twitter. 'Thatcherite dinosaur to lead UK EU exit group from home in France. Says everything!' tweeted Labour MP Paul Blomfield.

Lawson's comments infuriated Leave.EU and, at 1.30 p.m., a statement was put out by Arron Banks, Richard Tice and multimillionaire Jim Mellon, who was helping to bankroll the group:

> The announcement that Lord Lawson is 'leading' *the* campaign to leave the EU is wrong. He's leading 'a' campaign that is run by the 'Westminster bubble' from SW1. When are these politicians going to learn that this campaign cannot we [*sic*] won from SW1. It has to appeal to the people, not the small clique of Eurosceptic Tories. It would be better if the Eurosceptic Tories just 'shut up' as they are going to alienate the vast majority of people who will look at this campaign as a Tory stich-up [*sic*].
>
> The Leave.EU campaign is about the people of Great Britain, which includes Labour, Lib Dem, UKIP, Tories and anyone else who believes we should vote to leave the EU at the next referendum. If the Tories keep using hasbeens like Lord Lawson and the other Eurosceptic rabble then that will turn off supporters. So get back in your box, Nigel, and let the people support a people's campaign not an SW1 bubble brigade.

The email was angry enough, but seemed to miss the key point:

Conservatives for Britain had just publicly altered its position from 'Change or Go' to simple 'Go'. The Tory Eurosceptics, who had been decried by Nigel Farage less than a week earlier for not joining the fight, had now issued a call to arms.

With the amendments to the Referendum Bill secured, CfB had carried out its main parliamentary function and could drop the pretence that it was backing Cameron's renegotiation.

It wasn't just CfB that was changing its position. Over the summer, while Farage had been planning his tour and Tice had been mulling over mergers, Matthew Elliott had been sounding out the Business for Britain signatories to get a sense of who would be backing a Leave vote. Not only was he trying to get the political weight of senior business figures backing Brexit, he was also hoping to get something more concrete: donations. This was proving tricky, and one man was to blame.

'The biggest damage that Arron Banks did was preventing donors from stepping forward until the designation issue was settled,' said Daniel Hannan. 'To them it didn't look like a series of one-way howitzer blasts, it looked like a scrap. That's how it always looked to someone who isn't really paying attention: "Why can't you all get together?"'

Bernard Jenkin was encountering similar difficulties.

> It was very difficult because a lot of MPs, a lot of donors, kept saying, 'But why are there two campaigns? Why can't you work together?' They weren't really interested in the detail, they just thought, 'Surely there should be one campaign?', which was perfectly understandable. We had to keep explaining to people there was a very fundamental difference not of personality but of tactics, of strategy, that we needed a campaign that was going to be broadly heard and appeal to the wavering middle-of-the-ground voters, not just motivate the core vote – which is what UKIP tend to do.

According to Farage's advisor Chris Bruni-Lowe, the difficulties their Leave campaigning rivals were encountering were no accident. 'We said, "All you've got to do is muddy the waters so donors don't know who to fund. In the end they'll fund no one, but Arron's got the money so they'll blow Elliott out of the water and we can run a much more aggressive campaign,"' he said.

Jenkin raised the first cheque, totalling £50,000, from a business contact, and Elliott began putting the structure in place. Like his campaigning rivals, he was working on the premise that the referendum question would present yes/no options, and decided to rehash the logo used for the campaign against the euro – a lowercase 'no' in white font inside a red circle. He was even able to utilise a company he had registered in 2010 – 'No Campaign' – as the vehicle for the organisation.

All that changed when, on 1 September 2015, Cameron accepted the Electoral Commission recommendation that the referendum question should provide the choice of remain or leave, not yes or no. It was hugely disruptive.

Elliott said:

> Websites had been designed and all this sort of stuff and of course we had a perfect suite of having nocampaign.com, for arguments sake, and @nocampaign on Twitter, and the Instagram name, the right Facebook name. So it was all perfectly aligned. Then they changed the bloody question, and then we all scrambled round. Of course, voteleave.com was very quickly taken by somebody and they put one of these music videos on.

Indeed, anyone who logged on to voteleave.com found themselves redirected to the music video for Rick Astley's 1987 hit 'Never Gonna Give You Up' – a long-running internet joke known as 'Rickrolling'.

After a brainstorming session, Elliott and Cummings decided to go with 'Vote Leave, Get Change' as their new company's full name, and registered the business on 18 September. Elliott had now moved out of his Tufton Street base, and was able to rent two floors in the Westminster Tower building on Albert Embankment. Located at the end of Lambeth Bridge on the south side of the Thames, the building provides a perfect view of the Houses of Parliament, situated just across the river. The second floor of the office block was used by Vote Leave for phone canvassing and hosting media events. The seventh floor was home to Elliott, Cummings, Vote Leave researchers and other staff. The space had previously been used by TV news station Al-Jazeera, and had been completely stripped out when the company had left. The first few months of Vote Leave's time in their new offices was characterised by builders making the space suitable for the company – including constructing a boardroom and separate rooms for Elliott and Cummings.

'It seemed like an age,' remembered Elliott. 'We were working out of one half while the other was boarded up and bang bang bang, and all that sort of stuff, while they worked in the other half.'

It was while sitting among dust and building materials in late September that Cummings came up with the slogan that would come to define the campaign. 'Dom's initial hunch was to go for "Vote Leave, Get Change", and that was the initial sort of concept,' said Elliott, 'but then he had that sort of spark of inspiration: "Vote Leave, Take Control". It slightly evolved into "Take Back Control", which was the catchphrase for debates and what have you.'

The campaign was ready to go, but Elliott wanted to hold off launching until after the Conservative Party conference, taking place in Manchester from Sunday 4 October to Wednesday 7 October. 'We wanted to allow people to fly the flag and appear on CfB platforms at party conference,' he claimed – somewhat strangely given that Lord Lawson had already moved CfB to a 'Go' position three days before the conference kicked off.

On Friday 9 October, the worst-kept secret in British politics
was revealed and Vote Leave was launched. Ex-Tory treasurer
Peter Cruddas, former UKIP donor Stuart Wheeler and Labour
backer John Mills were all put forward as the big financial hitters.
Owen Paterson, Steve Baker and Kate Hoey also delivered supporting statements, and Carswell went the extra mile of writing a
comment piece for the *Telegraph* about why he was backing Vote
Leave over Leave.EU: 'Having fought and won two parliamentary
elections over the past year, I know the importance of appealing
to undecided voters. Everything I have learnt from my experience
of fighting and winning for UKIP in Clacton convinces me that
the Vote Leave campaign has what it takes to win.' He didn't quite
write the words 'unlike Nigel Farage', but the sentiment was clear.

Along with the platitudes and rallying cries from supporters,
Vote Leave also released a campaign video focusing on what it
believed would be the strongest argument to persuade undecided
voters: the cost of being in the EU.

After an opening shot of the River Thames, the camera focused
on the outside of St Thomas' Hospital. Within a few seconds, what
appeared to be bank notes started detaching themselves from the
building and flew up into the clear blue sky. As a map of Europe
appeared, a voice said: 'Every week, the United Kingdom sends
£350 million of taxpayers' money to the EU – that's the cost of a
fully staffed, brand new hospital.' The video then continued setting out what else that £350 million could be spent on: schools,
roads, railways, regional airports and even tax cuts. It ended with
a series of slogans flashing up over urgent, intense music, complete with pounding percussion: Vote Leave; let's take control;
let's save money; invest in the NHS; invest in science; get change;
the safer choice.

After being shown the video ahead of its release, Jenkin immediately picked up on what would be one of the most hotly contested
claims of the whole campaign: that the UK sent £350 million to

Brussels every week. Vote Leave were using the gross figure; after a rebate – which was applied before the money ever left the UK – the actual figure was just under £250 million a week. That, however, did not take into account that certain UK industries, institutions and areas received subsidies from the EU – amounting to £4.5 billion in 2015 – or £85 million a week.

'You've got the wrong number here, we are going to be in trouble,' Jenkin told the Vote Leave team once he had seen the video. 'It will be a rod for our own back,' he added. The Tory MP was told the matter had already been decided, and the £350 million figure was used by Carswell in his *Telegraph* op-ed and Hoey in her supporting statement released to the media.

In a press release sent out by Robert Oxley, Vote Leave's 'core message' was revealed:

> Technological and economic forces are changing the world fast. EU institutions cannot cope. We have lost control of vital policies. This is damaging. We need a new relationship with the European Union. What happens if we vote 'leave'?
>
> We will negotiate a new UK–EU deal based on free trade and friendly cooperation. We end the supremacy of EU law. We regain control. We stop sending £350 million every week to Brussels and instead spend it on our priorities, like the NHS and science research.
>
> We regain our seats on international institutions like the World Trade Organization so we are a more influential force for free trade and international cooperation.
>
> A vote to 'leave' and a new friendly relationship is much safer than giving Brussels more power and money every year.

At the bottom of the press release was a list of 'key staff', including 'Dominic Cummings – campaign director'. It had been just two months since Cummings had publicly and explicitly stated that he was 'NOT "running the NO campaign"' and would be helping 'in minor ways only' once the organisation had been created. Yet here he was – one of the 'key staff'.

Elliott was never in any doubt that Cummings would be staying on until the bitter end:

> Dom was always very clear, you know, if Karl Rove or David
> Axelrod or Lynton Crosby had volunteered their services
> to the campaign and the board felt that was appropriate, he
> would always be happy to move over to allow those big shots
> to take the hot seat, but none of them were going to do it.

Saving money. Science. The NHS. These were the areas that Vote Leave felt would win over the undecideds. Immigration and border control were not mentioned once in the video, or in Carswell's *Telegraph* piece.

Farage was utterly bemused by Vote Leave's campaigning focus, but was pleased they had now joined the fray – a move he felt he was responsible for thanks to his endorsement of Leave.EU at the UKIP conference two weeks earlier. 'Blow me down, within a fortnight, what happens? Vote Leave launches. Would it have launched if we hadn't launched in Doncaster? No,' said Farage.

> In fact, they probably would have been taken by surprise
> the following March. Why? Because Elliott's fear was that a
> lot of his long-term donors would not support a Leave cam-
> paign. Business for Britain was set up to keep us out of the
> euro, to campaign against excessive EU regulation, but not
> the radical step, as it was seen, of leaving the EU. They would
> have left it, and left it, and left it, and left it. Victory num-
> ber one for us was that we smoked out Business for Britain
> and not only had we got them to declare for out but they're
> immediately pushed on the Cameron renegotiation and find

themselves with nowhere to go but to start criticising him, so we were really pleased with that.

Banks too believes his actions had forced the hand of Elliott and Cummings:

> Taking away all of the heat and all of the passion, one thing we did do was force Vote Leave to start their campaign sooner than they wanted to start. They definitely wanted to wait until Dave got back and get started afterwards. They were very respectful of the Prime Minister.

Elliott, however, insists Vote Leave emerged at the moment he had always planned, and that he had always been very clear about his plans with Banks, Farage and others involved in Leave.EU. 'We were always open with people about our timings for things, I just think that people saw us as being sort of quisling Tories who were more concerned about keeping on the right side of David Cameron than getting Britain out of the EU,' he said.

Campaign launches seemed to be infectious: three days after Vote Leave went public, so too did Britain Stronger In Europe – the Remain organisation. At a brewery in east London, business-people, MPs and celebrities got together to unveil the organisation tasked with maintaining the status quo. Will Straw, son of former Labour Foreign Secretary Jack Straw, was Elliott's equivalent in the organisation, while hosting the launch was TV presenter June Sarpong.

One of the main backers of Stronger In was former Marks & Spencer boss Lord Rose, a one-time signatory of Business for Britain. Ahead of the launch, journalists were sent extracts of his speech for publication that morning. The line of attack was clear – according to Rose, those advocating Leave were 'quitters'. He was due to say:

The quitters have no idea whether we would be able to access Europe's free trade area, or what the price of admission would be. The quitters have no idea how long it would take to renegotiate existing trade deals or how difficult it would be to negotiate new ones outside the EU, let alone how inferior the terms would be. The quitters cannot guarantee that jobs would be safe and prices wouldn't rise. The quitters cannot explain how we could stop free movement and simultaneously keep our access to the world's largest duty-free market.

Yet when it came to his speech, Rose dropped the entire section, preferring instead to say that Eurosceptics would be 'taking a risk with Britain's prosperity'.

The most startling warning came from former police chief Sir Hugh Orde, who claimed that pulling out of the European Arrest Warrant would have dire consequences for the UK. While he was president of the Association of Chief Police Officers, Orde said, the Metropolitan Police was asked to find and arrest fifty murderers, twenty rapists and ninety robbers.

Orde continued:

> My experience tells me if you are a robber in another country, you are a robber in this country. If you are a rapist, you are a rapist, and if you are a murderer, you are by definition extremely dangerous … If I was a villain somewhere else in Europe and I was escaping justice, I would be coming here because it's going to take a lot longer to get you back.

It seemed Stronger In were not going to duck the fight over controversial issues.

With Leave.EU and Vote Leave now announced, Farage again tried to facilitate a merger of the groups. After the conference season had finished in early October, the UKIP leader sat down with Banks and David Wall, the secretary of the Midlands Industrial Council, to try to find some areas of compromise. Farage and Wall then had a meeting with Elliott, who repeatedly blocked any union.

'Elliott said, "I'm sorry but my board don't find Mr Banks's language and behaviour acceptable." And that was the first in an endless series of attempts to form big umbrellas, all sorts of things, none of which ever came to anything,' recalled Farage.

Bruni-Lowe, who was also in the meeting, remembered Elliott 'sat there literally in silence in the most weird way'. After hearing Farage's plan to focus the campaign on immigration and Turkey, Bruni-Lowe claimed Elliott said, 'I'm sorry, Dominic says we can't merge.'

Those at the top of Vote Leave clearly felt Banks and Farage needed to be kept at a distance because of their unpredictability and desire to run a campaign using tactics of which they did not approve. Little did they realise that those concerns should have been focused a little closer to home.

CHAPTER 16

All Phil Sheppard knew was that it was a 'secret mission' that had come from the top – the very top – and he had been asked to see if any of his undergraduate friends at the London School of Economics would be interested. Michael Dowsett, director of Conservatives for Britain, was the man doing the asking. He had been tasked with finding young, enthusiastic Eurosceptics, and Sheppard, president of Students for Britain, fitted the bill perfectly.

When Dowsett asked Sheppard if he could recommend anyone who would also like to take part, Peter Lyon was also recruited. Like Sheppard, he was a nineteen-year-old LSE student, and just as willing to do what he could to help the campaign to get out of the EU. With the two operatives selected, they were told to report to Vote Leave's HQ on the banks of the River Thames for further orders.

Waiting to greet them was Paul Stephenson, the campaign's communications director. Stephenson was a former Conservative press officer who went on to work in the Departments of Transport and Health. After leaving government, he joined the British Bankers' Association, before being poached by Matthew Elliott in July 2015 to join what would become Vote Leave.

The two students sat across from Stephenson and received

their mission: Vote Leave were going to create a company and install Sheppard and Lyon as directors. Using the company to secure passes, the pair would then be sent undercover to the Confederation of British Industry (CBI) conference on 9 November, when David Cameron was due to give the keynote address. The two would then disrupt the speech, highlighting how the pro-EU CBI was misrepresenting the views of UK businesses when it came to the referendum.

This was their mission, should they choose to accept it. The students both agreed, and on 26 October – two weeks before the CBI conference – the pair signed some paperwork making them directors of Lyon Sheppard Web Solutions Ltd. A website was even created, complete with a quotation from Steve Jobs on the home page: 'Here's to the rebels. Here's to those who will speak truth to power, who embrace change.'

The following Monday, the pair visited Vote Leave HQ for a final run-through. They were to take their seats among some of the most powerful CEOs in the country, and at 9.50 a.m. would stand up and chant 'CBI – voice of Brussels' while holding up a banner with the same words.

Vote Leave's frustration with the CBI had gone up a notch that very day, with Dominic Cummings claiming an oft-quoted 2013 survey that showed eight out of ten UK businesses backed remaining in the EU was unreliable. Cummings emailed a complaint to the head of the British Polling Council, John Curtice, and copied in YouGov boss Peter Kellner, Simon Atkinson of Ipsos MORI and Nick Moon, secretary of the British Polling Council. 'Bugger – at first glance the odious Cummings might be onto something. Survey looks pretty dodgy but luckily we don't need to rule on that. But my initial thought is that YouGov did not give as much info as they should have,' Moon responded, not realising he had hit 'reply all' – meaning that 'the odious Cummings' saw the message.

On the evening of 8 November, the night before they were to carry out their mission, Sheppard and Lyon were talking through the plan over Facebook's messenger service. The two students – still teenagers, of course – were nervous, but Sheppard tried to reassure his co-conspirator. 'We're going to do this – and remember all these Eurosceptic heroes like Tony Benn and Dan Hannan, they're going to be behind us,' he said.

The next morning the pair made their way to Grosvenor House in London's Mayfair. Arriving at registration, they gave their names and presented the only form of identification they had on them – their provisional driving licences. Looking round at the other men and women milling around the venue, the pair began to feel very self-conscious. Regardless of the fact that they were in their smartest suits, they were clearly the youngest people at the conference by quite some margin. Surely they would be rumbled before they got anywhere near the Prime Minister.

The pair made their way into the main conference room and sat about ten rows from the stage. They pulled out the notebooks Vote Leave had issued them with. Tucked inside was the banner they would brandish as the Prime Minister spoke. The original plan was to stand up and begin shouting at 9.50 a.m., about ten minutes into Cameron's speech. The rolling news channels would be tuned in by then and it would ensure maximum coverage. But, as the clock struck 9.40 a.m., Cameron was not on the stage. He was running ten minutes late, meaning the 9.50 a.m. protest time was now redundant. Sheppard texted Stephenson, and the teenager was told to now go at 10 a.m. At 9.55 a.m., the Prime Minister took to the stage and the BBC's deputy political editor James Landale, who was reporting on the conference, received a message from Stephenson, telling him to make sure his camera was trained on the two teenagers sitting a few rows behind him.

At 10 a.m., and with the BBC and Sky News channels providing live coverage of the Prime Minister's speech, the teenagers knew their moment had arrived. As Cameron was outlining the importance of running a surplus during long periods of economic growth, the pair pulled out the banner from their notebooks and made sure it was the right way round.

'At the time, just before I did it, I was really nervous, to the point where I almost didn't do it,' remembered Sheppard. But there was no chance of backing out, as Lyon was already on his feet. A second or two later, Sheppard joined him. 'I didn't want him to look like an idiot,' he said. The pair began chanting in unison 'CBI: voice of Brussels'. It was hardly a roar, but in the room of businesspeople listening respectfully to the Prime Minister, the sound carried quickly.

Cameron hesitated for the briefest of moments as he realised he was being heckled, before relaxing and taking control of the situation. 'We're going to have a debate in a minute, if you wait for a second you can ask me a question rather than interrupting what's a very good conference,' said the Prime Minister.

The pair continued: 'CBI: voice of Brussels! CBI: voice of Brussels!'

'Come on, guys,' said Cameron, clapping his hands together. 'If you sit down now you can ask me a question rather than making fools of yourself by just standing up and protesting.'

The audience applauded Cameron's polite but firm rebuke, and conference security staff made their way to the two protestors. As they were escorted out, Cameron said, 'Thanks, guys,' and gave them a wave. The incident lasted thirty-five seconds, but to the two teenagers carrying out the stunt, it seemed a lot longer.

Lyon said: 'It felt like it went on for so long before security came over, they seemed to have no idea what to do. It completely took them by surprise, but David Cameron played it off very well – which you'd expect him to.'

With the point made, the two left the conference centre and began giving interviews to the media outside. On Sky News,

Sheppard was open about how he and Lyon had managed to infiltrate the conference. He said: 'We got in because Vote Leave formed a company for us that was able to get us in.'

When asked how it felt to interrupt the Prime Minister, Lyon said: 'It was the most terrifying thing I've done in my life.'

With the protest completed, Lyon returned to university to attend a lecture on crime and punishment, while Sheppard went to an orthodontist appointment. Neither of them realised that their 35-second protest would trigger an internal battle that would almost destroy Vote Leave.

Later that day, Bernard Jenkin was having lunch with a political journalist who asked for his view on the protest. The Tory MP had had a busy morning and had yet to catch up with the latest news. 'I was initially rather amused,' he remembered. The journalist was surprised Jenkin knew nothing about it, especially as it was a Vote Leave operation. 'No, it can't be Vote Leave, I don't know anything about it,' he told his lunch partner.

'But someone called Robert Oxley has been briefing the lobby about it,' came her reply. Upon hearing that name, Jenkin realised it was indeed a Vote Leave stunt and hurriedly changed the subject. 'I thought it was juvenile, and for us it was embarrassing that our leader had been heckled by an organisation we were associated with,' he said later.

Elliott, who knew about the stunt, had no regrets – despite acknowledging that it was 'hugely controversial'. He believed that in order for the Leave side to win the referendum, it needed to be shown that the business community was split on the EU issue. 'I think the stunt sent an extremely strong signal to the CBI and also to other business groups that when they enter the European debate they should make sure they reflect all sides of their business supporter base, rather than piling in on one side,' he said.

A few minutes after changing the subject at his lunch with the journalist, Jenkin felt a buzz in his pocket and discreetly looked down at his phone. Flashing up on the screen was a message from Steve Baker, saying he had informed Dominic Cummings he no longer wished to be a board member of Vote Leave.

CHAPTER 17

'I think it was a bit childish. I think heckling people isn't the way forward,' said Arron Banks.

'So your organisation would never do anything like that?' replied Sky News journalist Kay Burley.

'I wouldn't say we wouldn't do anything like that…' was Banks's response.

The CBI stunt put the Leave.EU co-founder in an unusual situation – he was able to take the moral high ground in public over Vote Leave. Just twenty-four hours earlier, it was his campaign group that had been accused of inappropriate behaviour. The Leave.EU social media activity was fast gaining notoriety for its irreverent and provocative style. The campaign's official Twitter account in particular sometimes danced close to the edge of bad taste and hyperbolic claims. On 8 October 2015, it argued that if Germany continued to register 409,000 refugees every forty days then '3.7 million will arrive in a year'. On 16 October, it warned the UK to 'brace yourself for another influx' of migrants – this time from Turkey. On 23 October, Leave.EU mocked the acronym ascribed to the official Remain campaign ('What does BSE mean to you? Britain's Stronger in Europe or… Mad Cow Disease?'), while on 25 October it used the 600th anniversary of the Battle of Agincourt to claim, 'Britons have always triumphed in the face of adversity. Let's lead the charge once more and #LeaveEU.'

These tweets may have been a little odd or far-fetched, but they did not provoke any serious outrage. However, an image posted by Leave.EU on 8 November was deemed to have gone too far. To mark that year's Remembrance Sunday, the organisation tweeted a photo of a Chelsea Pensioner veteran examining the ceramic poppies in the grounds of the Tower of London. Along with the picture were the words 'Freedom and democracy. Let's not give up values for which our ancestors paid the ultimate sacrifice. #LeaveEU'. There was an immediate backlash, and Lib Dem leader Tim Farron said: 'Using Remembrance Sunday and our veterans to try and make a political point is crass.' Shadow Culture Secretary Michael Dugher also piled in, saying: 'Remembrance Sunday is the day when the whole country unites and comes together to honour the service and sacrifice of our veterans and our armed forces. It's not an opportunity or a day to advance a political platform.' Leave.EU realised they had gone too far and, after deleting the tweet, Andy Wigmore told MailOnline:

> Clearly it's provoked a bit of anti-feeling. The post was there to illustrate the democracy that people fought for and our freedoms. It was probably a little bit clumsy. Of course if it has caused any offence we would apologise. That was not the aim at all so we have taken it down. People's reaction to it was probably right.

Speaking after the incident, Banks suggested that the tweet wasn't as unpopular as it was being reported. 'My mailbag absolutely filled up with veterans and different people supporting us, so the press perception of it versus the public was very interesting,' he said. Tice agreed:

We did make a mistake but we took it down and we said sorry. Interestingly, it wasn't the veterans who complained. In fact, we had the opposite. The veterans said, 'You're quite right.' It was the liberal luvvies and Vote Leave who complained. Those who had fought and got injured in wars had no problem with it, and that explains the gulf between SW1 and the rest of the country. Arron always said from day one you can't win this from SW1.

When it came to producing the graphics, Banks was clear about what the aim should be: cause a fuss, as it gets more followers. He said:

The team were briefed to sometimes come out and be punchy and not back off. What we found was if you backed off, you got into more trouble. We just didn't care what the press thought. We realised as well that after the shock horror, the press moves on very rapidly to something else. Actually, it just dies quite quickly, but the publicity just gains you more followers and gains more interest.

Banks added: 'Our main approach to PR was to double down. If we got nailed on something our philosophy was to send up a distress flare somewhere else that takes the press attention away. Very Trump-style campaigning.'

Leave.EU continued in its irreverent manner, with other tweets including a picture of Father Christmas in handcuffs with the line 'Christmas is incompatible with EU law and shall be renamed the winter festival'. It wasn't just through its social media outlets that Leave.EU seemed determined to provoke a reaction. As he had shown with his angry statement after Lord Lawson announced he was taking over as Conservatives for Britain chairman, Banks was always happy to make a public dig at his Leave rivals. When the two-referendum idea was floated again in October, Banks released a statement saying: 'Suggesting two referendums is a cheap political trick and as a non-political campaign we support one referendum: in or out.' The CBI incident gave him an opportunity to really lay it on thick. 'If we are to gain the trust of the British people in this campaign then provocative stunts and schoolboy politics [are] not the answer. This is a serious debate about a very serious matter and we now have to conduct ourselves accordingly,' said Banks.

The businessman was fast becoming an almost constant presence in the media whenever the EU referendum was discussed. On the day of the CBI stunt, he appeared on both Sky News and the BBC, and on 13 November he appeared as a panellist on Radio 4's *Any Questions?* programme when it was broadcast from Basingstoke. His media appearances continued into the new year, with a five-minute profile package of him broadcast on *Channel 4 News* on 29 January. Two days later, he told the BBC's *Daily Politics* he expected there to be a 'coming together' of Leave.EU and Vote Leave. It was no accident that Banks was seeing his profile rise, and it was thanks to a tactic put forward by Chris Bruni-Lowe:

> I said to him to sue the BBC and say you're going to basically sue every media outlet. Issue them with legal notices saying that if you get one side on – Elliott – and don't get us on, you're going to prejudice the Electoral Commission. Of course the media haven't got a clue and started thinking, 'Oh God, are we?' and started giving Banks equal coverage despite him having no right to be given equal coverage. You had Banks becoming the most senior Brexit figure because he was just suing everyone.

Leave.EU weren't just focusing on the air war. Like Vote Leave, they too were forensically studying the Electoral Commission's criteria for official designation, and were in dialogue with the organisation to discover just what they needed to produce to demonstrate a breadth of support. Knowing that Elliott would be able to secure the backing of a large number of MPs, Leave.EU began focusing on the thousands of oft-forgotten elected officials in the UK: local councillors. More than 2,000 councillors were signed up to back Banks's outfit, the majority coming from the Conservative Party.

While Banks and Leave.EU were having fun generating head-lines, Nigel Farage was not holding back on his 'Say No to the EU' tour. As the events were filling up across the country, it became clear to Bruni-Lowe and Farage that they no longer needed to be constrained by UKIP and they quietly began to drop the party branding and just focus on the MEP himself.

'The branding means that Nigel's asked about councillors who say shit. On his own, he can say, "It's just me, guv,"' remembered Bruni-Lowe.

The refugee crisis that was engulfing much of southern Europe had been an underlying theme at many of the events since the tour kicked off in September. Indeed, UKIP MEP Tim Aker used a rally in Essex on 17 September to claim that it was German Chancellor Angela Merkel's decision to grant asylum to thousands of refugees that was causing the local roads to look unkempt.

At the meeting, Aker was asked by an audience member: 'The state of the grass verges, pavements and roads in Tilbury is dis-gusting. I pay my council tax so why isn't the grass being cut and why aren't the streets being cleaned?'

He replied:

> I just think the question with that is, why are we sending so much to the European Union that we have to ask these ques-tions? I mean, when you pay your taxes and you work hard

and all sorts, do you pay it for Angela Merkel to throw at the
European Union? And even today we [UKIP MEPs] voted
to stop the fact that the European Union is going to reset-
tle these refugees. Six thousand euros a pop. Where do you
think that's coming from?

On 16 November, the tour arrived in Basingstoke. It was just three
days after a terrorist attack in Paris, in which at least 129 people
were killed by a combination of suicide bombs and guns. The terrorist organisation styling themselves as Islamic State – or Daesh
– claimed responsibility. All of the attackers were EU citizens,
but at least some, including the leader Abdelhamid Abaaoud, had
visited Syria before travelling to France to carry out the deadly
attacks. For Farage, this was proof of his warning in the run-up
to the general election that terrorists would exploit the EU's
border-free Schengen zone to carry out attacks.

He told the audience in Basingstoke:

> This dream of the free movement of people, this dream for
> others of the Schengen area – it hasn't just meant the free
> movement of people, it has meant the free movement of
> Kalashnikov rifles. It has meant the free movement of ter-
> rorists, and it has meant the free movement of jihadists.

He went further, arguing that there was 'a problem with some of
the Muslim community in this country', and claimed research
suggested that British Muslims experienced a 'tremendous conflict and a split of loyalties'.

'We already have a fifth column,' he said.

The comments provoked uproar from other politicians, with
then Home Secretary Theresa May telling the House of Commons
the next day: 'British Muslims and indeed Muslims worldwide
have said very clearly these events are abhorrent.'

Labour's former shadow Home Secretary Yvette Cooper addressed the UKIP leader directly, and said: 'As Nigel Farage knows, people from Muslim communities across Britain and Europe have condemned the vile attacks in Paris. This is not the time to divide and denigrate our communities – that is what the terrorists want. Nigel Farage should retract these irresponsible and shameful remarks immediately.' It wasn't the last time Farage would generate controversy for comments relating to Europe's migrant crisis.

A week later, on Monday 23 November, Banks upped the pressure on Elliott by making a public plea for unity. He leaked an email he had sent to Elliott four days earlier to the *Telegraph*, in which the businessman tried to brush off past disagreements by claiming that since 'our respective campaigns have launched, there have been times when our respective competitive spirit has spilled over the top, which was perhaps inevitable, given the potential competition for the designation'.

He then explicitly set out a merger:

> It is time that we put all these disagreements to one side and remember our ultimate objective – leaving the European Union. As you know, we reached out to you in July and August, but your view then was to proceed on your own course. The two Leave campaigns have focused on very different things. Vote Leave produces great technical analysis such as the 1,000-page document 'Change or Go' and developed good links with big businesses.
>
> We have attracted 300,000 supporters in three months, a huge social media presence and increasing small donations from the general public. We have signed up over 1,300 cross-party local councillors from all political parties and over 3,000 SME businesses in the last three weeks alone. We have some 200 groups up and down the country.

In terms of uniting Leave.EU and Vote Leave we have no
prior conditions and believe that discussions should now
take place that reflect the complementary strengths that the
two organisations enjoy.

I have a simple view of life and this is my unequivocal message
moving forward – if you want to leave the EU, you are on our
side. We should be one winning team. I appeal to everyone
to move forward in that spirit and take on our real enemies.

The tactic was simple: by making the merger proposal public,
Banks was hoping those sympathetic to the idea in Vote Leave
would place even greater pressure on Elliott and Cummings to
facilitate a coming together of the campaigns.

The letter precipitated a meeting in early December involving Banks and Tice from Leave.EU and John Mills and Daniel
Hodson – a retired British banker who also worked as a trader in
the City of London in the 1990s – representing Vote Leave. It may
have been different Vote Leave voices, but the words were still the
same. No to Farage playing a role, no to focusing on immigration, and no to a merger.

By the end of December, relations had deteriorated to such
a degree that Banks was convinced Vote Leave had hired private detectives to follow him. He decided to 'turn the tables' and
set his own surveillance company, Precision Risk & Intelligence,
loose on Vote Leave.

Banks said:

I discovered I'd been trailed by a private investigator so basically someone was obviously trying to collect information
or do something. We figured out it was probably Vote Leave
or something to do with them, who knows. So we turned
the tables and did the same back. What I did was I wrote an
email to Elliott.

The email read: 'I have a personal investigator on my tail. You might want to watch out – I have a business that specialises in personal security and counter-intelligence … we have ex-MI5 and SAS operatives who specialise in counter-surveillance.'

Elliott took the email to be a warning that he and others were about to be put under surveillance. The email was leaked to the *Mail on Sunday* on 23 December, with a Vote Leave source saying: 'We believe that Arron Banks has been monitoring the Vote Leave office because he has been passing information about staff movements to people, and he has operatives tailing their top people.'

In the article, Banks denied the claim that he had set spooks loose on the rival Leave campaign, claiming Elliott had misunderstood what was supposed to be a warning that the In camp were using private detectives. His denial was just another piece of the psychological warfare against Elliott he was engaging in.

'For two weeks running they were terrified about it, they were shredding all their documents, they were absolutely terrified,' said Banks, adding: 'It was quite amusing because during Christmas, the Vote Leave lot were terrified of our team of former SAS and MI5 agents. Of course, when it appeared it just looked stupid. It looked like Vote Leave had lost the plot.'

When told Banks had admitted hiring the private detectives, Elliott wasn't surprised:

> The number of times he knew certain things, it was clear from emails he was sending to John Mills, and things that he ordinarily wouldn't have known. Having said that, it's difficult to know how much of that was the ExCom being leaky like a sieve or spooks following us around. I suspect a lot of the time it was the fact that ExCom and people were very liberal in forwarding emails.

Banks may have been happy playing with the minds of Vote Leave, but he was in full seduction mode when it came to UKIP. While Farage and thousands of councillors were already committed to backing Leave.EU, there were still twenty-one MEPs and the party's ruling National Executive Committee up for grabs. If these Ukippers split their support between the two Leave campaigns, it could effectively negate the claim that Leave.EU had the backing of the only officially pro-Brexit party in the UK. Farage was having the same concerns, but he knew he could not just instruct the MEPs and NEC to back Leave.EU. They needed to be convinced that Banks's campaign was not only the most likely to win designation, but the one that would put the UKIP voice front and centre of the referendum debate. 'We had to let people make their decision independently, but we knew the way they will end up wanting to back Leave.EU is the moment they see Banks's operation, they will be blown away,' said Bruni-Lowe.

It was decided to arrange for the MEPs and NEC to visit both organisations to see for themselves which campaign deserved their support. UKIP chairman Steve Crowther contacted Vote Leave to arrange a time, and it was agreed the party's MEPs and the NEC would go to Westminster Tower on Friday 22 January 2016. But first, they would go to Leave.EU.

Banks's attempts at wooing high-profile Ukippers hadn't got off to the best of starts. Carswell may not have been the most popular member of the party, but seeing Banks describe him as 'borderline autistic with mental illness wrapped in' at the UKIP conference did lead many in the party to question whether this was someone they could do business with. One of the most reticent was Suzanne Evans, who was still deputy chairman of the party when Banks asked to meet her on 2 November. Banks was planning to explain over lunch how Leave.EU would move forward, and also speak to her about a potential role in the organisation. The meeting was arranged for the private members' club 5 Hertford Street in Mayfair, and at 12.15 p.m., Evans was sitting at a table waiting for Banks. Half an hour later, Banks had still not arrived. Evans called and texted him, but got no response. He had forgotten about the meeting.

When it came to wooing UKIP's MEPs and its NEC, Banks made sure nothing would go wrong. On Wednesday 13 January, he ferried the entire group down to his plush manor house on the outskirts of Bristol. Some stayed in his country pad, while others were booked into lavish hotels nearby. Regardless of where they stayed, they all found a bottle of champagne awaiting them in their rooms. 'It was "Olympic bidding" type behaviour,' joked one MEP.

On the evening of the first day, the group were treated to a sumptuous dinner, and the alcohol flowed freely – more than one of the delegation had a sore head the next morning. On Thursday 14th, the group were shown around Leave.EU's headquarters and phone banks, and all their questions and concerns were dealt with. 'It was brilliant,' one MEP remembered.

The schmoozing was a tremendous success, and the MEPs and NEC left Bristol happy to throw their support behind Banks and Leave.EU. On Friday 22 January, the delegation descended on Vote Leave's HQ, knowing that it would take something special from Elliott and Cummings to convince them to endorse a campaign which, up to that point, had seemed disinterested in working with UKIP. The party was split into two groups, with the MEPs scheduled to go in first, followed by the NEC members.

Four days prior to the Vote Leave meeting, Banks deployed his 'mess with their heads' strategy and published a letter he had sent to Elliott accusing him of not really wanting to leave the EU.

After opening the letter by saying he was 'dismayed to see members of Vote Leave in the media recently advocating two referendums in order to somehow secure a better deal for the UK with the European Union', Banks turned the screw:

The actions of your colleagues and previous historic statements suggest you are committed to staying in a reformed
EU rather than campaigning for a Leave vote. It is incon-
ceivable that the Electoral Commission could award Vote
Leave the official designation while you remain committed
to reform through a second referendum.

Knowing there were currently tensions within Vote Leave over
the way the campaign was being managed, he zoned in on the
group's weak spot:

As I have said previously, the only person apparently standing in the way of a formal merger is Dominic Cummings.
With his latest comments suggesting the Prime Minister use
anything other than Article 50 of the Lisbon Treaty to ini-
tiate our withdrawal from the EU, he has become a liability
and a danger to both Leave campaigns.

He ended the letter by offering to 'extend my hand, again, for us
to open up talks about how we can move forward as one unstoppable campaign devoted to securing a Leave vote and only a Leave
vote in the one and only referendum we will have'.

The letter had the desired effect and, as the MEPs and NEC
entered Vote Leave HQ, their heads were filled with the notion
that they were about to listen to people who didn't really want to
leave the EU.

As they took their seats in the boardroom, John Mills welcomed them all and thanked them for coming. Elliott then stood
up and began by praising UKIP for the work it had done for the
Eurosceptic cause, and acknowledging the party's crucial role
in securing the referendum. He then began explaining the various groups Vote Leave had under its umbrella: Conservatives for
Britain, Labour Leave, Muslims for Britain etc. Farage arrived

about half an hour late – flanked by Bruni-Lowe and Michael
Heaver – and sat at the back of the room. Some of the MEPs were
bemused, wondering why Farage had brought his two advisors
along to a meeting that was supposed to be for MEPs only. With
the presentation over, the questions began.

Patrick O'Flynn, the sole UKIP MEP backing Vote Leave for designation, nonetheless gave the campaign's representatives a rough
ride over the notion of a second referendum. Cummings struggled to explain why he favoured the two-referendum approach,
but, according to Bruni-Lowe, said, 'We are advocating a second referendum because the person coming across to us from
the Tories wants a second referendum and we have to leave that
option open.' At least two MEPs in the room got the impression
that Cummings was talking about Boris Johnson. After O'Flynn
had quizzed Vote Leave over the second referendum, Heaver
jumped in and accused the organisation of ignoring Farage. 'Why
do you never retweet anything that Nigel posts on social media?' he
asked, followed by Bruni-Lowe reading out statistics of how many
times Douglas Carswell had been retweeted compared to Farage.
Some MEPs were angry about the intervention. One described the
pair as 'charmless and aggressive', and added: 'They weren't really
bothered about UKIP, they were bothered about Nigel. It was very
much about Nigel's ego and Nigel's pride.'

Some of the MEPs backed Farage and accused Vote Leave of
being little more than a Tory front. Voices began to be raised, and
eventually East of England MEP Stuart Agnew cut across Heaver
and called for calm. 'There was some embarrassment at their
behaviour,' said one MEP, a sentiment shared by another colleague:

> There were a lot of MEPs who weren't happy with the
> behaviour of Chris Bruni-Lowe and Nigel. A lot of us were
> embarrassed by what happened. They came in, sat at the back
> of the room and started shouting and screaming. The points

they made were valid but it was Stuart Agnew who had to take control of the meeting in the end because Vote Leave had completely lost control.

From Farage's point of view, the meeting had been a total success, and when the MEPs got together in Strasbourg at the beginning of February they all – with the exception of O'Flynn – agreed to support Banks when it came to designation.

The people at the top of Vote Leave weren't bothered by the decision of UKIP's MEPs and NEC. The meeting had been a distraction from a much bigger issue – whether Vote Leave would even still exist by the time the referendum arrived. Little did the MEPs realise it at the time, but Vote Leave was on the verge of completely disintegrating.

CHAPTER 18

'**Y**ou think it is nasty? You ain't seen nothing yet,' Dominic Cummings told the *Telegraph*. Like Arron Banks, he too preferred to double down in the face of criticism.

He went on: 'These guys have failed the country, they are going to be under the magnifying glass. Tough shit. We are going to be tough about exposing the failure of the establishment – they can bleat that it is nasty because they don't like scrutiny. It is going to be tough.'

Vote Leave's campaign director had no regrets over the CBI stunt – which was what worried Bernard Jenkin the most. The North Essex MP took Steve Baker's place on the company board and, for his first act, tried to establish just how the organisation he had helped set up had managed to smuggle two students into a conference for high-flying businesspeople. Jenkins asked the Vote Leave compliance committee, chaired by Vote Leave board member Daniel Hodson, to investigate the incident. After being assured that, while it was an act of subterfuge, it would not cause any long-lasting damage to relations with the CBI, Jenkin called for a meeting with Cummings to find out what else was planned. The conversation was 'robust', remembered the Tory MP.

'I just thought it important for the board to send a message to the executive that they are accountable, and if things like this happen there are going to have to be explanations and assurances. Dominic was absolutely livid with me,' he said.

Cummings felt the organisation needed to be nimble, willing to think outside the box and be unafraid to challenge orthodoxies – mirroring the view he had taken while working in the Department for Education. Jenkin read the situation slightly differently: 'It basically means he should be able to decide whatever he wants, when he wants, and nobody should interfere with it.'

He added:

> Dominic was making it quite clear there would be other stuff that would be much more radical. And if we weren't prepared for it, we had better *get* prepared for it. At the back of my mind was the whole question of designation. If Vote Leave was not regarded as a fit and proper person in corporate terms, we would not get designation.

It wasn't just Jenkin who was questioning the direction Vote Leave was travelling in. Labour for Britain – which had now become Labour Leave – was also getting frustrated. Despite going public at the beginning of October, Vote Leave was still very much a Westminster-based operation. For politicians like Kate Hoey, who were used to being involved in ground campaigns, it was enormously frustrating. One of the early flashpoints came at a meeting of the exploratory committee one afternoon in October.

'There were heavy criticisms,' remembered Brendan Chilton. 'It really came to a head when the Leave.EU campaign had done a national leaflet back in October. We turned up at that meeting and it was like, "What the fuck's going on?"'

Another person getting increasingly frustrated was Peter Bone. The Tory MP was one of the three – along with Tom Pursglove and Philip Hollobone – who had run their own mini-EU referendum in Northamptonshire in 2014. The Wellingborough MP was first elected to the Commons in 2005 and had spent ten years cultivating an image of a ground campaigner who took the fight to the doorsteps.

Looking back, he said:

> What was becoming clear was that Vote Leave was very good at the air warfare, and the research and all that, but had very little knowledge or interest in ground warfare. And the people like Steve Baker and Bernard Jenkin never had to fight for marginal seats, they weren't used to ground campaigns.

Around the time Vote Leave officially launched, Bone went over to Westminster Tower to meet with Cummings and Elliott to discuss how to get a ground campaign started, and what role he and Pursglove could play. After hearing 'all the right noises', Bone left the meeting feeling confident that Vote Leave were committed to the sort of campaigning tactics he was used to.

Another reason for Bone's optimism was the recruitment of Richard Murphy, the Conservatives' former head of field campaigning, who had spent eighteen years as an election strategist for the party. He was appointed Vote Leave's head of field operations and regional campaigning, and having him on board seemed to signal a commitment to taking the fight to the Remain camp on the doorsteps of Britain.

* * *

On 10 November – a day after being heckled at the CBI – the Prime Minister formally set out his demands for EU reform in a speech at Chatham House in London. He confirmed what had been leaked to *The Guardian* – namely that he would not call for an emergency brake on migration to the UK – and also admitted

that there would be wriggle room on restricting benefits to foreign workers. In the Tory manifesto, which was barely six months
old, Cameron had vowed to 'insist that EU migrants who want to
claim tax credits and child benefit must live here and contribute
to our country for a minimum of four years'.

In the Chatham House speech, he stepped back from such a
hardline position, and gone was the word 'insist'. 'I understand
how difficult some of these welfare issues are for other member
states. And I am open to different ways of dealing with this issue,'
said the Prime Minister. He followed up the speech by sending a
letter to European Council President Donald Tusk in which he
outlined his four areas of reform: economic governance; compet-
itiveness; sovereignty; and immigration.

The speech, and the follow-up letter to Tusk, was the tipping
point for Iain Duncan Smith. The Work and Pensions Secretary
had been given the impression that the so-called emergency brake
on migration would be a key part of the address. He was on his
way to his colleague Dominic Raab's constituency of Esher and
Walton in Surrey when he was called by one of Cameron's top
advisors to say the brake had been pulled.

Duncan Smith remembered:

> I got called by Ed Llewellyn at that stage to say: 'You know
> that emergency brake we've got in there? We've had to remove
> it from the speech.' I said: 'Why's that?' He said: 'Only because
> there's some technicalities and issues around it.'
>
> I just knew why they'd removed it: because Angela Merkel
> finally read the speech. The staff probably said: 'It's OK,' but
> then she then read it, I think, and I think she simply said:
> 'I can't back a speech which has this in it because this breaks
> one of our principles,' so we're back to square one again. From
> that moment on it was pretty much downhill because David
> Cameron didn't have a lot of options. I don't blame him for

this. What became apparent to me was the European Union didn't really take this referendum seriously.

In the Commons the next day, Tory MP Jacob Rees-Mogg spoke for many Eurosceptics when he took to his feet:

> This is pretty thin gruel – it is much less than people had come to expect from the government. It takes out a few words from the preamble but does nothing about the substance of the treaties; it deals with competition, for which the European Commission itself has a proposal; and it fails to restore control of our borders. It seems to me that its whole aim is to make Harold Wilson's renegotiation look respectable. It needs to do more; it needs to have a full list of powers that will be restored to the United Kingdom and to this Parliament, not vacuously to Parliaments plural.

Conservatives for Britain – which had been on a Leave footing since Lord Lawson took over as chairman in October – saw its numbers swell to well over 120 at a meeting on Tuesday 17 November to discuss the package.

Ahead of the meeting, Owen Paterson told the *Telegraph*:

> The Tusk letter was a once in a generation opportunity to seek fundamental change in Britain's relationship with the EU. The requests made by the Prime Minister will not secure a deal the British public deserve. The renegotiation process is effectively over and I will be focusing on campaigning for Britain to leave the EU.

It was the moment when Bernard Jenkin also publicly declared for Leave for the first time. 'My view is that the letter was a turning point. I am now fully signing up to vote "Leave", he told the

Telegraph, adding: 'I think most Conservative MPs will probably vote Leave.'

With Cameron's negotiation aims falling short of even the
relatively low bar he had set himself in May, many Vote Leave
supporters were anxious to get on with the job of campaigning.
Yet, it soon became clear that those running the show were not
prepared to sanction the kind of activity the group's members
felt was needed.

In mid-November, Richard Murphy quit Vote Leave after learn-
ing the campaign would initially be focused on digital activity,
with the ground game coming into play closer to the date of the
referendum – which had still not been revealed. Within a month
he was hired by Leave.EU as its director of field campaigning.
'Leave.EU have already set up over 300 local groups and they
are best placed to run an effective ground campaign. The campaign to leave the EU can only be won outside of Westminster,
so a vibrant, professional grassroots organisation is critical,' he
said in a statement.

Vote Leave's digital focus was partly tactical, but also a very real
illustration of the lack of money the organisation had to play with.

'I can understand why Richard Murphy felt those funding con-
straints in October/November because we couldn't print a million
correx boards and print five million leaflets and have, you know,
a thousand street stall packs by tomorrow and ten thousand
T-shirts,' said Elliott.

With no ground war on the horizon, some in Vote Leave tried
to seize the initiative and organise grassroots events. However,
it was at this level that the lack of cooperation between the two
Leave campaigns was starting to make a difference. 'You were
getting activists coming to us and saying, "Who do we support?
Whose orders do we follow?"' said Chilton. The Ashford councillor was so frustrated with the inactivity he wrote to all the
political parties in his area to try to coordinate some action.

'I said, "Any Brexiteers, there's a meeting tomorrow night in the Queen's Head pub, turn up." We got a group but only half the people were there, because Leave.EU were organising a training session on exactly the same night in a pub two miles down the road,' he remembered. Grievances were raised at the ExCom meetings, which, according to Chilton, 'did get quite heated on occasions because politicians were frustrated. There were very stern words and often those stern words were met with a "So what?" approach and "We're not doing it" – more so from Dom.'

As Labour Leave's General Secretary was worrying about the absence of a ground campaign, John Mills, Vote Leave's chairman, was questioning why there was such a determination not to work with Leave.EU. He understood that while Farage was not going to appeal to 'liberal-minded metropolitan people', the UKIP leader 'does have a very substantial pull with the sort of people who switch their vote, and he was clearly very good'.

He added:

> I certainly shared the view that you need two separate campaigns addressing different constituencies, but that you could have some sort of coordination, some sort of overarching body, that you wanted to avoid loads of resources going into competing designation applications, and that there really was a substantial role for those sort of UKIP-type of people, knocking on doors and acting as a ground war.

Mills tried to persuade the board there should be greater cooperation between the two campaigns, but found himself in a 'minority of one'. He said: 'Generally speaking, the rest of the board very much just took the line that was put forward by Matthew Elliott and Dominic Cummings, that there should be a sharp division.

Mills added: 'It rumbled on. I remember one particular meeting when I know I did put this quite strongly but obviously it was getting nowhere. You didn't need a vote from the board [on whether there should be a change in tactics] as it was quite clear that there was no support for it. Not much at all.'

It wasn't just those from the Labour part of Vote Leave's tent who were getting frustrated. Even some of the Tories who helped get the campaign off the ground were finding out it was not quite the organisation they had envisaged in the aftermath of the general election. Every Monday morning at 10 a.m., parliamentarians would descend on Vote Leave HQ for a briefing on the campaign's activities. David Campbell Bannerman remembered one incident in particular which to him summed up the way he and other Tories were viewed.

'You had a former Secretary of State, Owen Paterson, in this meeting, and Bernard Jenkin was behind me – he was one of the heads of Vote Leave at that point,' remembered Campbell Bannerman.

> The guys that were meant to be briefing us – Dominic Cummings, Matthew Elliott – were in a private meeting, though we could see them – with Dan Hannan and Doug Carswell. The four of them are in that meeting and we're being briefed by Victoria the campaign lady, and Bernard and Owen were looking, thinking: 'What the hell are they doing in that room? They're meant to be briefing us and the parliamentary meeting.' So it sent messages they weren't particularly bothered, they had more important things to do.

Paterson agreed: 'The exploratory committee became more and more just a fringe routine meeting which had to be gone through, and in the end it was dropped.'

There was one word Campbell Bannerman used to sum up the attitude of Vote Leave, and Cummings in particular: contempt. 'Vote Leave was regarded as having contempt for people.

Contempt was a word that kept coming back,' he said, looking back.

Again, Paterson agreed: 'There was no arguing: he was right, his ideas were right. He was so driven by his belief in his own ideas he was prepared to upset committed Eurosceptic MPs like Peter Bone and important Labour representatives like Kate Hoey.'

Tensions boiled over on Monday 7 December. It was one of the regular meetings between MPs and Vote Leave staff, this time with Cummings in attendance. Before the briefing began, the atmosphere was frosty. The previous day, the *Mail on Sunday* had run an article claiming that even if David Cameron was to back quitting the EU, Vote Leave wouldn't want him to head up its campaign. The article had a quote from a senior source at Vote Leave, complete with a word usually reserved to describe Nigel Farage:

> If Cameron thinks we'd want him leading the 'leave' campaign he's deluded. He's toxic on this issue and he would undermine the campaign. No one believes him on the EU any more. If there was a choice between who to put up in a television debate between Cameron and Boris, you'd want Boris every time.

Many Eurosceptic Tories were furious. Despite their wide and entrenched differences with Cameron over Europe, having their party leader described as 'toxic' by a campaign they were backing was a step too far. Just months before, he had won the Tories their first election since 1992, and they did not want to see such language hurled in the direction of the man who had secured such a feat. There was also a practical reason why you would not turn Cameron away from leading Vote Leave, if he so wanted. He was the Prime Minister, and on issues such as this, having the leader of the country as part of the campaign was deemed to be a bonus. 'Most of us thought, "Who the hell is briefing that we don't want the Prime Minister?" The Prime Minister is worth 20 per cent of the vote,' said Campbell Bannerman.

Peter Bone raised the article with Cummings. He had already been feeling deflated before he saw the article, as Vote Leave were putting out leaflets he knew nothing about. 'We were supposed to be there to do the ground work but then they produced a leaflet without even talking to me,' he said. Richard Murphy had quit just a few weeks before, and Bone was beginning to realise that the ground campaign he felt was essential if Vote Leave were going to win the referendum was nowhere near the top of the group's priorities.

He was also, like many others, struggling to understand why Vote Leave was refusing to work with Leave.EU and UKIP. 'We didn't see how we could win without having UKIP,' he said. For Bone, Vote Leave saying the Prime Minister was 'deluded' and 'toxic' was the final straw.

He remembered:

> The Prime Minister was saying that 'if I don't get the right deal, basically I'll lead the Out campaign', which I thought was great news, and that was slagged off by Cummings in the press. I didn't agree with that point of view, I thought that was a huge mistake and that was the thing that pushed me over the top.

Bone raised it in 'a pretty angry way', prompting Cummings to respond: 'I don't care, I don't care what you do, we're just going to go on and you can think what you think, I'm just going to do what the hell I want to do,' according to Campbell Bannerman.

With parliamentarians watching, Cummings continued to tear a strip off Bone. Paterson, who was in the room, said: 'He was gratuitously rude to Bone. Bone was a very committed backbencher who has got a group of MPs around him in Northamptonshire who get on with him very well and he was inevitably going to play a big role on the campaign. It was wholly and unnecessarily rude.'

Once Cummings had finished, Bone very quietly picked up his coat and left the room. It was the last time Bone was involved in Vote Leave, but not the last time he would be involved in a Leave campaign.

CHAPTER 19

Peter Bone was down, but he was not out. Vote Leave had never really suited him. He was a campaigner who felt comfortable manning a street stall, not a Westminster insider who could manipulate donors and the press. After walking out of Vote Leave, he could have gone across to Leave.EU, giving them some much-needed Conservative support. But why swap one campaign full of egos obsessing about designation for another? Sitting in his office in Portcullis House, decorated with posters and leaflets from previous victorious election campaigns, Bone and his political apprentice Tom Pursglove decided what was really needed was a new organisation entirely, which would focus purely on the ground campaign – one that would take the referendum out to the rest of the country. Public meetings, street stalls, leafleting, door knocking – all the tactics and techniques Bone was comfortable with. It would be a grassroots campaign, hence the name: Grassroots Out – often shortened to GO.

Bone said:

> We decided we would set Grassroots Out up to campaign at a grassroots level on a cross-party issue, because we knew that from our own area there were lots of people who were Labour, UKIP and non-aligned who wanted to do it.

I wanted to replicate what we were doing locally, which was having organised canvassing all the time. We thought if we could set up groups all round the country we could get a proper grassroots campaign, so that was the point of it.

Bone and Pursglove knew the failing of Vote Leave and Leave.EU was that they were both too tribal, and if their new project was to work it had to be cross-party from the off. A call went out to Kate Hoey, who Bone knew was getting just as frustrated with Vote Leave's lack of a ground campaign as he was. The proposition was music to Hoey's ears, and the three met in her office to iron out the details. It wasn't just Labour and Tory figures Bone wanted to get signed up to Grassroots Out: it was also Ukippers. Bone and Hoey were both very much in the camp that felt Eurosceptics from across the spectrum should be working together, not at cross-purposes. Bone and Pursglove met with Farage at the Blue Boar Hotel near St James's Park to discuss their venture, which was met with enthusiastic support from the UKIP leader.

There was one other failing that was also common to both Vote Leave and Leave.EU – they were both obsessed with securing the official designation. According to Bone, when Grassroots Out was formed: 'There was no intention of going for designation whatsoever. It never crossed our minds.'

On 16 December 2015, Grassroots Out Ltd was registered with Companies House, with Bone and Pursglove listed as directors. It was just nine days since Bone had walked out of Vote Leave.

With Tory, Labour and UKIP Eurosceptics all on board, Bone organised a meeting with representatives from Vote Leave to inform them of their plans, and to ask if anyone would like to be involved in the activities they had planned. Joining Bone in his office were Pursglove, Hoey, Brendan Chilton from Labour Leave, and John Mills and Daniel Hodson from Vote Leave.

'Everyone was in favour of that in the room, we all thought

it was marvellous because it finally meant these two warring tribes would have something to work through,' said Chilton.

On 4 January, the group was announced to the media, with supportive quotes from Bone, Pursglove, Hoey and Farage. 'At the moment, every day that passes while we are not organised at the grassroots is a wasted opportunity to spread our message on the ground, gifting the advantage to our referendum opponents. GO will help to redress that imbalance,' said Bone in an article for MailOnline.

Two days later, Pursglove, Hoey and Farage penned an article for the *Telegraph* in which they announced that Grassroots Out would hold a public meeting in Kettering, Northamptonshire, on 23 January. 'For it is only by leaving Westminster and taking the debate across the country that we will win,' the three wrote. Set to speak were Bone, Pursglove, Hoey, Farage and Tory MP Philip Hollobone, while the event would be chaired by UKIP MEP Margot Parker.

With Farage backing GO, it was no surprise that in its regular mail-out to supporters Leave.EU welcomed the new organisation, describing it as 'a group we look forward to working closely with in the run-up to the referendum'. The UKIP leader had spotted an opportunity to reboot his attempt at being a key player in the referendum. Instead of creating a group and hoping Tories and Labour MPs would back it – like Leave.EU – he would align himself with one created by representatives of other parties. But what to do about Leave.EU and Banks? He couldn't just drop them now Grassroots Out was on the scene. He decided to merge the two together, and Banks agreed to pump in some money to get it off the ground.

'Nigel didn't think we were going to win the designation without some form of political coverage and of course at Leave.EU we didn't have any Conservatives,' said Banks. 'So they came up with this idea of Grassroots Out as a way of bringing in Conservatives,

Labour and UKIP, as that would give Vote Leave a run for its money.'

Leave.EU co-chair Richard Tice was extremely enthusiastic. 'I thought it was great,' he said:

> It was a logical answer to politicians' frustrations. It was very easy to say Leave.EU is what it is and where it is in the whole thing and it made sense to say Grassroots Out was a vehicle for politicians who didn't agree with Vote Leave to come to help.

Keen to get support from his party, Farage invited Bone and Pursglove along to the UKIP MEPs and NEC away days in Bristol on 13–14 January. The Tory duo made a presentation to the UKIP delegation on the morning of the second day, emphasising that this group would not be going for designation and was merely a vehicle to organise ground campaigning and public meetings.

On Saturday 23 January, Grassroots Out hosted its first public rally at the Kettering Conference Centre. Before its 2 p.m. start time, Farage, Bone and Pursglove went for walkabouts in Wellingborough and Kettering to publicise their new group. Activists wore bright grass-green coloured T-shirts and waved balloons as the Brexiteers pounded the streets and posed for photographs. Farage lived up to his reputation and popped into the Little Ale House in Wellingborough for a pre-rally pint.

Also in Kettering was Chilton, who had caught the train up from London. He was supposed to be arriving with a cheque from Vote Leave as part of an agreement Mills had secured with Elliott to help get the group off the ground, but no money was handed over. Chilton says:

> I was instructed to go and meet Matthew Elliott by John to go and collect a cheque for £20,000 and to take it to the

first big rally in Kettering. I called Matthew the night before and said: 'When am I meeting you?' – in fact I had called him several times and text him but got no reply – and that Saturday morning I came into London, I was at St Pancras station, the train was due to leave in half an hour. I kept texting: 'Matthew, where's the cheque? Who's coming to give it to me?' and I never got that cheque.

Upon arriving in Kettering, Chilton met up with Hoey and the pair shared a taxi. On hearing that the money from Elliott had not materialised, Hoey was furious, but it also confirmed to her what she had been thinking for a while: she needed to quit Vote Leave. As the cab got closer to the conference centre, Chilton suddenly realised he had no idea what he was about to encounter. He had never met Farage, Banks or Andy Wigmore before, and the only things he had heard about them were negative.

Chilton recalled:

> Prior to getting involved with Leave.EU and Grassroots we had been told that Leave.EU and Arron and Nigel were devils with horns and we mustn't go near them. It was sort of like Plato's cave – we mustn't venture out! As we were going across to the rally ground, I said to Kate: 'What the bloody hell are we going to do now we're here? We're in the heart of the empire!' And she said: 'I don't know, we're just going to have to go with it.' We got there and they were nice as pie.

By the time the clock struck 2 p.m. and the speakers were ready to take the stage, two and a half thousand people had filled the conference centre. Along with the six names previously announced, DUP MP Sammy Wilson had been added to the line-up, giving the group an excuse to walk on to the stage to the theme tune from *The Magnificent Seven*.

Margot Parker spoke first, and fluffed her first line when she welcomed everyone to the 'Cottering Conference Centre'. Up next was Sammy Wilson, followed by Philip Hollobone (in a Union Jack sports jacket), Peter Bone, Tom Pursglove, Kate Hoey and then Nigel Farage – who ended his speech by getting the audience to shout: 'We want our country back!' As the standing ovation came to end, Farage indulged his showman side: 'All the speakers that were advertised have turned up and spoken, but I might just have one more speaker for you. One little surprise up our sleeve. Are you ready to welcome another guest? Well, I'm pleased, because we've got a big hitter,' he said.

After describing the next speaker as 'one of the most important people in the whole of this referendum campaign', Farage went for the big reveal: former Defence Secretary Liam Fox.

The ex-Cabinet minister had been on Farage's radar as someone he could do business with for many months, but it was after Fox's appearance on the BBC's *Andrew Marr Show* on Sunday 20 December that the UKIP leader had contacted him about sharing a platform together. Fox had announced he would be voting to Leave in the referendum and urged the pro-Brexit camps to 'speak with a much greater, much more unified voice than they have had up to this point'. When asked if he would share a platform with Farage, Fox was unambiguous in his reply: 'Oh yes, definitely.'

As Fox shook hands with Farage in Kettering, the UKIP leader leaned in and said: 'The *Marr* programme has come true.'

It was a hugely symbolic moment for the UKIP leader. 'It was very emotional for me, very emotional, because suddenly we'd reached out and beyond and the UKIP view was no longer insane. There were other people from other parties prepared to stand up and say those things. I felt very strongly about that,' he said.

At the end of Fox's speech, the eight members of the panel signed a document given the grandiose name of 'The Kettering Declaration': 'We, the undersigned, declare that in the weeks and months ahead we shall set aside party politics and work together towards our common goal of a free and prosperous United Kingdom outside the European Union, engaged with the wider world and governed by its own laws.'

The Kettering rally had been a tremendous success in the eyes of those involved. On a Saturday afternoon in Middle England, more than 2,000 people had turned out to hear from a truly cross-party panel of Eurosceptics about why they should vote to leave the EU.

'Yes, you're talking to the faithful, but it motivates them to get up and go and knock on another hundred doors in the following fortnight,' Tice reflected.

On Thursday 28 January, Bone, Pursglove and Hoey met with Banks, Mills and Elliott at 5 Hertford Street to discuss how the respective campaigns could all work together. 'At the end of the day it was Vote Leave that didn't want to come in, didn't want to merge. Leave.EU would have,' said Bone, before adding: 'That was hugely disappointing to me, Tom and Kate.' Mills was keen on some sort of joint working, but Elliott couldn't back any kind of merger that involved Leave.EU.

Although the campaign was aimed at reaching out beyond the Westminster bubble, it was still having an impact within it – mainly due to some garish merchandise designed by Richard Murphy (who had been seconded from Leave.EU to Grassroots Out to run its campaigning division). The most notorious of his creations was a Grassroots Out tie, consisting of black and bright-green stripes with the campaign's logo sprinkled liberally over the top. Several Tory MPs wore the notable neckwear to Prime Minister's Questions on Wednesday 3 February, and Bone even offered one to David Cameron as an incentive to come and speak at a rally in London planned for 19 February. 'The honourable gentleman is always very generous with his time, with his advice and now also with his clothing. The tie is here – I feel the blazer is soon to follow,' responded Cameron with a smile.

Grassroots Out might have been having fun with their eye-catching outfits, but not all Eurosceptics were fans. 'We'd be ten points ahead if it wasn't for those idiots in the green ties,' one senior Vote Leave MP remarked.

The next rally was scheduled for Friday 5 February in Manchester. Farage, Bone, Pursglove and Hoey all spoke, as did UKIP MEP Louise Bours, John Boyd from the Campaign Against Euro Federalism, Tory MP William Wragg and political commentator Simon Heffer. The two big speakers were Graham Brady, chairman of the Conservative backbench 1922 Committee, who was annoyed that Farage got a standing ovation and he didn't, and former Tory leadership contender David Davis.

It was after the Manchester rally that the decision was made to change the *raison d'être* of Grassroots Out. Bone, seeing the growing popularity of GO, thought his organisation was in a much better place to secure designation than Leave.EU, and suggested that plan of action to the UKIP leader. Farage said:

> I thought, 'Woah, hang on, I didn't agree to support this if you're on some sort of mad ambitious course.' I was a bit hesitant. It was a Friday night. I thought what Bone had said was important. I didn't know if it was important for good reasons or bad reasons, but I knew it was important.

The next day, Bone and Farage thrashed out the idea in a meeting with Richard Tice, and decided to go for it. 'That little kite that Bone had put up last night in Manchester is right and it's right because we start from fresh, there's no baggage, there's no artillery war,' said Farage. On the Sunday, Farage approached Banks, who agreed to throw Leave.EU's support behind GO. 'It was amazing. Arron's generosity in this was amazing,' said Farage.

Banks may have been enthusiastic to begin with, but as time went on he regretted getting involved in GO. 'The big mistake was doing the GO thing, as that distracted us from our core campaign, which would have got stronger and stronger,' he said. 'If I had my time again I wouldn't have done that. We would have done our own rallies and pulled people in as they all came to see Nigel, really.'

Despite putting his hand in his pocket and helping finance some of the rallies, Banks's involvement with GO did not get off to the best start. He cost the campaign group significant support among Conservative MPs thanks to an interview he gave to *The Times*, which came out the day after the Manchester rally.

The interview took place in the Carluccio's restaurant at Heathrow Airport just before Banks jetted off to South Africa. A few glasses of Pinot Grigio loosened his tongue more than usual, and Banks proclaimed that his Leave rival Elliott was more interested in getting a peerage than in winning the referendum: 'He wants to be Lord Elliott of Loserville,' he said.

Banks also gave a small window into his relationship with Andy Wigmore: 'Every morning Andy starts with an impression of one of the people from the campaigns, like Matthew. "Oh, Arron, I want to suck your earlobes, Arron." His "Matthew" is brilliant. "Oh, Arron, this is such a distasteful situation." These people are jokes!'

Those comments may have bordered on the ridiculous, but it was what he said about David Cameron that really caused a furore: 'Anyone who can use their disabled child as a prop to show that they're human is in my mind a dreadful person,' said Banks. Cameron's first son, Ivan, had been born with a combination of cerebral palsy and severe epilepsy, leaving him requiring 24-hour care. Ivan died in 2009, aged just six.

Speaking later, Banks said:

> Well, of course that was all over *The Times*. Elliott photo-
> copied *The Times* and sent it to every Tory MP saying what

a disgraceful bunch of people these people are, you can't
trust them, they're horrible people, look what they said
about the Prime Minister. Then Bone reckons he lost virtually every Tory MP as a result.

Farage was also furious, remembered Banks: 'I had a call from
Nigel saying, "What the fuck are you doing?" and he called me
moronic – "What a moronic thing to do!"'

When asked if he regretted the comments, Banks said: 'Nah,
I don't regret it because it's true. When you are worth £70 million
you don't have to rely on the NHS for your disabled child and to
have your wife in the [party conference] audience crying is just
a bunch of bollocks.'

After they announced their intention to go for designation on
Tuesday 16 February, all eyes turned to the third Grassroots Out
rally, planned for Westminster three days later. It would be held in
the Queen Elizabeth II Centre on the day Cameron was expected
to finalise his deal with Brussels, and then officially announce
the referendum date – meaning Cabinet ministers would be free
to campaign for Leave. With the rally just a minute's walk from
Downing Street, speculation was rife that this group – which
had been active for just a month – had secured a high-profile
speaker to address the crowds that night. It had – just not the one
people expected.

CHAPTER 20

Peter Bone's departure and subsequent creation of Grass-roots Out were not the only problems facing Vote Leave as 2015 turned to 2016.

There were now arguments over the behaviour and attitude of Dominic Cummings, the lack of a merger with Leave.EU and a perceived slighting of a number of Tory Eurosceptics who felt they should be playing a higher-profile role in the campaign.

A senior Vote Leave member remembered Cummings would attend meetings with MPs but 'would spend his whole time on his iPhone, and his attitude seemed to be: "How long is this meeting going on for? I am a busy person, I've got things to run."'

Tory MEP David Campbell Bannerman felt marginalised, and said: 'I was pretty pissed off with Vote Leave's contempt and isolation. I always felt I was sidelined, not listened to. I'm not in it for the ego but I just thought if you're being treated with contempt then you are wasting your time.' Brendan Chilton from Labour Leave shared office space with Vote Leave in Westminster Tower and was disheartened by how he could see the organisation behaving. He said:

> They would spend just as much time running around monitoring the tweets of Leave.EU as they would on Stronger

In Europe, it was pathetic. We'd be sitting there and we'd think: 'What the bloody hell are we involved with here?' The enemy are Stronger In, yet we've got briefings coming out on Leave.EU, it's pathetic. It was tit-for-tat, six of one and half a dozen of the other.

It wasn't just Vote Leave's behaviour towards Leave.EU that infuriated Labour Leave, but also how they were being treated. John Mills, who was chairman of Vote Leave at this point, remembered the feedback he was getting from his Labour colleagues based in Westminster Tower:

I don't think there was any real policy issue differences, it was just that I think that the Labour people felt that they weren't terribly welcome at Vote Leave, and you know it wasn't wholly a Conservative organisation, but it was kind of a Conservative tone on balance. They just weren't made terribly welcome and they didn't like it.

On 23 December, *The Times* ran an article laying out the tensions for all to see, and the finger of blame was pointed squarely at Cummings:

MPs expressed concern about the direction of the Vote Leave campaign after one of its leading figures was suspected of using it to pursue a vendetta against the prime minister. Two senior Tories today suggest that Dominic Cummings, a former aide to Michael Gove who is running the campaign, should be sacked if he uses it to attack Mr Cameron. They have intervened after Vote Leave organised a protest against the prime minister at the CBI conference last month. There is also dismay at the level of briefing against Mr Cameron, following suggestions that he would not make a good frontman for the 'out' campaign should his renegotiation with the EU fail. This issue is understood to be causing tensions between senior Vote Leave figures and Conservatives for Britain, the group that is shepherding Tory MPs opposed to EU membership.

The two Tories cited were Sir Alan Duncan – who would actually go on to back Remain – and Andrew Percy, MP for Brigg and Goole, who was a member of the Eurosceptic group Better Off Out. 'The referendum campaign must be conducted on the issues and not on the basis of personality,' Percy told *The Times*. 'The Prime Minister is entitled to his view just as those who support leaving the EU are entitled to ours and both campaigns should conduct themselves with respect for those in the other side. I won't be involved in any campaign that is being used to settle old scores.'

A Vote Leave source hit back:

> This campaign isn't personal for anyone. Top Vote Leave staff were campaigning on the EU before David Cameron was even an MP. When the Prime Minister dropped promises on the EU that he made as recently as last year it is clear he can't be trusted on the EU. We will continue to explain that to people.

As a board member who was also chairman of the ExCom group, Bernard Jenkin was hearing the grumblings loudest of all and decided to try to tackle the concerns as best he could. 'In the run-up to Christmas there was lots of discussion about the style and culture of Vote Leave and how it was going to go forward,' said Jenkin.

> The conversations were always quite tricky because Dominic was absolutely determined not to be accountable. I can only put it like that. Dominic has many, many extraordinary

qualities, such as his insight into voter behaviour and his
understanding of the very limited information you get from
focus groups and polls, and then the ability to synthesise
that information effectively in order to create messages that
would have an effect. He also has an absolutely fantastic
grasp of the legal, constitutional, economic and geopolitical
significance of us being in the EU and being outside the EU.
But managing him was a challenge.

Jenkin may have shared concerns over the style and tactics of
Vote Leave, but there was one matter he resolutely agreed with
Cummings on: there should be no merger with Leave.EU. But
that view wasn't shared by many in the organisation, who couldn't
understand why there wasn't one unified campaign. This constant
complaining was frustrating for Matthew Elliott. The activist was
using all his charm and connections to try to woo some big names
over to Vote Leave – and these people were clear that they didn't
want it to be a UKIP-led campaign.

Elliott recalled:

> Dom and I were having lots of conversations with Cabinet
> ministers and conversations with senior businessmen, so
> we knew what sort of campaign they wanted – a non-UKIP
> based campaign – and we had a good reason to believe that
> some of the senior guys would be coming on board.

The problem for Elliott was that he could not tell people this was
happening, for fear it would leak into the press: 'You can't then
turn around and say: "Actually, stick with us, I had a great dinner
last night with an ex-Cabinet minister, you know he was really
up for this."'

He added: 'It's easy to forget how sensitive it was for Cabinet
ministers. I had Cabinet ministers around my flat in Brixton for

lunch for the weekends to have the chats with them and talk through the campaign.' Elliott was in the tricky position of being accused of not carrying out any significant activity, yet he was forced to carry out arguably the most significant activity in secret.

Even Douglas Carswell, the UKIP MP who had been willing to risk his entire political career to help support Elliott in running the Leave campaign, was starting to get a bit worried about what was actually going on.

He said:

> I used to look and think, 'These ruddy Conservatives, when are they going to actually come to the fight?' It's all very well me trying to say, 'I'm representing UKIP with this group,' but when's the ruddy cavalry arriving? I remember feeling at times immense frustration that, yes, I knew that these people had to be leading the charge, but where the heck were they?

The new year offered little respite from the disagreements – and the tension was now extending beyond the concerns of Eurosceptic MPs and starting to influence the donors. Vote Leave was already having difficulty extracting money from anti-EU supporters who wanted to keep their cheque books closed until one of the campaigns was given official designation, but the feedback surrounding Cummings's behaviour was also causing people with money to think twice about handing over much-needed cash.

In mid-January, Jenkin received a telephone call from Elliott after a meeting with donors. 'He said: "Dominic's got to be moved to a different role because he's becoming an obstacle to raising funds,"' recounted Jenkin. Mills agreed, and a plan was put together to remove Cummings from the campaign director role but keep him on as an advisor.

A showdown meeting with Cummings and the rest of the board was set for Tuesday 26 January, but what Jenkin didn't realise until he got into the room was that Cummings was well aware of the plot.

'Dominic organised an insurrection amongst his staff at Vote Leave, amongst key media people mainly. And basically he threatened to blow up the whole campaign if he couldn't be the campaign director,' said Jenkin.

He added: 'Cummings convinced the rest of the board that they were all going to resign and there wouldn't be a campaign, it would just fold up and there would be no people. The result was the board basically crumbled and John Mills was left with very little authority.'

Cummings had seen off the so-called coup, leaving Elliott still facing major problems with donors. Morale remained extremely low, particularly among the Labour members of Vote Leave.

'We were on the cusp of complete destruction at that point,' said Jenkin. To make matters worse, it became clear that Mills would soon be resigning from the board – leaving Vote Leave without a chairman just weeks before David Cameron concluded his renegotiation. After discussing the issue with Elliott, Jenkin approached Lord Lawson in Parliament and asked him to take over as chairman. The former Tory Chancellor – who had already turned down a previous approach from Elliott – reluctantly agreed, but on one condition: Elliott and Cummings had to go from the board.

Cummings, of course, was not happy about the ultimatum, and resisted any attempts to force himself and Elliott out. Lawson would not budge over his conditions either, leading to yet another stalemate. In an appearance on the *Sunday Politics* on 31 January, Steve Baker sounded a bleak note as he was quizzed on the inner wranglings in Vote Leave:

> It's very, very late in the day to be making such a profound change but, given the severe concerns of my colleagues, it's quite clear there are going to have to be material changes

in Vote Leave in order to carry parliamentarians with the campaign. There's going to have to be a greater degree of involvement with parliamentarians so that they feel they're meaningfully helping to shape the campaign in order to win the core and the swing voters we need.

Campbell Bannerman, who wasn't on the board, was trying his best to find out what was happening, as all he and others were hearing was that Cummings had been sacked. He said:

> I was getting these phone calls from Steve [Baker] and others while all this was going on and it was slightly comic: 'Has he been fired or not fired?' or 'Where are we?' It just kept going on and on. It was like a Houdini act and he managed to get out.

It fell to Jenkin to lay it out in plain language to Cummings. The Tory MP happened to be in Baker's office when Elliott rang to discuss how to move forward, and Jenkin took his opportunity to speak to the Vote Leave pair:

> I had a very difficult conversation with Matthew and Dominic to persuade them that they just had to bite the bullet and do this. I don't think Dominic really ever forgave me for it. I said, 'Look, if you don't agree to do this I think this whole campaign is going to collapse and it will be over, there is no option.' Dominic, very gamely, finally submitted and it saved the campaign.

A compromise was reached. Cummings and Elliott would stay on in their respective roles as campaign director and chief executive but stand down from the board. Elliott later downplayed the reshuffle, and said:

That was basically part of a broad restructure. If you notice
Dom and I set it up as the first two directors, then the idea
was that we would always have a board, where the executives sit in attendance but don't actually sit on the board as
leading directors. If you look at any charity, that's how it's
set up – trustees are sort of non-executive and not paid to
do what they do.

While the Tory members of Vote Leave were happy with the way
the matter had been resolved, the Labour representatives were not.
Tensions had already been exacerbated by Labour Leave holding
its own campaign launch on Wednesday 20 January.

As Brendan Chilton put it:

We had our little mini-launch in January, which some people in Vote Leave objected to because we were part of their
campaign – 'We've already launched, why are you launching again?' they said. We knew we need our own identity in
all this if we're to win Labour voters. Unfortunately, relations
broke down because we were very ambitious, we wanted
huge leafleting agendas, ground wars going on, and the strategy of Vote Leave, while commendable in some respects,
didn't have the focus on the ground war which we felt
was important. There was also then clashes of personality,
there were growing concerns that the two main Leave campaigns weren't working together.

The introduction of Lawson as the new chairman did little to
quell fears that Vote Leave was essentially a Tory campaign with
a few Labour people tacked on simply to appear cross-party for
the purposes of designation.

On Tuesday 2 February, Mills, Chilton, Hoey, former Labour
minister Nigel Griffiths and trade unionist John Sweeney met

to air their frustrations. The meeting was a blood-letting. Hoey was furious with Vote Leave's constant refusal to work with any of the other campaigns or UKIP, and announced she was quitting Labour Leave. Mills managed to persuade her not to make the decision public, something she reluctantly agreed to. Chilton, Griffiths and Sweeney told Mills they would work for Vote Leave for another three weeks – to just after the conclusion of David Cameron's renegotiation with Brussels – then think again. It wasn't as if they didn't have another offer – Banks had promised Labour Leave £30,000 a month plus an office across the River Thames in Millbank Tower at no charge – on the condition that the organisation switched its support from Vote Leave to Leave.EU. Such a move would ruin Vote Leave's claim to be a cross-party campaign group, and strengthen the hand of Leave.EU when it came to applying for official designation.

After the meeting, Mills fired off a furious email to Elliott and Cummings, beginning by rebuking Vote Leave's campaign director for a text message about Griffiths.

> [The meeting was] not helped by a text sent by Dominic I think yesterday with another disparaging comment about Nigel. Dominic – What on earth are you doing, generating more and more ill feeling like this entirely unnecessarily? I thought you had promised to stop doing this sort of thing. Don't you realise that this kind of behaviour puts more and more damaging and unnecessary strain on everyone? It certainly makes my life more difficult, entails me spending more and more inordinate amounts of time pacifying people and defending policies in some of which I don't really believe, and wearing down such credibility as I still have, because of the need to undo the damage to relationships which your insensitivity causes.
>
> The bottom line is that Labour Leave are fed up with

the way they have been treated by VL [Vote Leave] and the
intransigent and insensitive – from their perspective – policies
it pursues – unfortunately typified by the remark referred
to above.

The email went on to list the flare-ups from the meeting, and ended
with a clear warning:

> LL [Labour Leave] is as sick of all the divisions there are
> in the Leave camp as many other people, and if nothing is
> done between now and the end of February to improve rela-
> tions with Leave.EU – which incidentally now has wider and
> wider trade union support, which is a big pull for LL staff –
> there will be another crunch point.

The warnings went unheeded, and on Wednesday 4 February,
Hoey told *The Spectator* she had quit the campaign group. 'I have
made it clear I was not prepared to work with Vote Leave,' she
said. In an interview published in the *Telegraph* the next day,
she went even further in her criticism.

Citing Elliott and Cummings as the reasons for her departure,
Hoey said:

> It's about style of campaigning and it's about the lies some
> of them have been saying. They are always trying to do
> down Leave.EU by saying it's a UKIP front. We have been
> working now for a while with all these people and it's not
> true. This week, there have been a few emails exchanged,
> just showing Dominic particularly at his most strange.
> We have been pushing to get back some kind of unity.
> But every time there have been discussions going on and
> things have been doing quite well, there is some vitriol and it
> all stops again.

With Hoey gone, Labour Leave's position within Vote Leave was hanging by a thread – and, with it, the chance of the campaign securing designation as the official Leave campaign. The pressure to make amends was on, especially as, finally, the Cabinet cavalry were coming.

CHAPTER 21

I t had been almost two months since David Cameron had set out his negotiation goals at Chatham House, and Eurosceptic members of his Cabinet were getting restless. On 18 December 2015, just over a month after the speech, the Prime Minister travelled to Brussels for more face-to-face talks with EU leaders. In a statement after the summit, the Prime Minister effectively announced the referendum vote would be in 2016 – with some time in June the most likely date.

While the negotiation aims and date of the referendum were starting to become clearer, the issue of whether Cabinet ministers would be able to campaign with their consciences instead of toeing the government line was still a matter of debate. Before the Commons broke up for Christmas, Iain Duncan Smith told Cameron he needed to be decisive about the issue:

> I said to him, 'You need to make a feature out of this because you're going to have to do it, so why don't you do it as a positive rather than a negative? Just say you're going to do it and not have it dragged out of you.' He kept saying, 'I'll think about it.'

It wasn't just those inside Cabinet telling Cameron to suspend collective responsibility. Graham Brady, chairman of the backbench 1922 Committee, penned an article for the *Telegraph* on 19 December in which he said: 'It has made sense for collective responsibility to apply during the renegotiation but as the negotiations draw to a close, the Cabinet and other ministers should be given the freedom to express their views. As in the 1975 referendum, the Cabinet must be given the "freedom to differ".'

On 27 December, former party leader Michael Howard added his voice to the growing clamour, telling the BBC: 'When it comes to the campaign, if there are Cabinet ministers who feel strongly that we should vote to leave the EU, they should certainly be allowed to do so without losing their seat in the Cabinet.'

Yet Downing Street were only offering vague assurances over the matter, and there were fears that even if Cameron did lift collective responsibility, it would only be in the short campaign ahead of the vote – meaning ministers would be tied in to supporting a deal they didn't agree with until virtually the eleventh hour.

By the first week of January 2016, Leader of the Commons Chris Grayling and Northern Ireland Secretary Theresa Villiers had had enough. The pair may not have been the highest-profile members of Cameron's top team, but their Euroscepticism was well-known around Westminster – and the Cabinet table. Daniel Hannan was a particular fan of Villiers, who had joined the government as a Transport minister in 2010: 'The first thing she did was to take the EU flags off all the buildings under her ministry's control. Now can you imagine any male politician doing that and then not telling anyone? I only know about that because a civil servant told me,' he said.

On Sunday 3 January, Grayling called Cameron's chief of staff Ed Llewellyn and demanded a meeting with the Prime Minister for the following day. He was going to give him an ultimatum: publicly commit to lifting collective responsibility as soon as the deal is done, or accept his resignation.

On the morning of Monday 4th, Grayling met with Cameron in

Downing Street and set out his position. The PM was not entirely surprised by Grayling's ultimatum, but did not give any ground initially. He asked Grayling to come and see him again that afternoon. In the meantime, Villiers called Cameron and issued a similar demand. Cameron was boxed in. To lose one Cabinet minister would be embarrassing; to lose two would be damaging.

Cameron, fearing a mass walk-out of Eurosceptic Cabinet ministers, agreed to the demands, and in the Commons the next day gave the assurance many had been waiting for. Speaking from the Despatch Box, he said:

> My intention is that at the conclusion of the renegotiation, the government should reach a clear recommendation and then the referendum will be held. But it is in the nature of a referendum that it is the people, not the politicians, who decide.
>
> As I indicated before Christmas, there will be a clear government position, but it will be open to individual ministers to take a different personal position while remaining part of the government.

The relief among Cabinet ministers on the Leave side of the argument was palpable. Since his appointment after the general election, Culture Secretary John Whittingdale had been mulling over whether he would sacrifice a job he loved for a cause he believed in. As well as being a Maastricht rebel in the 1990s, Whittingdale had served as political secretary to Margaret Thatcher from 1988 to 1992 – meaning he was by her side as she drew up the infamous Bruges speech in which she set her face against further European integration.

He said:

> Would I have resigned from Cabinet if I had been told that I had to support the renegotiated package if I remained in the

Cabinet? I would have found that incredibly hard. I wouldn't want to give up this job but on the other hand, I was told I was throwing my career away in 1992 because of my views on Europe and I've always been consistent and I can't see how I could change that now.

Grayling was the first out of the blocks to hint he was preparing to vote to leave. In an article for the *Telegraph* on 13 January, he claimed: 'Simply staying in the EU with our current terms of membership unchanged would be disastrous for Britain.' It was the first time a Cabinet member had spoken so openly about wanting the UK to quit the EU. On 4 February, Whittingdale followed suit, telling *The House* magazine:

I have a track record where I've been highly critical of the way the EU works and I have opposed measures for closer integration and it certainly needs reform. I hope the Prime Minister will get that agreement and then I'll look at it when he comes back with it.

When asked whether he would rule out breaking ranks with the Prime Minister on the issue, he said: 'I wouldn't.'

The next EU summit was pencilled in for 18 February and, leading up to the Brussels meeting, Cameron embarked on a frenzy of activity as he tried to shore up his renegotiation. On Friday 29 January, he held talks with European Commission President Jean-Claude Juncker over whether the UK could hold back in-work benefits from EU migrants. This 'emergency brake' – which would only affect access to welfare – would allow the UK to stop paying benefits to new migrants if public services were under excessive strain.

As well as needing permission from other member states before the brake could be activated, the proposal was potentially open to a legal challenge, as it discriminated against foreign workers. Iain Duncan Smith, who was involved in the Downing Street discussions over this measure, repeatedly warned that Brits could be affected by this change.

He said:

> I was sat quite deeply in those benefit negotiations throughout, and they kept trying every permutation of 'Could we introduce this stuff but not introduce it also for British citizens?' and everything else, and I said: 'Well, you're going to have tens of thousands to a hundred thousand British citizens adversely affected by this, and I don't think that's a very good message for us to say that we've gone for reform of the European Union but, by the way, we are going to give a bunch of British citizens a good long kick while we're at it' – it's not really saleable. You'll be astonished how Downing Street turned itself into knots over this and I kept looking at them all and my team kept coming back saying: 'This doesn't work, lots of British affected' until my team put forward a proposal. I said at the end of the day the best thing you can do is treaty change.

On Sunday 31 January – after failing to reach an agreement with Juncker over the deal in Brussels – Cameron invited European Council President Donald Tusk for dinner in Downing Street. Over a meal of smoked salmon, beef with vegetables, and pear and apple crumble, the two tried to iron out their differences, with the emergency brake the main area of disagreement. It was a relatively quick discussion, with Tusk only staying in Downing Street for an hour and forty-five minutes, but it was enough time for the Prime Minister to get agreement that the current levels of immigration from the EU – 265,000 a year according to the most recent figures – would be sufficient to trigger the brake. 'This is a significant breakthrough, meaning the Prime Minister can deliver on his commitment to restrict in-work benefits to EU migrants for four years,' said a Downing Street spokesperson.

Cameron may have been feeling optimistic, but Tusk was clearly enjoying the drama: 'No deal yet. Intensive work in next 24 crucial. #UKinEU,' he tweeted upon leaving No. 10. Throughout the next day, UK officials worked with EU counterparts to try to nail down exactly what would be part of the final negotiation. At 5.44 p.m. on Monday 1 February, Tusk teased those waiting to see what was in the deal: 'Tomorrow around noon I will table proposal for a new settlement for #UKinEU. Good progress last 24 hours but still outstanding issues,' he tweeted.

2 February was a crucial day for Cameron's negotiation, and the morning papers were not kind. 'Is that it then, Mr Cameron?' was the *Daily Mail*'s headline, while *The Times* ran with: 'Cabinet rift as Cameron softens deal on migrants'. At 9 a.m., Boris Johnson appeared on radio station LBC for a phone-in show. For Johnson, one of the key changes he had been hoping to see was the reassertion of the sovereignty of the UK Parliament over the EU. Cameron's negotiations seemed to be offering only a pooled veto: the UK would be able to block proposed EU laws, but only if it could persuade 55 per cent of the other members to sign up in agreement.

'A red card that needs thirteen other countries waving it too is not a win. A democracy would have an outright veto,' said UKIP's Gawain Towler. On LBC, Johnson revealed his own scepticism about the deal – after engaging in some typical sarcasm: 'I am, unfortunately, not able to give you a full read-out because I haven't yet been able to absorb the full, quivering magnitude,' he said about the draft package on offer.

When asked about the red card system, Johnson replied:

> I think what would be better would be if we had a brake of
> our own that we were willing to use and that we were more

willing to say: 'Britain's an independent sovereign country
and we don't agree with this particular piece of regulation or
legislation and we want to stop it', and that's what we should
be able to do.

While Johnson was on the air, the Cabinet gathered in Downing
Street for its weekly meeting. With the draft deal all but signed
off, Grayling felt that collective ministerial responsibility should
be lifted immediately. He repeatedly tried to catch Cameron's eye
as the meeting progressed, until eventually the Prime Minister
relented and allowed him to speak. After Grayling asked whether
now was the time to allow ministers to speak out, Cameron shut
him down, telling him there were still details to be sorted out and
'we don't want you tying yourself up in knots'.

Duncan Smith shared Grayling's frustrations and, away from
the Cabinet table, spoke to the Prime Minister.

> I said: 'This is wholly wrong,' and we had a slight falling out
> over it at the time. It was very much my view that it was just
> not good, it was bad faith from the government to still keep
> us trapped in the Cabinet while you were busy selling some-
> thing about the referendum which we couldn't comment on.
> That was it really, and at that point I felt a bit upset by their
> behaviour.

With Cabinet over, Cameron left Downing Street and travelled
not to Parliament to give a formal statement on the deal, but to
Chippenham in Wiltshire, where he would make a speech on the
renegotiation. As he left No. 10, lobby journalists entered to get
an advanced look at what was being proposed, which would be
revealed by Tusk later that morning.

With what was becoming his usual Twitter flourish, Tusk
published the draft deal at 11.35 a.m. with the words: 'To be, or

not to be together, that is the question… My proposal for a new settlement for #UKinEU'. The main pillars of the deal were: an emergency brake on in-work benefits, with 'gradually increasing access' for up to four years if migration was placing pressure on member states; child benefit would now be paid at the equivalent rate of the country where the youngster lived, rather than the UK level; no more UK bailouts of the Eurozone; a red card system which would allow national parliaments making up more than 55 per cent of votes on the council to be able to veto EU legislation; and an end to 'ever-closer union' for the UK.

At 1 p.m., as Cameron began delivering his speech on the deal in Chippenham, his long-suffering Europe Minister David Lidington was fielding angry questions on the draft agreement in the Commons. Steve Baker decided to forgo any forensic analysis of the package and went straight for a headline-grabbing intervention: 'This in-at-all-costs deal looks funny, it smells funny, it might be superficially shiny on the outside but poke it and it's soft in the middle. Will my Right Honourable Friend admit to the House that he has been reduced to polishing poo?'

Lidington responded: 'No, I don't, and I rather suspect that whatever kind of statement or response to a question had been delivered by me or any of my colleagues from the Despatch Box my Honourable Friend would have been polishing that particular question many days ago.'

At that same moment, Cameron was trying the polish the deal in Chippenham: 'I can say, hand on heart, I have delivered the commitments that I made in my manifesto.'

The Prime Minister then gave it the most full-throated endorsement he could think of: 'If I could get these terms for British membership I would opt in to the European Union,' he said.

The next day, the Prime Minister was at the Despatch Box in the Commons preparing to outline the deal to MPs – many of whom were angry that he had waited a day to face their scrutiny.

It had not been a good morning for the Prime Minister, who had endured another terrible set of front pages. While the *Express* headline, 'Cameron's EU deal is a joke', was to be expected – the paper had long called for the UK to quit the EU – even outlets that didn't usually splash on politics gave him a kicking. 'EU are joking' said the Metro, while *The Sun* mocked up Cameron as *Dad's Army*'s Captain Mainwaring along with the headline: 'Who do EU think you are kidding, Mr Cameron?' The only piece of solace was on the front of *The Guardian*, which led on Home Secretary Theresa May backing the deal.

In the Commons, all eyes were on Boris Johnson. It was clear that his calls for parliamentary sovereignty to be restored had not been met, but it was still not known whether he would go the extra inch and actually campaign for a leave vote. An appeal for him to commit to remain came not from the Tory benches, but from the opposition, when Labour's Alan Johnson, who was leading his party's campaign for a Remain vote, got to his feet. After pointing out that Boris Johnson's father, Stanley, and his brother, Tory MP Jo, had both committed to Remain, he asked Cameron to 'have a word with his Honourable Friend to tell him about the importance of family solidarity and of joining the swelling ranks of Johnsons for Europe'.

A few moments later, the former London Mayor stood up to ask Cameron a question:

> Since you have been so kind as to call me, Mr Speaker, perhaps I may ask the Prime Minister how the changes resulting from the negotiation will restrict the volume of legislation coming from Brussels and change the treaties so as to assert the sovereignty of this House of Commons and these Houses of Parliament?

Cameron responded:

> Asserting the sovereignty of this House is something that we
> did by introducing the European Union Act 2011. I am keen
> to do even more to put it beyond doubt that this House of
> Commons is sovereign. We will look to do that at the same
> time as concluding the negotiations.

The Prime Minister ended his answer with a passionate flourish: 'I am not saying that this deal is perfect. I am not saying that the European Union will be perfect after this deal – it certainly won't be – but will the British position be better and stronger? Yes, it will.'

Boris Johnson, who was sitting next to arch-Eurosceptic Bernard Jenkin, leaned back in his seat at the back of the Commons with a slight frown on his face.

With the draft deal in place, Cameron embarked on a mission to try to convince as many of his Cabinet as possible – and Johnson – not to campaign for Leave after the negotiation was signed off at the European summit in Brussels scheduled for 18–19 February. One of the key people he wanted on board was Justice Secretary Michael Gove. As rumours started to appear in the press that Gove was leaning towards Leave, Downing Street began applying pressure on him to declare for Remain. In the run-up to a speech the Prime Minister was due to give on prison reform on Monday 8 February, Cameron's chief of staff Ed Llewellyn called Gove to discuss the topic – it was, after all, in his remit as Justice Secretary. As the conversation came to an end, Llewellyn asked Gove if he could clear up the rumours that he was planning to vote Leave. According to a source, Gove replied: 'Sorry, I can't do that, I'm genuinely torn.' The Justice Secretary then explained that if it wasn't for the fact that it was his old friend David Cameron putting the deal forward, he would definitely be campaigning for Leave. 'Llewellyn was quite shocked', said the source, 'and told Michael he better come in and see the boss.'

Gove went in to see Cameron after the prison reform speech had been delivered, and the pair were joined by Chancellor George Osborne for the crunch meeting. According to a source, Cameron appealed to Gove's sense of loyalty, reminding him that he had helped build the modernising Conservative agenda and that a split over Europe would undermine the whole project. The Justice Secretary left the meeting still undecided about what to do, but favouring a Leave vote.

Boris Johnson was also afforded a Downing Street meeting that week, but instead of the No. 10 treatment he was granted an audience with Cabinet Office Minister Oliver Letwin in No. 9. On Thursday 11 February, Johnson and Letwin discussed the plan to return sovereignty to the UK Parliament, but, like Gove after his meeting with Cameron, the London Mayor left unsure of which way to vote, but also leaning towards Leave.

Those at the top of Vote Leave were watching the activity taking place across the River Thames with a keen interest. Dominic Cummings had been in contact with the Justice Secretary about coming out for Leave for 'several weeks', according to Matthew Elliott, but Gove had offered no guarantee that he would be joining the campaign.

There were, however, four of Cameron's team who were definitely going to campaign for Out – Iain Duncan Smith, Chris Grayling, Theresa Villiers and John Whittingdale. The four began meeting in Duncan Smith's spacious office to discuss tactics for announcing their decision. Whereas the ExCom committee would meet under a painting of King Charles I in Owen Paterson's office, the Cabinet ministers conducted their plotting in view of a stuffed toy cockerel – the mascot for Duncan Smith's beloved Tottenham Hotspur. 'I convened it as the senior Cabinet minister, as I thought collectively we should be talking, because we were isolated at that moment and it's important to know if we do something we should do it together. That was the plan,' said Duncan Smith.

One of the key discussions was when exactly the four would be able to break from collective responsibility and start campaigning. If Cameron finalised the deal on Friday 19 February, it could be another three days until the next Cabinet meeting – giving the Prime Minister even more time to talk up his deal while they were gagged. After pressure from Duncan Smith and Graham Brady, Cameron agreed to hold a Cabinet meeting on Friday evening upon his return from Brussels.

As the week leading up the Brussels summit began, it was still no clearer as to whether Johnson and Gove would be joining Duncan Smith, Whittingdale, Grayling and Villiers in campaigning for Leave. On Tuesday 16th, Gove and his wife Sarah Vine went for dinner at Johnson's Islington home. As Vine revealed in her *Mail on Sunday* column, the two MPs spent much of the night talking about the deal, and whether the 'red card' achieved by Cameron really did signify a return of sovereignty to the UK. According to Vine, Johnson was 'very agitated, genuinely tortured as to which way to go'.

During the dinner, Johnson received a phone call from Letwin to further explain the sovereignty deal. Referring to Gove, Johnson said: 'I've got the Lord Chancellor here,' before putting Letwin on speakerphone so he could set out the reasons for backing the negotiation to both of them simultaneously. The phone call made little difference to Gove, who was past the point where he could be convinced of the virtue of the deal. For him, it was just a matter of whether he was willing to sacrifice his friendship with Cameron.

The time for making a decision was fast approaching and on Wednesday 18th, the day after the dinner with Gove, Johnson visited Cameron in Downing Street. Wearing a Transport for London woolly hat, Johnson was kept waiting outside the famous black door for a good thirty seconds before being let in at just before 10 a.m. After an hour of talks with Cameron, in which he again

pushed him over sovereignty issues, Johnson left, telling journalists: 'I'll be back – no deal as far as I know.'

At 1.20 p.m. on Thursday 19th, Cameron stepped out of a car in
Brussels to begin the final steps in getting the deal rubber-stamped
by the twenty-seven other EU leaders. The Prime Minister knew
securing a robust agreement – and being seen to have fought the
good fight in doing so – was essential to give the Remain side a
boost in the polls. Public opinion at that moment seemed to be
evenly split, and of the six opinion polls conducted since the draft
deal had been announced, Remain was ahead in three, while Leave
was in the lead in the other three.

Any hope Cameron had of a quick agreement evaporated
quickly, and at 9 p.m. he was still locked in talks with his foreign
counterparts, discussing the mechanics, morality and legality of
the 'emergency brake'. Unfortunately for Cameron, there was the
small matter of the migration crisis continuing to affect countries
in eastern, southern and central Europe, meaning discussion of
the UK's renegotiation was suspended for five and half hours. At
4.30 a.m., Cameron left the venue to get some sleep, before returning at 9 the next morning.

While Cameron was battling against a lack of sleep, Gove and
Johnson were fighting with their consciences. Both were coming under equal pressure from Downing Street, who knew that
should one fall in line, it might stop the other from breaking rank
as well. On the Thursday evening, when Cameron was settling
down to a marathon dinner with other EU leaders, Osborne was
speaking to Gove, again trying to convince him to back the deal.
The Justice Secretary told the Chancellor he was '99 per cent' certain he would vote Leave. Osborne asked if there was anything
he could do to encourage the 1 per cent that would campaign for
Remain, to which Gove replied, 'No,' adding that this was something he needed to work through himself.

By Friday morning, Gove had made up his mind. As close a

friend as he was with Cameron, and as much as he did not want to undermine him, he simply could not advocate a Remain vote in the EU referendum. He would be campaigning for Leave. Gove planned to tell Cameron of his decision face to face as soon as the Prime Minister returned from Brussels, and he set about drafting a lengthy statement explaining his decision.

As Cameron was working on his EU deal and Gove was preparing his statement explaining his decision, the other Cabinet ministers planning to campaign for Leave were putting together their own plan of action. At 11 a.m., Duncan Smith was joined in his office by Grayling, Whittingdale and another high-profile Conservative prepared to call for Leave: Priti Patel, the Employment Minister, who attended Cabinet. Although a Conservative Party member in her teens, Patel's first job in politics had been with the Referendum Party – the single-issue vehicle set up by Sir James Goldsmith in the mid-1990s. As the name suggested, its sole policy was to secure a referendum on the UK's EU membership. Patel acted as the party's head of press, but after the election – in which the Referendum Party failed to win any seats – she moved back to the Conservatives as a press officer for new leader William Hague. Elected to the Commons in 2010, she quickly established a reputation as a no-nonsense Thatcherite, with strong right-wing views on law and order. Given her Eurosceptic past, it was no surprise she was prepared to vote Leave.

Duncan Smith, Whittingdale, Villiers, Grayling and Patel: they were the five preparing to call for Leave as soon as Cameron returned. But at that moment, no one was sure about Gove and Johnson. Duncan Smith had been to see Gove just days before the meeting in his office: 'He told me he was torn, genuinely torn. I thought he would probably stay,' he said, before adding: 'I didn't know what Boris was doing. I spoke to Boris on a couple of occasions and he said he was seriously thinking about it, so that was all still in the air at the time.'

As the day wore on, the rumours and speculation that had been the currency in Westminster for much of that week intensified. It was not just a matter of who would declare for Leave, but how they would do it. Grassroots Out had organised a rally in the Queen Elizabeth II Centre for that evening, and promised a special guest. With the venue just a minute's walk from where the final Cabinet meeting was due to be held, hacks were speculating that a Cabinet minister would address the expected thousands of Eurosceptics. If true, it would be hugely symbolic, and put the Farage-backed campaign in pole position to get the official designation.

Over in Brussels, talks were taking so long that a planned English breakfast to finalise the deal turned into an English lunch, and then an English dinner. At 4.23 p.m., Cameron announced that as 'negotiations are continuing into this evening ... a Cabinet meeting won't be possible tonight'. German leader Angel Merkel was clearly fed up with waiting for an English meal of any description, and at 5.45 p.m. popped out of the talks to get some chips from a nearby café. As the German leader was filling up on fries, the Queen Elizabeth II Centre was filling up with people. While 1,500 Eurosceptics made their way through the glass doors at the front of the building, word leaked out of a potentially game-changing moment in the EU referendum campaign: Gove was going to campaign for Leave. The BBC's Laura Kuenssberg and the Huffington Post's Paul Waugh both received tip-offs about the Justice Secretary's plan.

Gove was baffled as to how the news got out. A source close to the new Leave advocate said the leak had not come from his team, and they believed that Downing Street had leaked the story to try to bounce Gove one way or the other. No. 10 denied this. Either way, one of the two big cats was out the bag – and all eyes now turned to Johnson.

At 7 p.m., the Grassroots Out rally kicked off with documentary maker Martin Durkin appealing for money to help fund his latest project, *Brexit: The Movie*. He was followed by the usual

Eurosceptic suspects: David Campbell Bannerman, Peter Bone, Tom Pursglove, Kate Hoey and others. The venue was so rammed that Tory MP David Davis struggled to get past security, as did ITV's political editor Robert Peston.

In Brussels, EU leaders finally sat down for their English dinner at just after 8.30 p.m., with a deal seemingly agreed. By the time Nigel Farage took to the stage in London, Lithuanian President Dalia Grybauskaitė tweeted: 'Agreement #UKinEU done. Drama over.'

The drama was not over in London, though. Throughout the evening, journalists at the Grassroots Out rally had been speculating about who the special guest might be. It was clearly not going to be a Cabinet minister, seeing as collective responsibility was still in place. It was not only hacks who had been intrigued. Earlier that day, Whittingdale had asked his Eurosceptic Cabinet colleagues if they had secretly signed up to appear. 'We were all sat there saying: "It's not me, it's not me" – it turned out it was none of us. The rumour was it was Chris Grayling but it was never Chris. It was bollocks actually.'

At just after 9.30 p.m., Farage ended his speech by highlighting the cross-party focus of Grassroots Out. 'Our last speaker tonight very much proves that point. Our last speaker tonight is without doubt one of the greatest orators in this country.' At the back of the room, a cry of 'He's an anti-Semite' went up from a member of the audience. Some turned round to see who the shout was aimed at, and their eyes fell upon George Galloway.

The left-wing firebrand was an even more controversial and divisive figure than Farage. After sixteen years as a Labour MP, Galloway was kicked out of the party in 2003 for suggesting UK troops should 'refuse to obey illegal orders' in Iraq. He then joined Respect, winning the seat of Bethnal Green and Bow in the 2005 general election. His notoriety in the eyes of the public grew with an appearance on *Celebrity Big Brother* in 2006, in which he performed a dance routine while wearing a skin-tight red leotard, and asked a fellow contestant, 'Would you like me to be the cat?' before miming licking a saucer of milk in a role-playing game. He lost his seat in Parliament in 2010, but returned after winning the Bradford West by-election in 2012. He had long criticised the foreign policy of Israel and its behaviour towards Palestine, and in 2014 he 'declared Bradford an Israel-free zone' in a speech in Leeds. 'We reject this illegal, barbarous, savage state that calls itself Israel. And you have to do the same,' he said.

Despite deep and significant political differences with Nigel Farage, the pair had always got on well at a personal level. Farage first met Galloway after they appeared on the BBC's *Question Time* show together in Edinburgh in 2013. The UKIP leader said:

> I sat and had a long talk with him after *Question Time*. It was very interesting. I thought: 'I disagree with this guy funda-mentally but he's the only person in this room I want to talk to.' He's self-made in many ways of what he does. Interest-ing, bright, fantastic orator, some of his views I find really difficult but some of mine he probably finds really difficult, that's the way human beings are.

Farage had decided to call Galloway to ask if he wanted to appear at the rally after seeing him proclaiming his Euroscepticism on the *Sunday Politics* show on 7 February. 'I organised it a week before but didn't tell anybody. I spoke to lots of people but George was very much a part of my thinking for doing that,' said Farage.

Wearing his trademark fedora, Galloway took to the stage to a mixture of boos and applause. His appearance was too much for some people, and a hundred or so of the 1,500 people in the room walked out. 'He's a despicable person,' one man said, while another added: 'We need proper people, proper democrats. He won't do us any good.' A third man said simply: 'I can't stand the

man.' Fearing a mass walk-out, some organisers told security staff
to 'shut the doors' to keep people in, although this was ignored.

Standing at the back of hall was Arron Banks, who had a simple reaction to seeing the controversial figure take to the stage:
'Holy fuck!'

Those who did stay for Galloway's speech lapped it up. The
former MP told the audience he was on the stage that night 'in
memory of the late great Right Honourable Tony Benn', that he
didn't want to 'subcontract out' the UK's foreign policy to Romania
and that he wanted a return of parliamentary sovereignty.

Referencing the breadth of political views on the panel,
Galloway ended with a line that made Farage visibly chuckle: 'Left,
right, left, right, forward march to victory on the 23rd of June.'

Farage might have been enjoying it, but Campbell Bannerman
was not happy. 'That was a huge mistake,' he said.

Banks had moved on from his initial shock and enjoyed
the speech: 'Nigel is the best speaker I've ever come across but
Galloway ran him a pretty close second. That was pretty sensa-
tional. It looked like a third of the audience were going to rush
the stage and rip Galloway to pieces.'

Farage wasn't bothered about the people who left when Galloway appeared, and had no regrets about inviting him to speak.
'Some Jewish people were upset, I know that, I get that,' he said,
before adding:

> What was even more remarkable was the number of sort
> of UKIP types who gave him a standing ovation … What it
> showed was there was an audience out there that listened to
> George. Far bigger than Mr Hannan. He was the only root we
> had to try and start a conversation in the Muslim community.
> Muslims for Britain? That was a fucking joke that Elliott set up.

While Galloway was lapping up the applause in Westminster,

David Cameron was finally able to confirm that a deal had indeed been struck in Brussels. Taking to Twitter at 9.44 p.m., the Prime Minister said: 'I have negotiated a deal to give the UK special status in the EU. I will be recommending it to Cabinet tomorrow. Press conference shortly.' Standing before the media, Cameron confirmed what he had achieved: no more UK bailouts of Eurozone countries; protection for UK businesses; new powers to stop criminals coming to the UK; a seven-year emergency brake on migrants claiming in-work benefits; and an exemption for the UK from ever-closer union.

He also said that the planned Cabinet would now be held on Saturday morning – the first Saturday meeting of the Cabinet since the Falklands War. Cameron had his deal; he now had to sell it – and the first customers would be his own ministers.

At just before 10 a.m. on Saturday 20 February, David Cameron's Cabinet filed into Downing Street for what would be a historic meeting. Duncan Smith could not keep the smile off his face as he walked up to the door of No. 10. Patel managed to keep her emotions hidden a little better, but a small smile did eventually break out as she made her way up Downing Street. Gove elected not to undertake the walk in front of the waiting media, and instead was dropped off right outside the door by a black Land Rover. Duncan Smith, Whittingdale, Villiers, Grayling and Patel already had their exit plan in mind – as soon as the meeting was over, they would travel to Vote Leave's HQ and pose for photographs. They knew Cameron would be giving a speech in Downing Street that would dominate the news coverage, and it was important to get across as early as possible in the campaign that not everyone in government backed him. Division was key. One source close to the Cabinet ministers said:

> There was a talk at first of there being a press conference, but we thought they wouldn't be ready for that, it just had to be

a statement of 'Here's a picture we give out to the papers that has everybody together showing a united front' – boom. At first IDS wasn't that keen to do it because he was doing an interview with [BBC political editor] Laura K and wanted that to be his exclusive. But we said: 'OK, it won't be interviews, it will just be a picture,' so he agreed too.

One person who wasn't aware of the plan was Gove, who had missed out on the meetings in Duncan Smith's office. After Duncan Smith 'collared' him on the way into Cabinet, Gove agreed to join the others in their photoshoot.

With the Cabinet members seated, Cameron kicked off proceedings by setting out the deal. Each member of the Cabinet then took it in turns to announce whether they were for Leave or Remain. Chancellor George Osborne was first, followed by Gove. 'Prime Minister, I can't support this,' said the Justice Secretary. Foreign Secretary Philip Hammond was next, and then Duncan Smith. 'I made the point that it is possible for us to stay together over this,' he remembered:

> At that stage the Remainers all thought they were going to win quite easily so they were indulgent of us. They all kind of smiled and said, 'Yes, yes, off you go and you do your usual nonsense over Europe,' but it was clear and obvious to them they were going to win.

After all the members of the Cabinet had spoken, Cameron left the room to prepare for his press conference outside 10 Downing Street, where he would confirm that the referendum would be held on 23 June 2016.

As he was getting his notes together, the Vote Leave Six left No. 10 by a back door that led straight out onto Whitehall. Waiting for them was Steve Baker in his Jaguar, ready to whisk them across to Vote Leave's HQ just over the Thames. There was a moment of confusion when Energy Secretary Amber Rudd – not realising what was happening – left through the same door and almost found herself smuggled into a car bound for Westminster Tower. Also waiting on Whitehall was Gove's advisor Henry Cook, who hadn't been told that his boss would be making the trip to Vote Leave. Not everyone could fit in Baker's Jag but, as Villiers was Northern Ireland Secretary, meaning she had a designated government driver and car at all times for her own protection, Gove hitched a ride with her.

Once the short drive to Westminster Tower had been completed, the six split themselves across the three small elevators in the building and went up to Vote Leave's floor in the office block. 'There was a feeling [that] this was an extraordinary moment,' remembered Whittingdale. The group walked into Vote Leave's HQ to applause from activists. Grayling gave a brief speech, saying that that morning's Cabinet had been 'deeply civilised' and both sides had agreed to have 'a mature, sensible, grown-up, friendly debate about these matters over the next few months'.

The group then signed a giant campaign board and posed for a photograph. The plan worked perfectly, and the front pages of the next day's *Sunday Times* and *Sunday Telegraph* ran the picture of the Vote Leave Six brandishing their banner, as opposed to a photo of David Cameron outside Downing Street.

With the deal signed off, the referendum date confirmed and the Cabinet divided, there was just one outstanding question left to be resolved: what would Boris Johnson do? Duncan Smith sent messages to Johnson after the Vote Leave Six had gone public, asking him when he would also be declaring, and for which side. 'I do remember that I got the impression he was going to join us,' said Duncan Smith. Johnson spent Saturday in his Oxfordshire home working on his column for the *Telegraph*, in which he would announce with 'deafening éclat' his decision. He was actually

writing two columns – one backing Remain, and one rooting
for Leave. He was unsure which one to send over to the *Telegraph* for
publication, but after re-reading the Remain article he realised
the only argument he had put forward was that of showing loyalty to Cameron. For Johnson, that was not a good enough reason.

On Sunday 21 February, Cameron appeared on the BBC's
Andrew Marr Show to talk up his deal. It wasn't long before Marr
pressed him on Johnson's position, and asked the Prime Minister
if he had a message for the London Mayor. Cameron replied:

> I would say to Boris what I say to everybody else, which is
> that we will be safer, we'll be stronger, we'll be better off inside
> the EU. I think the prospect of, you know, linking arms with
> Nigel Farage and George Galloway and taking a leap into
> the dark is the wrong step for our country, and if Boris and
> if others really care about being able to get things done in
> our world then the EU is one of the ways in which we get
> them done.

By the time Johnson had returned to his London home on Sunday
afternoon, he knew what he had to do. Word began to leak out
that he had decided to back Brexit, and the media descended
on his Islington home. At just before 5 p.m., Johnson walked out
of his front door to face the cameras. Nine minutes earlier, he had
texted Cameron to tell him of the decision.

In his faux-stuttering manner, while running his hands through
his neater-than-usual shock of blond hair, Johnson said:

> I will be advocating Vote Leave – or whatever the team is
> called, I understand there are many of them – because I want
> a better deal for the people of this country, to save them
> money, and to take back control. That's really I think what
> this is all about. What I won't do, I'll just stress, what I *won't*

do, is take part in loads of blooming TV debates against people from my party.

Johnson was for Leave, but, crucially for Elliott and Cummings, he was also for Vote Leave. Just a month earlier, Cummings had been fighting to keep control of the organisation he had helped create. Now he had the most popular politician in the country in his ranks, as well as a bevy of Cabinet ministers: the Vote Leave Six was now the Vote Leave Seven. Whereas Farage's surprise that week had been producing George Galloway, Cummings had managed to land the biggest political fish of them all in the shape of Boris Johnson. But there was still one more person Cummings wanted to complete his Vote Leave operation.

CHAPTER 22

On 28 January 2016, Baroness Shirley Williams gave her final speech in Parliament. At the age of eighty-five, the former Labour Education Secretary, co-founder of the Social Democratic Party, and Liberal Democrat peer had certainly lived a colourful political life. In her last address in the House of Lords, Williams called for 'greater public sector imagination', praised the introduction of the Open University by the Labour government in which she served in the 1960s and talked up the 'great public institutions' of the BBC and the NHS. She also spoke of one of her other great passions – Europe:

> There is one great issue left – it is the reason I am retiring – and it is the most central political question that this country has to answer. It will arise later this year in the shape of the referendum on our relationship with the European Union. Regardless of your own views, Members of this House will know that all my life long I have been passionately committed to the idea that the United Kingdom should be not only a part but a leading part of the European Union. The future demands that of us. We have to contribute to the huge issues that confront us – from climate change through to whether we are able to deal with multinational companies

which wish to take advantage of us – and we can do that only
on the basis of a much larger body than our own Parliament,
important and significant though that is.

The issue of the UK's role in Europe had been one of the cat-
alysts for her and three Labour colleagues – Bill Rodgers, Roy
Jenkins and David Owen – splitting from the party in 1981 and
forming the Social Democratic Party. Despite the 1975 referendum producing an overwhelming vote for staying in the then
Economic Community, the Labour leadership of the early 1980s
was arguing for a withdrawal. Speaking to the Huffington Post UK
in 2015, Williams said: 'We had a genuine sense of being betrayed,
really betrayed, and that was what was for us almost certainly the
single most decisive factor … It was nothing to do with equal-
ity and all the rest of it, all that we accepted, but on Europe we
were outraged.'

In 2016, Williams was as passionate about staying in Europe
as she had been in 1981, but another member of the 'Gang of Four'
most certainly was not.

David – now Lord – Owen had been ploughing his own political furrow since 1988, when he refused to endorse the SDP's
merger with the Liberals to form the Liberal Democrats. After
being made a peer in 1992, he sat as a crossbencher until donating more than £7,500 to Labour in 2011, after which he switched
to being an 'independent social democrat'. Unlike Williams, his
view on the European project had drastically changed in the forty
years since the last referendum.

He set out his initial concerns over the EU in a 2012 book
titled *Europe Restructured? The Eurozone Crisis and Its Aftermath*.
By the time David Cameron was carrying out his renegoti-
ation at the beginning of 2016, Owen was a confirmed Outer.
He announced his decision to vote to leave in an article in *The
Sun* on 24 February: 'To remain in the EU is in my judgement

a more dangerous option for British security in its deepest sense – economic, political, military and social – than remaining in a dysfunctional EU dragged down by a failing Eurozone. Remaining in the EU is risking more than leaving,' he said.

Vote Leave were delighted to have Labour's former Foreign Secretary on board, but it wasn't Lord Owen that Dominic Cummings was so keen on securing: it was the peer's close friend, Gisela Stuart.

The German-born Labour MP for Birmingham Edgbaston had decided not to play a prominent role in the EU referendum campaign, despite her deep-seated Euroscepticism. Unlike many on her side of the argument, Stuart was genuinely waiting to see what deal Cameron could return with from Brussels. She was hoping in particular for a recognition that there should be a two-speed EU – with some countries choosing to be part of the Eurozone, and others, like the UK, having a looser arrangement. 'It is not "British exceptionalism", she said,

> it is a recognition [that] this is a legitimate choice that a number of states in the European continent will take. Up to that point I would have said: 'You know what, you can probably work on that', so my involvement with all of this did not happen until after he came back with the deal.

Stuart might have been waiting for Cameron's return, but Cummings was keen to get her involved in Vote Leave much earlier. The Labour voices in the campaign were making no secret of the fact they were not happy with the way the organisation was being run, but Cummings needed them to prove Vote Leave was truly cross-party. Cummings had come across Stuart during the No to AV campaign, and had earmarked her as someone he would like involved in Vote Leave.

Just before Christmas 2015, Cummings and Stuart met in one

of Parliament's tea rooms, and the Vote Leave campaign director asked her to come over and join his team. Stuart declined. But the pressure kept on coming. Paul Goodman, the former Tory MP who had worked with Stuart on Parliament's *The House* magazine, also urged her to get involved in the campaign. On 17 January, Goodman published an article on the ConservativeHome website asking 'Where are Labour's Eurosceptics?' – illustrated with a picture of Stuart. 'Where is Gisela Stuart, a convinced Eurosceptic with real knowledge of the issue, as a former UK Parliamentary Representative to the European Convention that produced the European Constitution?' he wrote. Over a lunch shortly afterwards, Goodman could still not persuade Stuart. 'I just kept saying: "No, no, I'm not doing this,"' she remembered.

With Cameron's deal nearing completion, one more person sat down with Stuart to try to convince her to play a role in the campaign: Lord Owen. 'He is the one person which I genuinely could not say no to,' she said. Lord Owen was not just a political friend, but a personal one. Owen had been close to Stuart's late husband Derek Scott, who had died of stomach cancer in 2012. Scott had worked for Labour Chancellor Denis Healey in the late 1970s, before joining Owen on his SDP journey in the 1980s. In the 1990s, Scott re-joined the Labour Party, and served as an economic advisor to Tony Blair when he was in Downing Street. He was one of the fiercest opponents of the UK joining the euro, and predicted the political and economic instability the single currency would cause on the Continent. As Scott's cancer became terminal, Owen was one of the 'two key people' who helped notify friends and associates of his impending death. 'He was an absolute stalwart,' Stuart said.

With such a strong bond, it was no surprise that Owen should carry the greatest influence over Stuart's thinking. In the middle of February, while Eurosceptic Tory Cabinet ministers were planning their escape from collective responsibility and Labour Leave

were plotting theirs from the grip of Cummings's campaign, Owen
sat down with Stuart in a Lords tea room.

Stuart recalled:

> David took me to a dark corner and said two things that
> were very important: one was that he was going to come
> out for Brexit. Now, to me, this is a very significant step for
> someone like him. He also pointed out to me that as my
> day job was to be a politician, and this is about the most
> significant decision this country is going to take for dec-
> ades to come, sitting on my hands really wasn't something
> I could do.

It was a forceful argument, and 'it also happened to be very true',
she said.

Realising she had no choice but to get involved, Stuart initially planned on forming 'a small group' focused on defence and
security issues. Yet after looking into the shenanigans at Vote
Leave, and speaking to the current chairman Lord Lawson, she
became acutely aware of the need for a Labour MP at the top of
the campaign group. She said: 'It was at that stage chaired by Nigel
Lawson, which was just, you know, the wrong signal if you were
to prove to the Electoral Commission that this was cross-party
and inclusive.'

Her timing was fortuitous. While the Cabinet ministers and
Boris Johnson had just joined the fray, there were serious concerns over the future of Labour's representation in Vote Leave.
Brendan Chilton and his comrades were in the process of taking
up Arron Banks's offer to come and work in his offices in Millbank
Tower, just across the River Thames from Vote Leave. The arrival
of the Vote Leave Seven, who were all Conservatives, further convinced Chilton that Labour voices would not play a significant
role in Cummings's plans. That contrasted with Banks and Farage,

who recognised that millions of Labour voters, particularly in
Labour heartlands, could not be reached by Conservative voices.
Chilton said:

> From the very start, one of the first conversations I had with
> Arron was the vital nature of the Labour vote in this. In
> some ways you can discard the Tory and UKIP vote because
> we've got them. He understood the need for the Labour vote
> and the need for Labour people delivering Labour messages
> and so we hit it off.

With Vote Leave's campaign team having changed dramatically
in the space of a few weeks, the board was restructured. Having
delivered the stability he was tasked with providing, Lawson stood
down as chairman and left the board – although he remained on
the campaign team. Stuart was asked to take over and on 13 March
it was announced that she would become chairman of Vote Leave.
John Mills would stay on as deputy chairman, meaning the organisation had Labour figures in two of the highest roles. As well as
acting as chairman, Stuart was also made co-convener of the campaign committee – sharing the role with Michael Gove. Other
members of the committee included all the other Cabinet members: Boris Johnson, David Owen, Douglas Carswell and Daniel
Hannan. Yet the real power lay in the 'core group' which would
meet on an almost daily basis to discuss the campaign. This was
composed of Gove, Stuart, Elliott, Cummings, Johnson and former Labour MP Ian Davidson.

The reorganisation signalled an end to the so-called coup
against Cummings that had been launched earlier in the year,
and those at the top of Vote Leave were undoubtedly much hap-
pier with the new arrangement. Bernard Jenkin, who had led
the efforts to try to solve some of the problems in the organisation, said:

The whole dispute was hugely draining of energy and momentum, which was painful and frustrating for everyone, but the outcome was positive. The result was that we established proper governance and the authority of the board over the campaign. This was hugely important for Vote Leave's reputation with donors and with the Electoral Commission. The board was still too big to function effectively as a whole, so it relied very heavily on the chairman – Nigel Lawson and then Gisela Stuart; the compliance committee chairman Daniel Hodson, the chairman of the finance committee, Jon Moynihan, and the designated 'Responsible Person', Alan Halsall. They really put in the hours and they all did a fantastic job, so we were able to optimise the very considerable abilities of Matthew, Dominic and the team.

In the days leading up to the announcement of the new board, Vote Leave embarked on a flurry of media and campaigning activity. It kicked off on Friday 11 March with Johnson giving a speech at a logistics company's warehouse in Kent. He even hopped into the cab of a specially branded Vote Leave heavy goods vehicle, taking it for a short drive down the forecourt while journalists looked on in amusement. The same day, Priti Patel addressed a reception of business leaders in the east of England, while Iain Duncan Smith also met entrepreneurs in the West Midlands.

On Saturday 12 March, Vote Leave organised 'Take Control Day', which involved more than 400 street stalls, canvassing sessions and leafleting drops. The organisation also projected the words 'Vote Leave, Take Control' on the Angel of the North, and 'Let's take back control – Vote Leave' onto Edinburgh Castle, Cardiff Castle, the Gateshead Baltic Flower Mill and the White Cliffs of Dover. Even Matthew Elliott donned a Vote Leave baseball cap and helped stuff flyers through front doors.

In the three weeks since Cameron's deal and the arrival of the Cabinet ministers, Vote Leave had evolved from an essentially passive Westminster-based operation – mainly focused on courting the media and MPs – to a proper campaign organisation. Elliott and Cummings had kicked into top gear just as the decision on which campaign would win the official designation was due to be made.

CHAPTER 23

'**S**lap her!'

On hearing the name Suzanne Evans, the UKIP activist delivered a rather blunt verdict on how to handle the increasingly problematic party member.

The comment was out of keeping with what up to that point had been a good-natured UKIP spring conference in Llandudno, north Wales. Party activists and officials descended on the picturesque town with its sweeping bay for their seasonal get-together on Saturday 27 February. Coming just a week after Boris Johnson, Michael Gove et al. had broken cover and declared for Leave, there was a sense that now the referendum campaign was really under way.

The conference was taking place in the Venue Cymru, with the keynote speech from Nigel Farage set for midday. As with all political conferences, there were a number of fringe events scheduled alongside the main events, and those entering the venue that morning were handed numerous flyers outlining what was on offer. One was for a Vote Leave event with Suzanne Evans, Douglas Carswell and Tory MP David Jones – who was also a former Welsh Secretary. It was set for 11 a.m., and would take place at a hotel along the seafront.

Also planned for 11 a.m. was a Grassroots Out fringe event,

224 — OWEN BENNETT —

which would be hosted by Farage inside the conference centre. UKIP's head of press Gawain Towler claimed the clash were purely coincidental – 'We were always going to have one, but it was a happy timing,' he said – but rumours persisted that the event had been called just to scupper the Vote Leave meeting.

At just after 11 a.m., Evans delivered her speech to a room of journalists and the braver party activists who had decided to shun the Farage fringe. Any notion that this Vote Leave event would be about building bridges with UKIP quickly disintegrated when Evans began referencing a report called *How (Not) to Talk about Europe*, produced by think tank British Future.

Sitting alongside Carswell, she said: '[The book's] poll found that the two least trusted voices on Europe are Tony Blair, which isn't surprising, and also Nigel Farage. You might not like it, and I don't like it either, but that is what the book says.'

Discussing how best to convince undecided voters to back leaving the EU, Evans added: 'They say really, even if you love Nigel Farage and you love UKIP, it's best not to mention it unless somebody else mentions it instead.'

Turning to UKIP's main campaigning issue – immigration – Evans added: 'This book suggests that those people who are concerned about immigration have already made their mind up, they are going to vote to leave.'

She also cited claims that the presence of the UKIP logo on campaign tools could turn people off from the Eurosceptic cause:

> UKIP campaigners were handing out these bags thinking it was a great idea, but even people that wanted to leave the EU wouldn't take the bags as they had UKIP on it. Now, you might think that's daft, but would you take a bag that had a Tory logo on it?

It was an astonishing attack on UKIP's leader and its campaign strategy, delivered on a day when the party was getting together to refine its message ahead of the referendum.

Evans's comments were published on the internet within the hour, prompting the activist to proclaim 'slap her' when her name was mentioned within earshot later that day.

By the time Farage sat down with journalists outside a pub in the town at 3 p.m., he was exasperated. Referring to the fact that the survey Evans had mentioned was produced in 2015, Farage said:

> The facts are all desperately wrong and cooked up and there is a very significant wall of data which shows that actually the immigration issue and security issue is by far – by about three to one – the issue upon which undecided voters will make their minds up. So to quote something that was done during a general election when people were thinking about different issues is just wrong. As far as her saying that, well, she's an ordinary member of UKIP, she can say what she likes. I couldn't care less.

Farage's views were drawn not just from his experiences of campaigning across the country, but also from the results of the huge opinion poll Chris Bruni-Lowe had been carrying out. Three months earlier, Bruni-Lowe had commissioned another 10,000-strong poll to make sure Farage was hitting the right spots when it came to campaigning. Of those undecided or considering switching their vote, regaining control of the UK borders was the top issue, with 37.9 per cent ranking it as the argument which would most likely influence their decision. The second highest ranked was the fact that leaving the EU would 'save the UK money which could be spent at home' – which was chosen as the main reason by only 17.7 per cent. When respondents were asked to pick their top three issues, immigration and border control was selected by 61.9 per cent.

Sensing Farage was in a punchy mood, the journalists asked if he would support Vote Leave if it got the designation. He began his reply sarcastically: 'Yeah, I think a double referendum is a super idea! And let's not discuss immigration and we don't really want to leave at all! It'd be great! I'd love it!' he said, before continuing:

> We are committed to a genuine cross-party campaign, the most cross-party campaign that has ever been put together in British politics – and by the way an alliance that hasn't finished building either – that is pulling the left and right together, and this idea that you can win the referendum by being middle-class Conservatives is just b—

Farage stopped himself from saying 'bollocks', and ended the sentence with the words 'not right'.

As for Carswell, Farage pretended not to know who he was. 'Who? ... Oh, I remember, I met him once.' After being reminded of the identity of UKIP's only MP, Farage added: 'He can do what he likes, I don't care. I've not got time, I'm not interested.'

Peace was certainly not breaking out between the rival groups, and designation day was fast approaching. With Cameron's EU deal now in place, Grassroots Out stepped up its campaigning activity. An 'Action Day' was pencilled in for Saturday 5 March, with more than 500 street stalls planned in villages, towns and cities across the UK. Farage may have been convinced that Evans was 'desperately wrong' to claim UKIP branding would turn people off, but others in the party seemed to agree with her. An email sent out to activists ahead of the Action Day by UKIP's West Midlands regional organiser, Andrew Illsley, contained advice remarkably similar to Evans's warnings. 'No UKIP logo's [*sic*], literature, rossettes [*sic*] must be visible on the day,' he wrote, in bold type.

Grassroots Out continued its group campaigning the following weekend, running its own Super Saturday alongside Vote Leave's

Take Control Day. After months of criticism that there was no ground campaign, both organisations were now out on the ground with branded flyers, T-shirts, pens, hoodies and even condoms ('The safer choice' and 'It's riskier to stay in' were the slogans printed on the Vote Leave-produced contraceptive packets).

In market towns and metropolitan cities, activists were focusing their energies on attacking the real enemy: Stronger In. But at the top of the campaigns, the old tensions still remained. On Monday 14 March, UKIP peer Lord Pearson emailed both Vote Leave and Leave.EU asking for a truce. 'We are not even collaborating about our core messages, whereas the Remain people are sleek, ruthless and on message,' he said in the email, according to the *Financial Times*.

Pearson received no response, as both groups were at that moment frantically putting together their respective bids to be chosen by the Electoral Commission as the official Leave campaign. Each group had to demonstrate a range of abilities, including: breadth of support among campaigners; how they planned to represent other campaigners; how they would use the benefits of being appointed the designated campaign; how they would fund their campaign.

As the designation documents were being put together, it became even clearer how vital the appointment of Gisela Stuart was to the Vote Leave board. A series of emails between Labour Leave members showed just how far relations between the two organisations had deteriorated. On Wednesday 16 March, Elliott was forced to explain to John Mills why a letter that had gone out to supporters asking for funds implied that Labour Leave was still backing Vote Leave, when it had decided to be neutral. 'This letter was drafted and signed off weeks ago,' said Elliott.

> It takes mail houses a long time to print, collate and post big mailings, so this is essentially several weeks old, even though

it has only just landed in the past few days. You can tell that it
was written a few weeks ago because it doesn't mention
Gisela being chairman of VL or Frank [Field] being on the
campaign committee. These appointments happened after
the letter was written.

The Vote Leave chief also pointed out in his email that while
Labour Leave was officially claiming neutrality in the designation battle, Nigel Griffiths, Kate Hoey and Brendan Chilton had
publicly promised to back GO.

Mills forwarded the email on to Hoey – copying in a number of people, including Griffiths – and added his own thoughts
about how members of Labour Leave should be behaving.
He wrote:

> Another difficult issue, in terms of keeping everyone together,
> is what we should do about paid staff siding one way or the
> other on the bodies seeking designation and here we have a
> particular difficulty round Nigel and his position in GO. I am
> not at all suggesting that Nigel should not stay with Labour
> Leave as he has been a longstanding and valuable member of
> our group but there clearly is a problem with paid staff having
> formal positions in the competing organisations and being
> paid by funds coming at least in part from the other camp.
> Can I therefore propose, if Nigel wants to retain his present
> position in GO which I very much expect he will, that as
> from the beginning of April 2016 he should be paid by GO
> and not by Labour Leave? Can you please confirm that this
> would be acceptable?

The email prompted a furious response from Griffith. After
rebuking Mills for only copying him into the email and not contacting him directly ('You discuss my future and my intentions

with others, without ever contacting me about it – most dishon-
ourable,' he wrote), Griffiths tore into Vote Leave:

> Your Vote Leave mailing was a disgrace and I am sad that you
> have become an apologist for Elliott and Cummings, who
> even used the Vote Leave target mailing to puff themselves
> up and tell the world what wonderful organisers they are –
> they just can't help themselves.
>
> My statement which you refer to was on behalf of Labour
> Leave after Kate and Brendan contacted me on 4 February
> and informed me that they were both leaving Vote Leave
> because they had [had] enough of the lies and bullying, and
> both had been in discussion with Arron Banks to set up
> Labour GO.
>
> And the failure of Vote Leave managers to act against
> the Vote Leave member of staff who threatened people who
> crossed him, saying, 'I'll put your name on the sex offenders
> register' tells us all what sort of people they are.

Hoey did not hold back in her views either, telling Mills:

> You have personally allowed the Labour Leave operations
> to be deliberately sabotaged by VL staff. Taking away the
> Twitter access, Facebook and now even Brendan's email.
> Words fail me but I so agree with Nigel about the utter
> nastiness of VL staff. I too am sorry that you seem to be
> in the pocket of Elliott and Cummings and that none of
> the Lab members of the VL board are prepared to stand up
> to them.
>
> VL may win designation but you have long lost the
> moral case to win it and I have grave doubts about your two
> henchmen being able to work with anyone other than their
> chosen little elitist lot during the referendum period.

I see absolutely no point in meeting as you nave [*sic*] wasted
so much time of Brendan and the others in 'promises' that
you have never fulfilled.

Hoey, Chilton, Griffiths and other Labour Leave members were
now more than happy to add their names to Grassroots Out's
designation application. Yet despite the support of many Labour
Eurosceptics, Grassroots Out, which was applying for designation
under the name the GO Movement, knew they were at a disad-
vantage by not having the support of any of the Cabinet ministers
who had come out for Leave.

Richard Tice, who had been appointed chairman of GO
Movement, was realistic about the group's chances of securing
designation. He said: 'We win on breadth and depth, but we lose
on the establishment. If they vote for the establishment, we lose.'

Indeed, such was Tice's fear of the establishment that he and
other members of GO began to suspect their phones were being
hacked. 'We had a Grassroots Out board meeting where phones
were left outside,' he recalls. 'You might say that was total para-
noia, but there's some bad stuff out there.'

At just before 2 p.m. on Monday 21 March, ten days before the
designation applications had to be submitted to the Commission,
Arron Banks sent a message out through Leave.EU's mailing list,
appealing for support for GO:

> We transcend the British political spectrum at all levels from
> members and group leaders, to councillors, MPs and MEPs.
> With prominent figures in the Conservative Party, Labour,
> UKIP, DUP, TUV, the Liberal Democrats and the Respect
> Party all on board, the GO Movement is in <u>pole position</u> to
> win designation, however… **We need your help to get us
> over the line.** One of the criteria the Electoral Commission
> will look for when assessing our application is the 'breadth

of support' we can show for our campaign among activists.
At this crucial point in the referendum campaign ask you to
do two things [sic].

Readers were then invited to sign a pledge supporting GO, and
also email the Electoral Commission directly, calling on them to
award designation to the campaign.

The tactic was simple: the more people who emailed in, the
greater the 'breadth of support' it demonstrated. It didn't quite
go to plan.

At 7 p.m., just five hours after asking people to bombard the
Commission with support for GO, Banks sent out another email.

The enormous strength of the mass movement we have built
was clearly demonstrated today, when 7,500 of our supporters
wrote to the Electoral Commission endorsing our bid for
designation in the space of just two and a half hours, a level
of support so high that their servers couldn't cope!

Instead of embracing this incredible demonstration of
people power, however, the Commission has declared that
it will disregard any direct representations it receives from
ordinary members of the public.

The Commission had reminded Banks that it was down to the app-
licants to demonstrate their breadth of support within the formal
application, not through direct lobbying. It would not be the last
time Banks unleashed his Leave.EU followers on unsuspecting
players in the referendum campaign.

On Thursday 31 March, Nigel Farage, Tom Pursglove and
Peter Bone donned their lime-green and black Grassroots Out
ties and led a group of around fifty activists and supporters to the
Electoral Commission's headquarters near the Barbican in central London. They were there to deliver the group's designation

application; instead of just submitting it by email, the group had brought along a paper version. More than ten boxes, filled with messages of support, were handed over to the Commission, while a Labour GO-branded bus was parked up on the street outside. GO-branded T-shirts, hoodies and flags were on display and, as usual, Farage revelled in the limelight. 'The designation document was a bloody masterpiece. Eighteen separate properly identifiable political organisations including the New Communist Party of Great Britain,' he said. The GO gang were in high spirits. They were convinced they had submitted an excellent application.

The 222-page document focused on two main areas: the sheer number of supporters GO had, and the fact it was not an 'establishment' campaign. It proudly listed the political parties it had the support of: Liberal, New Communist Party of Britain (which Andy Wigmore had had to join in order to persuade them to sign up), Respect, Traditional Unionist Voice and UKIP. Yet those five political parties had just one MP between them: Douglas Carswell, who was backing a different organisation. The document listed forty MPs who had 'attended Grassroots Out events, participated at Grassroots Out Task Forces or are receiving our regular campaigning bulletins or direct mailings', including John Redwood, David Davis, Liam Fox and Chris Grayling as evidence of its reach and support. However, these MPs were not necessarily endorsing the application. Davis got a mention again in the document when GO suggested its three-pronged team for any planned TV debates. 'Our potential line-up of Kate Hoey, Nigel Farage and David Davis is one that would leave our rivals quaking in their boots. No other campaign can put forward such an experienced, well-regarded, cross-party team,' said the document.

Differences with Vote Leave were repeatedly flagged up, with 'the factional infighting between groups' referred to as one of the 'weaknesses' GO wanted to address: 'Approaches have been made to all "Leave" campaigns, and the offer stands – particularly in relation to the "establishment" Vote Leave organisation. Clearly, not being part of the establishment will be perceived as a weakness to some. However, the nature of the "Leave" family is diverse and complex.'

GO promised that 'by taking the campaign out of SW1, we will win the referendum door by door, vote by vote', before issuing a warning about what would happen if its rivals were awarded designation.

> There is a genuine threat that we would not be welcomed into the Vote Leave structure in the event of them being awarded the lead status, despite GML [Go Movement Ltd] offering to merge with them to form a unified entity on numerous occasions, unfortunately to no avail. We have, however, put in place the framework and processes that would allow, and indeed enable us, to easily incorporate Vote Leave into our movement and utilise their expertise. As one of the pillar groups, Vote Leave would be able to operate independently within the umbrella, using its £700,000 on their specific 'air war' activities – a realistic sum of money to achieve this.

The document was full of photographs, graphics, biographies of key players and examples of plans carried out and what was yet to come.

Vote Leave's designation application was a lot more sombre. Running to just seventy-seven pages, it shunned graphics and photographs and contained only text and tables. It clearly set out its regional director structure and talked up its local coordinators – 30.9 per cent of whom were UKIP supporters. Although not mentioning them by name, Vote Leave dismissed its rival's claim that high volumes of social media engagement indicated genuine support:

> Social media is a relatively weak indicator of an organisation's active supporter base. By contrast our 43,544 registered

supporters are each individuals who have pledged their will-
ingness and availability to support actively our campaign,
and provided us with their contact details. We believe that
these supporters represent a meaningful resource for our
campaign, which we are well prepared to build upon. We do
not regard any number of fleeting endorsements generated
on social media (for example, Facebook 'likes' or Twitter re-
tweets) as comparable to this resource.

Alongside the 121 MPs backing Vote Leave (108 Conservative, eight
DUP, four Labour and one UKIP), the campaign also claimed the
support of 1,594 councillors 'either verbally, in writing or online'.

Also revealed in the document was one of the few examples
of actual collaboration that had been taking place between the
various groups involved on the Leave side of the argument. It
had gone almost unnoticed, but every Monday morning David
Campbell Bannerman would chair a contact group which brought
together a range of representatives from groups such as Better Off
Out and the Freedom Association. Another regular attendee was
Brian Monteith, the head of press for Leave.EU. After Grassroots
Out was formed, they too sent along representatives. The idea
for the group came from Campbell Bannerman, who proposed
it even before the 2015 general election as a way of getting all
the Eurosceptic groups talking to each other. As the campaign
went on, it became a vital forum for exchanging plans and strategy. 'What the contact group did was try and avoid conflict
i.e. Nigel and Boris in the same town at the same time,' said
Campbell Bannerman. 'It was very much like "What are you
doing?" "Well, Better Off Out is running this campaign on fish
for this month for these places." "Oh, that's interesting, oh, hang
on, we're doing something similar there at the same place maybe
we better pull that" or whatever.' Despite the fact that Campbell
Bannerman had actually endorsed GO for designation, this

contact group had taken off when he was part of Vote Leave, so it was included in its application.

After months of battling, splitting and arguing, the designation documents were in, and both campaigns faced a two-week wait before discovering which organisation had won the fight.

Of course, neither campaign downed tools during this period. GO continued with its public meetings, holding rallies in Glasgow on Thursday 7 April and Bournemouth on Saturday 9th and visiting Gibraltar on Monday 11th. As well as the Bournemouth meeting, that Saturday was also designated another action day for GO campaigners, with two million leaflets produced for distribution.

Vote Leave was also producing leaflets, and found itself in hot water over one in particular. A double-sided flyer sent out to millions of voters was headed up 'The UK and the European Union: THE FACTS' and contained eight claims about the UK's relationship with Brussels – including that the EU has control over Britain's borders and the UK has no trade deals with countries such as Australia and New Zealand.

However, the only place on the leaflet where it was made clear that the document was a piece of campaigning literature produced by Vote Leave was in small font on the back.

On Tuesday 5 April, Labour MP Chris Bryant wrote to the Electoral Commission asking them to investigate whether the leaflet broke campaigning rules. He said: 'Vote Leave are actively seeking to deceive people by presenting campaign material as being independent when it is in fact campaign propaganda.'

It was not the first time Vote Leave had stoked controversy that week with its campaigning behaviour. On Tuesday 29 March, the campaign published an 'EU Most Wanted' dossier, listing fifty criminals who had committed offences in Europe but were able to come and settle in the UK before reoffending. Top of the list was Arnis Zalkalns, the Latvian who had served a seven-year prison sentence in his own country for murdering his wife in 1998.

He was believed to be the killer of fourteen-year-old schoolgirl Alice Gross in west London in 2014, but hung himself before he could be arrested. Of the fifty criminals in the dossier, forty-five had committed serious offences, including nine murders and seven rapes. Vote Leave, which had repeatedly branded the Stronger In campaign 'Project Fear' for its economic warnings, was accused of 'scaremongering of the worst kind' by its Leave.EU opponents. Vote Leave's Robert Oxley hit back by saying: 'It is a bit rich from campaigners who constantly do Britain down to throw around words like "scaremongering".' Vote Leave was happy to have the row – if Stronger In was trying to argue the toss about murderers and rapists from the EU coming to the UK, it would only further cement the point in the public's mind that murderers and rapists from the EU *had come* to the UK. All publicity was good publicity. It was a tactic they would deploy again and again throughout the campaign.

What hadn't generated such good publicity for Vote Leave was Boris Johnson's appearance in front of Parliament's Treasury Committee on Wednesday 23 March. The Mayor of London was in particularly loquacious form as he sat down to be grilled by the committee's chairman, Andrew Tyrie. But, after holding forth in his usual entertaining manner, Johnson found himself quietly but firmly brought back down to earth by Tyrie. The committee chairman pointed out that, despite Johnson's previous claims, there were no EU laws banning children under eight years old from blowing up balloons – there was instead a requirement to put a safety warning on the product's packaging – and there was no ruling saying that teabags could not be recycled; that was instead a rather draconian interpretation of EU law by Cardiff Council. Tyrie also told Johnson that his claim about rules regulating the size of 'euro-coffins' was 'a figment of your imagination'.

Johnson ended the two-and-a-half-hour session by claiming: 'I've demolished the questions I've been asked,' but there was a sense that the London Mayor had not lived up to his billing as the Brexit frontman. His appearance on the BBC's *Andrew Marr Show* on Sunday 6 March had generated a similar reaction, with an exasperated host telling him, 'It's not the Boris Johnson Show, it's the *Andrew Marr Show*,' after the Brexit campaigner tried to ask and answer his own questions. Commentators were damning in their criticism, with *The Sun*'s Trevor Kavanagh – who was extremely sympathetic to Brexit – claiming the Mayor's performance 'may have damaged both Brexit and his dream of becoming our next Prime Minister'. He added: 'This was the moment for a forensic response from the leader of the Out campaign. Instead Boris disappeared in a cloud of waffle.'

The Scottish Conservatives' leader Ruth Davidson was also distinctly unimpressed: 'Is it just me or is Boris floundering here? Not sure the bumble-bluster, kitten smirk, tangent-bombast routine is cutting through,' she tweeted.

With Vote Leave seemingly struggling to find its groove, and GO's rallies repeatedly drawing the crowd, Banks and Farage were confident heading into the week of the designation announcement that the campaign they were backing would be victorious.

However, the pair's fear that they were going to be denied official status because of an establishment-led conspiracy received an unfortunate boost just days before the announcement.

On the afternoon of Tuesday 12 April, two days before the Electoral Commission was due to reveal its decision, Vote Leave's press office was having a practise run. A press release was drafted responding to a victory announcement, and sent out to members of the communication team for proofreading. Unfortunately, it was sent to the 'all team' email address, instead of the 'all press team' account. More than 120 members of Vote Leave staff had an email drop into their inboxes telling them Vote Leave had been awarded official designation. Some of those staff were at that moment sitting in a meeting of the parliamentary council in

Westminster – a forum for MPs and peers to ask questions about how the campaign was going and raise any issues they had. One of those at the meeting was Matthew Elliott, who remembers the confusion the press office mistake caused. He said:

> One of the members of staff was sitting in the parliamentary council, saw this come through, thought it was a real press release rather than a draft because it didn't say test or draft or anything like that, and I think he was sitting next to the guy who is the chairman of the National Convention for the Tories [Steve Bell]. 'We got the designation! It's such good news!' they said.

Before Elliott could tell his staff that the email had been sent in error, Bell had taken to Twitter to share the happy news. 'Great news @vote_leave has official designation for Leave in the EU referendum roll on #independence', he wrote.

'Politics is down to cock-up rather than conspiracy usually,' Elliott reflected. 'It was a cock up.' The Electoral Commission moved quickly to confirm that no decision had been taken, but Arron Banks was far from happy. Within hours he sent out a press release arguing that 'I know the Conservative Party is one of entitlement but celebrating two days early takes the biscuit'.

He also said: 'That such a senior figure in the Conservative Party would issue a self-congratulatory tweet about the formal referendum campaign designation process ahead of any announcement is deeply worrying and gives me cause for concern about the credibility of the whole procedure.'

Banks's anger on Tuesday 12th was nothing compared to his mood on Wednesday 13th.

At just before 3 p.m., Banks was having tea at Claridge's in Mayfair with Andy Wigmore. Across St James's Park, Peter Bone was getting his hair cut in Parliament's hair salon, located just next to one of the restaurants in the historic building. Also getting a quick chop at the same time were Tom Pursglove and David Davis, while Nigel Farage was driving on the A26 just outside the French town of Arras as he journeyed back from Strasbourg to London. All believed the Electoral Commission would be announcing its decision the next day, but that afternoon it took everyone by surprise and revealed its verdict early.

After being marked out of a possible 52 points, Vote Leave's application scored 49, whereas GO tallied 45. Vote Leave would be the official Leave campaign for the referendum.

The scores were tight, and Vote Leave's victory seemed to come in two key areas. First, they 'better demonstrated the depth of representation in their support from those campaigning, including at a regional and local level'. Secondly, and perhaps most crucial of all, Vote Leave would support other campaigning organisations without requiring them to 'deliver messages or activity on their behalf'.

In its announcement, the Electoral Commission highlighted David Campbell Bannerman's contact group, which had 'the specific intended purpose of allowing an exchange of views between campaigners'.

It added: 'By contrast, the approach from "Go Movement Ltd" is based on other campaigners signing formalised agreements as "affiliates" but there is no established mechanism for supporting campaigners who do not wish to sign these.'

Commenting on the decision, Claire Bassett, chief executive of the Electoral Commission said:

> After careful consideration, the Commission decided that 'Vote Leave Ltd' better demonstrated that it has the structures in place to ensure the views of other campaigners are represented in the delivery of its campaign. It therefore represents, to a greater extent than 'Go Movement Ltd', those

campaigning for the 'Leave' outcome, which is the test we
must apply.

There was an irony that the organisation which had so strong-
gly resisted any kind of merger should be the one praised for
having structures in place to make sure other campaigns' voices
were heard.

The decision prompted mixed reactions from those on the
losing side. Farage, dishing out orders from his car in France,
instructed that a conciliatory message be tweeted out. 'I congrat-
ulate @vote_leave on getting designation,' it read. Matthew Elliott
responded within minutes: 'Thank you @Nigel_Farage. We are all
focused on winning together on June 23 #TakeControl.' Bone and
Pursglove heard they had lost thanks to a television in the hair
salon being tuned into Sky News, which flashed up the decision.
Bone was disappointed, but not surprised. 'Did I think we should
have won designation? Yes. Did I think that was a foregone conclusion? No,' he said. In an interview with the BBC less than an
hour after the announcement, Bone also struck a non-aggressive
tone, insisting that GO would continue despite not winning designation, and that there wasn't really a lot of difference between
his organisation and Vote Leave anyway.

One person who was not looking to build bridges was Arron
Banks. He was furious with the ruling, and within half an hour
Andy Wigmore was telling journalists the decision would be challenged in the courts. In an email to Leave.EU members, Banks
said: 'The tweeting by Steve Bell, the chairman of the Conservative
Party Convention, that Vote Leave had been given the designation
the night before of [sic] the official announcement smells of political corruption from our high-minded establishment and cannot
be allowed to pass without challenge.'

There was even a suggestion that applying for a judicial review
of the decision could set the referendum date back until October,

'but if we are to avoid the most important vote of our lives being rigged then I feel duty bound to take this course of action', said Banks. After consulting with legal experts, Banks announced he would reveal his decision on whether to proceed with the legal challenge at noon the next day.

With the email sent out, Banks and Wigmore decided there was only one more thing they could do that evening: get as drunk as possible. 'We went out on a monumental bender of monumental proportions,' said Banks. Richard Tice joined the pair for the early part of it but called time very early. Banks and Wigmore did not call time until 7 the next morning, having hit posh wine bars in Mayfair before ending up 'in a gay club somewhere as it was the last bar left. We went everywhere, it was a lot of fun, but boy, I was absolutely totalled when I came back,' recalled the businessman, adding: 'We were drunk as skunks.'

After having a shower and catching up on sleep, Banks met with Farage at 3 p.m. – he had slept through his self-imposed twelve o'clock deadline – to discuss whether to proceed with the legal challenge. Farage remembered that Banks was 'absolutely devastated. He was very upset. He cares about things, not like these cold, calculated, lifeless types.' The UKIP leader tried to calm him down, telling him that being the designated campaign was not the be-all and end-all in any case, and as the GO group was so well established it could carry on campaigning regardless. Also, as a political party officially campaigning for Leave, UKIP were able to spend £4 million during the campaign, alongside the £700,000 GO could invest.

As Banks put it:

> The thing that swung it for us was the fact that in a lot of
> ways being the designated campaign wasn't a happy place to
> be. We had the money, we were already going, we had the
> call centre, a huge supporter base. If we're the designated

campaign, we're probably be highly restricted in what we
can say or do.

After spending another day mulling it over, Banks sent an email
at just after 5 p.m. on Friday 15 April informing Leave.EU supporters that he would not be pursuing legal action.

Bone – who had been against any kind of legal action from the
very start – was relieved, especially as Banks's actions had made it
look like he was in charge of GO. 'For whatever reason, there was
a huge view that Arron Banks was running GO, and it was not
true,' said Bone. 'Basically, whilst he funded some of the events,
he never put money into our bank account, for instance. So he
just funded events, which was great. He was Leave.EU, which
was part of the GO Movement umbrella; he was never ever part
of Grassroots Out.'

Observing from afar, Douglas Carswell believed GO's association with Eurosceptics keen on getting designation distracted it
from the group's main focus of ground campaigning:

> They launched Grassroots Out and I thought, 'OK, great,
> good, if they do what they say on the tin – fantastic.' Where
> I think they made a serious error of judgement was when
> they allowed their organisation to become a vehicle to allow
> other people to apply for designation. I think that was a seri-
> ous error of judgement.

Allowing George Galloway to appear on a GO platform was, for
Carswell, 'exhibit A' of the organisation being tarnished by those
appearing under its banner. 'I've dined with many people but I
always use a very long spoon and I don't think they used a long
enough spoon,' he said.

Chris Bruni-Lowe, who did not agree with Carswell on
many points, echoed his analysis regarding the Respect leader.

According to Bruni-Lowe, the reason GO failed to get the designation was 'basically because we went with Galloway'.

Those at the top of Vote Leave were not just delighted with the victory, but also relieved that the whole tortuous process of battling for designation was finally over. 'Getting the designation was probably more difficult and more stressful than actually the post-designation period,' said Elliott. However, if those at the top of Vote Leave believed their rival campaign would now be starved of the oxygen of publicity because of the Electoral Commission's decision, they were very wrong. After all, there had to be a good reason why Nigel Farage was suddenly not all that bothered about his group not getting designation...

CHAPTER 24

'**L**et's give the NHS the £350 million the EU takes every week.' It was Vote Leave's first billboard of the campaign, and it was clear. All the money the UK currently handed over to Brussels would be given to the NHS if the country voted for Brexit. Never mind the fact that the £350 million was a disputed figure, or that Vote Leave were a campaigning group, not a government-in-waiting; the pledge was made and sent out on Friday 15 April – two days after Cummings's outfit had been awarded designation. The message was unequivocal and not open to interpretation, yet over the coming weeks and months Vote Leave and its supporters would repeatedly try to water down and clarify that claim. While the billboard may have raised a few eyebrows in Westminster and among Stronger In, it failed to capture the public's imagination – at least at first.

Besides, on that Friday, there were higher-profile events taking place, such as Boris Johnson's speech kicking off the referendum campaign at a rally in Manchester. To applause and laughter, he told activists gathered in the Old Granada Studios: 'We are passengers locked in the back of a mini-cab with a wonky sat nav driven by a driver who doesn't have perfect command of English and going in a direction, frankly, we don't want to go.' Indeed, such was his confidence, he even instructed supporters to sabotage

Channel 4 News's Michael Crick's live analysis of the event. 'Some chap from the media is trying to do his piece to camera … shut up … can someone go and interrupt Crick at the back there?' said Johnson. One activist obeyed Johnson's instruction, and tried to stand in front of Crick's camera while the bemused journalist tried to address the nation.

Nigel Farage was also generating some headlines that Friday thanks to a trip to Downing Street. The UKIP leader was personally returning one of the government's information leaflets, which had been sent to all 27 million homes in the country. The document, entitled 'Why the Government Believes That Voting to Remain in the EU is the Best Decision for the UK' had cost £9.3 million to produce and distribute – completely smashing the £7 million spending limit the Electoral Commission was enforcing for both sides in the campaign. However, the leaflet was being sent out before designation had been awarded, meaning the money spent did not count towards the official total. Leave campaigners were outraged. Boris Johnson said the leaflets were a 'complete waste of money' and 'crazy', while Graham Stringer suggested they had only been produced to distract attention from embarrassing questions about the Prime Minister's late father's tax arrangements, which had been raised in the Panama Papers leak.

Tory MP James Wharton summed it up best when he told the BBC that a colleague had been unhappy that the leaflet was not 'sufficiently absorbent for the use to which they wanted to put it'.

Even Labour leader Jeremy Corbyn – who was supposed to be on the same side as the government – was not happy, with his spokesman calling on the same money to be given to the Leave side so it could set out its case in a similar fashion. 'Jeremy is of the view that there should have been an even approach to the information so people can make an informed decision,' his spokesman said.

Farage sensed he could turn the leaflet into an opportunity to

generate some headlines for himself, and so arranged to personally deliver his copy of document to 10 Downing Street with the
words 'Return to Sender' scrawled on the front.

Grassroots Out also kept doing what it did best – rallies outside the Westminster bubble. On Monday 18 April, and arranged
at just four days' notice, an event was held in Stoke. Alongside
the usual suspects of Farage, Peter Bone, Tom Pursglove and Kate
Hoey was another speaker – Chris Grayling. The Cabinet minister, who had taken over running Vote Leave's contact group from
David Campbell Bannerman, decided now was the time to bury
the hatchet with the rival campaign.

Grayling was the first Cabinet minister to share a stage with
Farage, and at the rally he said:

> This is, after all, a campaign that is about people and not about
> party. That's why I am standing tonight as a Conservative
> Cabinet minister alongside two people who would normally
> be firm adversaries politically.
>
> I have campaigned vigorously against Nigel Farage and
> UKIP at elections – but in our desire to leave the European
> Union, we are united. He has as long a track record in fighting
> to leave the EU as anyone in this country, and tonight we stand
> side by side and for the next few weeks we have common
> purpose for our country.

'Applause for him, that was good skills,' said UKIP's head of press
Gawain Towler. Farage was also delighted, and the pair even
shared a car ride back to London from Stoke.

After spending almost a year trying to avoid any association
with Farage, those at the top of Vote Leave were not happy that
within days of getting the designation one of their Cabinet ministers was sharing a stage with the UKIP leader. However, as the
event had taken place on a Monday night in Stoke, Vote Leave

'didn't think it was worth a big row over, so we let him do it', said one campaign source close to the Cabinet minister.

Indeed, Grayling's appearance with Farage was largely over-shadowed by a speech from Chancellor George Osborne earlier that day in which he attempted to put a personal cost on Brexit for UK households. According to Treasury analysis, if the UK adopted a Canada-style trade agreement with the EU after Brexit, it would cost each household an average of £4,300 per year by 2030. This fig-ure was reached by using a number of wild assumptions. First, that the UK's gross domestic product (GDP) value would only grow by 29 per cent because of Brexit, rather than the 37 per cent the Treasury currently predicted. Secondly, GDP was then equated to household income – a move out of keeping with traditional economic analysis. Finally, Osborne based his assumption on the number of UK households in 2016 – meaning he was assum-ing there would be no change in the number by 2030. If this was Project Fear, it simply did not make sense. The Brexit-backing former Chancellor Lord Lamont said:

> They say economists put a decimal point in their forecasts to show that they have a sense of humour. The Chancellor has endorsed a forecast which looks fourteen years ahead and predicts a fall in GDP of less than 0.5 per cent a year – well within the margin of error. Few forecasts are right for fourteen months, let alone fourteen years. Such precision is spurious, and entirely unbelievable.

It would not be the first government stunt to backfire in the cam-paign, or even in that week, but before any more hyperbole could be unleashed from Downing Street, it was time for Dominic Cummings's moment in the sun.

The Vote Leave campaign manager had been summoned to appear before the Treasury Select Committee, which had fast become a one-stop shop for holding the referendum campaigners to account. It had already given Boris Johnson a rough ride, and on 3 March it managed to get Stronger In's Lord Rose to admit that workers' wages would rise if the UK left the EU ('I am deeply grateful to Stuart Rose for all the help he gave us,' Gisela Stuart later joked). On the afternoon of Wednesday 20 April, Cummings sat down in front of the Treasury Select Committee and set about bamboozling, challenging and quibbling with his interrogators for more than two hours.

The session kicked off with a discussion about the cost of regulation to the UK economy, but it wasn't long before committee chairman Andrew Tyrie zoned in on Vote Leave's headline claim: that the UK sends £350 million to Brussels each week.

After Cummings asserted that, according to the Office for National Statistics, the UK sends £19.1 billion to the EU every year, Tyrie reminded him that that wasn't strictly true, as there is a rebate of £6 billion.

'The money stays in the UK for the whole of this period. It never leaves the UK or crosses the exchanges,' said Tyrie.

Cummings was having none of it:

> When you are sitting in your slippers talking to Mrs Tyrie, looking at your bank statements, and it says X amount of money is debited from your account, that means that it has gone from your account, does it not? It is pretty clear what that means. The debiting is exactly what the ONS says here. It is debited from the UK. In table 9.9 of the ONS, that is what it says.

Tyre responded: '£19 billion is not the figure that we pay across the exchanges; we pay £13 billion across the exchanges.'

Cummings hit back: 'We are debited £19.1 billion according to the Office for National Statistics.'

An increasingly exasperated Tyrie tried again: 'That is an accounting procedure, but the money never leaves the UK, Mr Cummings.'

The Vote Leave campaign chief volleyed back: 'What happens on your bank statement when you are debited £19? That means that you are debited £19. That is what the ONS says we are debited – £19.1 billion.'

The rows continued:

> TYRIE: You are saying in your literature, in hospitals, that
> we can give a lot more money to hospitals, are you not?
> You are distributing literature to that effect. You are doing
> that, are you not?
>
> CUMMINGS: No, we are not. We have not distributed any lit-
> erature whatsoever to hospitals.
>
> TYRIE: I have a piece of literature here with your logo. Is this
> a pirated piece of literature? It says, 'Vote Leave. Take con-
> trol.' It is badged as your literature. It says, 'Help protect
> your local hospital.' It has here at the bottom, 'Vote Leave.
> Take control.org.' Is that not your organisation?
>
> CUMMINGS: It looks like it is one of our leaflets, yes.
>
> TYRIE: So you are distributing these things to hospitals. This
> was picked up from Guy's Hospital.
>
> CUMMINGS: I saw that story, I think, on a website.
>
> TYRIE: I have one of the leaflets here, yes.
>
> CUMMINGS: Yes. I saw that story on the website last week. We
> do not have a clue where that has come from. It certainly
> was not done by us.
>
> TYRIE: So is this pirated?
>
> CUMMINGS: No. Well, I have no idea. I very much doubt it.
>
> TYRIE: I just want clarity.
>
> CUMMINGS: I am giving you clarity.
>
> TYRIE: You have not yet on many of the points that I have been

asking. Let me go through some very simple questions. Did your organisation print this leaflet?

CUMMINGS: It looks likely that we did, but I cannot tell about any individual leaflet.

TYRIE: You do not know which leaflets might be printed by your organisation. You are running a campaign and do not know—

CUMMINGS: You are misunderstanding what I am saying.

TYRIE: I do not think you are understanding the question. I am asking a straightforward and simple question. We are getting down to very simple questions. Is this a leaflet of your organisation?

CUMMINGS: Do you mean that design of leaflet, or that individual leaflet?

TYRIE: I am asking you if this leaflet is one of your organisation's leaflets.

CUMMINGS: Yes, it is.

It wasn't just campaigning literature that Cummings was determined to argue over. When asked about whether the UK should retain access to the single market after Brexit, Cummings challenged the premise of the question.

CHRIS PHILP: Does that mean – and this is really a 'yes' or 'no' question – you think we should not be a member of the single market, whether in or out of Europe?

CUMMINGS: What do you mean by the single market?

PHILP: I mean the single market that we currently trade in and that Norway trade in. It is a 'yes' or 'no' question: should we be part of the single market or not?

CUMMINGS: The single market is defined by the European Union as including membership of the euro and Schengen.

PHILP: That is not true, as we are currently members of it

and are neither euro nor Schengen members, so that is
clearly untrue.

CUMMINGS: Exactly; that is the point. However, that is how
the European Commission and European Court of Justice
define the single market.

PHILP: We are currently members of it and that is not how
it is operating. It is a very simple question that you are
persistently refusing to answer.

CUMMINGS: You are confused about what the single market is.

PHILP: We are currently a member of it. Norway is currently
a member of it. Other EU members are members of it,
whether or not they use the euro. It is a very simple question. Should we be a member of the single market or not:
yes or no?

CUMMINGS: The single market is a political project from
Jacques Delors and it encompasses…

It was a window into the world of Dominic Cummings, and evidence that, while he was blessed with an extraordinary analytical
brain, he seemed to relish picking fights with as many people
as possible.

Daniel Hannan, who was a fan of Cummings, later admitted
that 'in retrospect Dom might have been a little bit less combat-
ive. Your goal in that situation should be to get through it without
generating any headlines. However, that's the package you get with
Dom. You won't find me criticising him at all.'

With Cummings's aggressive performance doing little to round
the edges of a Vote Leave campaign that was already proving spiky
– contested figures, the dossier of criminals, Johnson instructing
supporters to silence TV reporter Michael Crick as he tried to file a
piece to camera – Remain were feeling positive. Of the five opinion
polls conducted between the date of the campaign officially kicking
off on 15 April and 19 April, Remain were ahead in four of them.

On Friday 22 April, Downing Street deployed someone it believed would push Remain even further ahead in the polls: Barack Obama. The US President was on his valedictory tour of Europe and, having already expressed support for the UK staying in the EU, he was set to make another intervention in the debate. The visit was well-trailed in advance, and Boris Johnson decided to hit Obama with a pre-emptive strike in order to undermine the President's credibility. Writing in *The Sun*, the Mayor claimed a bust of Winston Churchill – Johnson's political hero – had been removed from the Oval Office on 'day one of the Obama administration'.

'No one was sure whether the President had himself been involved in the decision,' Johnson wrote. 'Some said it was a snub to Britain. Some said it was a symbol of the part-Kenyan President's ancestral dislike of the British Empire – of which Churchill had been such a fervent defender.'

The article provoked outrage in the media, with the reference to Obama's 'part-Kenyan' heritage drawing most of the fire. Labour MP Chuka Umunna called the comment 'beyond the pale', while shadow Chancellor John McDonnell accused Johnson of 'dog-whistle racism'. Farage decided to come to Johnson's aid and, appearing on BBC Radio 4's *World at One* that afternoon, claimed that Obama 'bears a bit of a grudge against this country' because of his 'grandfather and Kenya and colonialisation'.

By the time Obama appeared alongside the Prime Minister in Downing Street at just after 5 p.m., it seemed the US President had done his job. The two most prominent Leave figures were questioning the motives of the country's closest ally based on his father's nationality – not a good position for a campaign which insisted that reengaging with the world was one of the key reasons for leaving the EU.

At the press conference, Obama decided to dole out what he believed to be some home truths to Leave campaigners who claimed the UK would be able to secure a trade deal with the US soon after Brexit.

'They are voicing an opinion about what the United States is going to do; I figured you might want to hear from the President of the United States what I think the United States is going to do,' he said,

> and on that matter, for example, I think it's fair to say that maybe some point down the line there might be a UK–US trade agreement, but it's not going to happen any time soon because our focus is in negotiating with a big bloc, the European Union, to get a trade agreement done.

Obama added: 'The UK is going to be in the back of the queue.'

The line had been delivered, and it was as unambiguous as Downing Street had hoped it would be. 'Obama has detonated. That sound you hear is panicking Brexiteers running for shelter and returning fire with pea shooters,' was the verdict of the *Daily Mirror*'s Kevin Maguire. 'We expected a hand grenade or two from Obama. He has instead detonated a battlefield nuclear device,' tweeted the *Sunday Times*'s Tim Shipman.

What was riling many Leave campaigners, besides the intervention itself, was Obama's choice of language. Appearing on BBC Radio 4's *Any Questions?* that evening, Nigel Farage said: 'No American would say "back of the queue". Americans don't use the word "queue", Americans use the word "line".' The UKIP leader took that as proof that the line had been drafted by Downing Street, and earned a round of applause as he said it was 'shameful' that Obama was 'talking down Britain'.

Despite the row over the language used, the Remain camp were confident Obama's intervention would provide them with a boost in the polls. Stronger In's Head of Comms James McGrory could not hide his delight, and tweeted: 'I'm going to say it. The Obama presser couldn't have gone better. It has made my day to see how angry it has got the Leave campaigners.'

However, a survey by YouGov carried out on the day of his visit seemed to show the opposite effect. While his net approval rating in the UK was 56 per cent, almost the same number – 53 per cent – thought it was 'inappropriate' for Obama to express a preference on how the UK should vote in the referendum. This seemed to be carried through to voting intentions, as of the eight opinion polls carried out from the day of his visit to the following Friday, Leave was ahead in five of them.

Obama may have detonated, but at that moment it appeared to be a suicide bombing.

CHAPTER 25

T he queue stretched from the cinema's entrance deep into Leicester Square. It was made up of gentlemen in tuxedos and smart suits, while the women were wearing posh frocks and elegant dresses. In a cordoned-off area just outside the cinema, photographers took snaps of the VIPs arriving on the red carpet.

'Is it for *The Jungle Book*?' one tourist asked. It wasn't a bad guess. After all, the Odeon in Leicester Square was the home of film premieres, and the live-action remake of the Disney classic was about to be released in cinemas. However, it wasn't Sir Ben Kingsley, Bill Murray or Scarlett Johansson walking the red carpet on the night of 11 May 2016, but Nigel Farage, Kate Hoey and Lord Lawson. They had turned out for the premiere of *Brexit: The Movie*, a documentary directed by free-market advocate Martin Durkin.

Watching from a balcony above the cinema's entrance were the film's producers, David Shipley and Hunter DuBose – two corporate finance advisors who had spent almost a year bringing the project to the silver screen. It had not been an easy process, and the story of *Brexit: The Movie* is a perfect demonstration of the difficulties many faced when dealing with Vote Leave.

One evening in June 2015, Shipley and DuBose were enjoying a steak and a bottle of red wine at the Guinea steakhouse in London's Mayfair. The pair were avowed free-market libertarians, and as such were opposed to the regulation-heavy European Union. Over the meal, they discussed what they could do to help the Out campaign in the promised referendum. The duo were interested in policy and think tanks, not campaigning, but realised they had to take a more active approach to their politics in order to help achieve the outcome they desired. 'We knew this was a once-in-a-lifetime, constitutionally significant question that will never happen again,' said DuBose. They had already met with Matthew Elliott, whom they knew through Business for Britain, and offered to help in any way they could.

Over the steak and wine, the pair talked through a variety of ways of getting involved, before DuBose remembered someone he had first met a few years ago – Martin Durkin. The filmmaker was famous for producing programmes that attacked the consensus on global warming, and also for the sympathetic Thatcher documentary *Margaret: Death of a Revolutionary*, in which he theorised that the Tory Prime Minister had actually been a working-class hero. DuBose and Shipley agreed that a film about the benefits of Brexit might arm Eurosceptics with the facts needed to help them win the referendum.

At an Institute of Economic Affairs event later that summer, the pair approached Durkin with their idea. 'We gave him a pitch and before we'd even finished he said, "There should be a movie,"' remembered DuBose.

After holding meetings with Durkin and members of his production company, Wag TV, the two were confident the project could be a success. All they needed now was funding and help with refining the message. They got in contact with Elliott again. 'He was at that point the only person we knew involved in the Leave campaigns. We said: "We're making this film, we'd really like it if this film was informed by what you think [are] the most persuasive messages that [are] going to make it as effective as possible,"' said Shipley.

Elliott was initially happy to help and Dominic Cummings was despatched to attend planning meetings. After two such meetings, each lasting between two and three hours, the pair were even more excited about the project.

'Dominic was very engaged, he was forthcoming, contributing a lot, contributing ideas,' said DuBose.

Shipley agreed, and added: 'I remember after those two meetings turning to Hunter and saying: "It's funny, I don't understand why people say such nasty things about him. He seems like a really smart guy and [is] being really helpful."'

By the beginning of January 2016, the project had a production cost attached to it: £300,000. The pair had already tapped up all of their Eurosceptic contacts asking for donations, and decided to ask Elliott and Cummings if they could point them in the direction of any rich Brexit supporters who might be willing to contribute. The four were having a conference call to discuss the progress of the film when DuBose said the two words Cummings and Elliott did not want to hear: Arron Banks.

DuBose said:

> During the phone call I said, 'Just so you know we're having a conversation with Arron Banks tomorrow, do you have any insights you can give us about what his trigger points will be to make him want to help us?' There was just stone-cold silence at the end of the phone. Matthew said, 'You can't speak to Arron,' and out came this vitriolic rhetoric. The key message was 'Farage is toxic, Arron Banks is toxic, they will destroy this campaign. They will turn voters away from Leave and make them vote Remain.'

Shipley added: 'The other key message was "If you let them near this film they will make it their film and they will claim publicly it's theirs."'

The pair were shocked. They had been so focused on getting the project off the ground, they had not been paying attention to the various scraps between the groups.

DuBose said:

> At that point we didn't really understand how venomous the politics were between Leave.EU and Vote Leave ... Naively, we thought we're all working towards the same goal here, we're all trying to achieve the same outcome; we took a businessman's perspective. Our thought was, 'Surely if we all want the same objective, let's collaborate and make all this happen.'

Despite being taken aback by the strength of feeling coming from Vote Leave, the pair decided to stick with them. They had no reason to disbelieve the claims about Farage and Banks made by Elliott and Cummings. However, something strange then happened. 'They just disappeared,' said DuBose. 'Over the course of four or five months, from the day of that phone call until about a week before the premiere, we sent email after email, phone call after phone call to Matthew, but got nowhere.'

Shipley and DuBose decided to launch a public Kickstarter for the film, and hoped to crowdsource £100,000 from small donations. But as the clock ticked on, it looked like the project was going to miss its funding target. With Vote Leave seemingly no longer interested, the pair decided to go against Elliott's advice and contact Leave.EU. Andy Wigmore came to a meeting in the pair's Berkeley Square office, and they were astonished by his attitude.

DuBose said:

> They were incredibly supportive, they couldn't have been more different. They made a really meaningful donation to the budget of the film: they donated £50,000, which I'm

pretty sure came straight from Arron's pocket. They put a
huge amount of effort behind their social media support. At
every point, they emphasised we were an independent project. They never once suggested or even hinted at trying to
influence or interfere with the creative or editorial process.

With Banks on board and the finances sorted out, production
on the film began. Running up to the film's premiere on 11 May,
the pair repeatedly tried to contact Vote Leave to ask for help in
promoting the documentary. DuBose and Shipley even went to
Vote Leave HQ for a meeting with Robert Oxley and the campaign's national organiser, Stephen Parkinson. One source recalled
the meeting being particularly tense, with Elliott unhappy that the
two producers were in the office. 'I've seen emails on those lines,'
said Elliott later:

> I must have been particularly stressed that day. I certainly
> didn't mean to be rude and wasn't aware that I was being
> rude. When I joined the meeting, it was to encourage them
> and be in the meeting, it wasn't to control what was going
> on or anything like that. I think it was close to when we were
> handing in designation and if you remember the final days
> ticking up to both sides handing in their designation forms,
> there's huge competition in the sense of 'Which side does
> Kelvin Hopkins support' etc.

Indeed, that meeting was mentioned in Vote Leave's designation document to back up the claim it was working with *Brexit:
The Movie.* 'Our contact with Wag TV has been productive and
cordial,' the document said, 'and would continue if we were designated as the lead campaign.'

It was not a description Shipley and DuBose recognised based
on their dealings with Vote Leave since January.

Elliott later admitted to keeping the project at arm's length, and said:

> We were very fearful that if we worked with them too hand-in-glove, their spending might be considered against our £7 million. The second point was that we, quite understand-ably in a sense, weren't in control of the editorial side of it, and what was in there and the research and the facts and figures and what have you. We were always afraid that things which we hadn't 100 per cent verified or checked or felt able to defend would all of a sudden be ascribed to us as a campaign.

While all of these production and marketing battles were going on, Durkin had his head down and was frantically making the film. The seventy-minute documentary featured prominent Eurosceptic campaigners such as Daniel Hannan, Steve Baker and Douglas Carswell giving their takes on why the UK should back Brexit. The film contrasted previous periods of low regulation in British history, such as the Industrial Revolution, with today, and surmised that the UK economy was being strangled by the laws coming out of Brussels. Through the use of stereotypes, it also contrasted the workers of Europe with the tiger economies of Asia.

A review of the film on the Huffington Post said:

> The film itself focused on regulations, trade and EU waste – and stereotypes. An Italian umbrella factory was portrayed as shoddy with workers more concerned with snogging a curvaceous woman than making quality brollies. A French-man was, yep you guessed it, wearing a beret, a striped top and had a string of onions round his neck. The growing eco-nomic powerhouse of Asia was portrayed by two men being good at maths.

While the film talked a lot about regulation, there was one topic that was not mentioned at all: immigration.

The night before the premiere, Wigmore was shown the film for the first time. He was not happy. Banks said:

> Andy saw the film and said, 'I can't believe what I've just seen, there's no mention of immigration in it at all and there's only one short clip of Nigel in it. It's basically Vote Leave propaganda.' Andy was apoplectic, given that we'd just funded the bloody thing and we were trying to get the message out about control immigration and the Australian-style points system.

Farage's aide Chris Bruni-Lowe had a more succinct take on the film. 'The Brexit movie was shit, it was all libertarian rubbish, it was the worst thing I'd ever seen made,' he said.

With Farage getting just a few minutes of screen time, a row broke out over whether he should introduce the film at the premiere as planned. According to one source, Durkin was angry that Farage's aides had been so dismissive of the film, and didn't want him to introduce a piece of work he didn't believe in. Banks and Wigmore decided not to attend the premiere at all, despite Banks having invested a great deal of money in the project.

Those who did attend – including Farage – thoroughly enjoyed pretending to be part of the movie industry for the evening. Champagne was served before the 1,700 guests took to their seats, and the audience played their part in proceedings by booing every time Ted Heath's name was mentioned and cheering when Farage and Hannan appeared on the screen.

Shortly after the premiere, the film was put up online so people could view it for free, and it secured well over 2 million views on YouTube alone by the time of the referendum on 23 June.

Yet, for all the glitz and glamour of the premiere in Leicester Square, it wasn't *Brexit: The Movie* that made the headlines that

evening. Nigel Farage, who had spent a year being slammed as
toxic by the Eurosceptic 'posh boys', had seen the campaign he
supported fail to get designation, had been ignored, overlooked
and undermined by opponents supposedly on his side of the argument, was about to send Vote Leave into near meltdown. It would
put another nail in the coffin of the Tate Plot, and prove that, like
Carswell, Farage could play the long game too.

At 10 p.m., as the VIPs from the *Brexit: The Movie* premiere
were drinking champagne at an after-party, ITV announced it
would be hosting a prime-time referendum debate show featuring David Cameron and Nigel Farage. It would be broadcast at
9 p.m. on Tuesday 7 June, and would see the UKIP leader facing
questions from a studio audience for half an hour, followed by the
Prime Minister undergoing a similar interrogation.

Vote Leave was furious and, an hour and fifteen minutes after
the announcement, an email was fired out with the kind of language and sentiment normally associated with Arron Banks.

It read:

> The establishment has tried everything from spending tax-
> payers' money on pro-EU propaganda to funding the IN
> campaign via Goldman Sachs. The polls have stayed fifty
> fifty. They're now fixing the debates to shut out the offi-
> cial campaign. ITV is led by people like Robert Peston who
> campaigned for Britain to join the euro. ITV has lied to us
> in private while secretly stitching up a deal with Cameron
> to stop Boris Johnson or Michael Gove debating the issues
> properly. ITV has effectively joined the official IN campaign
> and there will be consequences for its future – the people in
> No. 10 won't be there for long.

The Vote Leave response provoked some mocking (after all, they
were supposed to be the sensible campaign) and even forced ITV's

political editor to defend himself against claims of bias: 'So, & I can hardly believe I need to say this, I never campaigned for the euro & ITV is wholly impartial in EU referendum debate,' tweeted Robert Peston.

'The whole point of us getting designation was basically to make sure it wasn't Nigel Farage in the debates,' said Elliott. Although he had had no idea that ITV were in negotiations with Farage, he was aware that Downing Street had been on manoeuvres in the few days leading up to the announcement. After a period of seeming non-engagement from Cameron's team with broadcasters over the format of the debates, or even whether the Prime Minister should be involved at all, suddenly 'there was a flurry of activity', said Elliott:

> Craig Oliver [Downing Street's director of communications] all of a sudden started hitting all the broadcasters to talk terms of the debates, essentially trying to bamboozle the process and present a fait accompli – they must be done in this way, David Cameron will not be debating anybody else – all these different sorts of rules and regulations.

It seemed to Elliott that Downing Street had specifically requested to take on Farage, a view shared by UKIP's Douglas Carswell. Having helped Vote Leave secure the designation, the Clacton MP was furious that ITV had selected the UKIP leader for the show:

> What is the point in having a designation process if one side and the broadcasters then choose who's going to be the spokesman on both sides? Imagine if you had a general election and ITV got to decide who should speak for each party? Imagine if you had a football match and the manager of one team got to pick the players of the other? It's absolutely insane.

Carswell added:

> You cannot allow Downing Street to spend £9.3 million on
> propaganda, you can't allow them to use the machinery of
> the state. You would never tolerate a general election where
> the incumbent government decided who the spokespeople
> were for each party and that is precisely what happened and
> it was an absolutely disgraceful ITV fiasco.

What Vote Leave did not know was that ITV had been in conversation with Farage since the beginning of the year, when the UKIP
leader had sat down with ITV's director of news Mark Jermey in a
restaurant at St Pancras station. Farage was on his way to Brussels,
but he, his personal press officer Michael Heaver and UKIP's head
of press Gawain Towler found time for a meeting with the TV
executive before departing on the Eurostar. The network had
asked for a sit-down to get a flavour of what Farage would be up
for in terms of debate formats in the run-up to referendum day.
The lunch was very much a brainstorming session, as at that point
the referendum date was yet to be officially announced.

A few weeks later, Heaver was asked to go into ITV headquarters
to see Jermey for a one-on-one meeting. 'I remember Jermey said,
"We think we can do it, we think we can get Cameron *v.* Nigel,"'
said Heaver, who suddenly realised he was about to broker a
huge political event. 'I'm sitting there thinking, "Fucking hell, I'm
twenty-six years old, a working-class boy," and I knew I was about
to help set up the most-watched, biggest part of the whole fucking referendum campaign. It felt quite historic. This is serious shit.'

After a couple more meetings – including one after Vote Leave
had been awarded designation – ITV went quiet until Heaver got
an email 'out of nowhere' to say that Downing Street had agreed to
take part in a show. The conditions were that Farage and Cameron
would not share the stage at any point, and the UKIP leader would

face the audience first. Heaver and Farage agreed. The UKIP leader's spokesman did not buy the idea that Downing Street chose Farage because they felt the MEP would damage the Brexit cause. 'If he's that easy, why didn't Cameron do him one on one and make him look stupid?' said Heaver. Reflecting on receiving the email, he added: 'It was frantic, they confirmed all the details and were going through it with No. 10 and confirmed it with us. And then ITV said to me about two or three o'clock, "We think we've got it and at ten o'clock tonight we're going to announce."' The spokesman decided to miss that evening's *Brexit: The Movie* premiere so he could be fully prepared for the news breaking.

Heaver, Farage and Towler were the only Brexit campaigners who knew what was coming, meaning that those at the top of Vote Leave found out about the debate at exactly the same time as everyone else. However, the ferocity of the Vote Leave statement was not intended simply as a threat to ITV, but also as a warning to the BBC.

The next morning, executives at the broadcaster were due to meet to finalise the terms of the corporation's own debates. The BBC had announced in February plans for what would be the largest political campaign event in the UK – a debate at Wembley Arena on 21 June. There had been reports in the press in March that the BBC was hoping for a four-on-four debate, with Boris Johnson, Nigel Farage, Iain Duncan Smith and George Galloway representing Leave, up against George Osborne, Alan Johnson, Tim Farron and Caroline Lucas for Remain. The story was strongly denied by the BBC, but Vote Leave was becoming increasingly worried that the broadcaster would ignore the designation protocol and request that Farage take part – as ITV had done.

Elliott said:

> The reason why we were quite strong that evening against ITV was partly trying to get ITV to change, but also to fire

a warning shot across the bows of the BBC for the next
morning, so when they were sitting round working out what
to do and thinking: 'Should we go with Nigel, he's better
box office than anyone Vote Leave can put up', they would
be scared off it.

ITV did not change its mind, but the BBC did seem to be edging
away from including Farage in its Wembley showpiece. Leave.EU
became so irked about the potential exclusion of the UKIP leader
it took the bizarre step of publishing the personal telephone numbers of the BBC's head of Westminster Robbie Gibb, as well as
Elliott, Cummings and Robert Oxley from Vote Leave, and UKIP's
Douglas Carswell.

It then emailed supporters asking them to lobby for Farage's
inclusion. The email, signed by Banks, Andy Wigmore and
Richard Tice, read:

> Nigel Farage, a charismatic campaigner with over twenty
> years' experience and leader of the only major, UK-wide
> party dedicated to Brexit, absolutely needs to be part of the
> debate.
>
>   It will be completely unacceptable if Matthew Elliot [sic]
> and Dominic Cummings, the backstairs crawlers behind the
> creaking Vote Leave machine, are allowed to sideline UKIP
> entirely, as they tried to with the planned ITV debate, in
> favour of a handful of Tory ministers who have only been
> part of the Brexit movement for five minutes.

The stunt did not go down well, and Leave.EU sought to wind
Carswell up further by publishing a private message he sent them
asking for his contact details to be removed from its website.
'Note from @DouglasCarswell. Only asked public to tell him
we want Nigel at BBC debate. So much for Direct Democracy!'

the Leave.EU Twitter account posted, along with a screenshot of Carswell's message.

Banks, Wigmore and Tice may have been having fun, but the action was certainly not approved by UKIP. 'I don't know a single person in our group who hadn't said, "Don't do it" when they floated it. Everybody. We thought it was a joke, it was so bloody outrageous,' Towler remembered.

Speaking afterwards, Banks said:

> I thought it was great. Robbie Gibb had 61,000 emails from our supporters saying he should include Nigel in the big debate. Apparently his phone went into meltdown as he had three or four thousand phone calls. Rob Oxley put out a wonderful tweet saying, 'An angry phone call lasts a few minutes, class lasts forever'. We killed ourselves, I couldn't stop laughing for about half an hour. Nigel calls Andy and says: 'What are you going to do next, throw bricks through their window? I quite like Robbie, poor Robbie.' Andy replied: 'You are the leading Brexit politician in the country, what right do they have to keep you from the debate?' Nigel said: 'What are you going to do next? You're only one step away from ISIS. Are you going to put bricks through their window?' Carswell went ballistic. His phone melted down, it was hilarious.

Despite – or maybe because of – Leave.EU's direct lobbying, Farage was not chosen for the Wembley debate. Yet he would get his moment in the spotlight on 11 June, giving Vote Leave an anxious month ahead.

CHAPTER 26

While those at the top of Vote Leave and Leave.EU were arguing with television executives and sending out aggressive emails, the actual campaign to get the UK out of the EU was still going on.

Wednesday 11 May was not only the day of the *Brexit: The Movie* premiere and the announcement of the Farage/Cameron ITV show, it was also the first time the Vote Leave battle bus hit the road. Aboard the 36-seat coach were Boris Johnson and Gisela Stuart and, as the bus pulled into Truro, a crowd of people brandishing Vote Leave banners gathered to greet the politicians. Johnson spent the day in full 'Boris' mode: he waved a Cornish pasty in the air, clutched a bunch of asparagus and claimed it would be more delicious outside the EU, and even gave an ice cream to an unsuspecting member of the public. But it was not Johnson's antics when off the bus that provoked a storm: it was what was emblazoned on the side of it: 'We send the EU £350 million a week, let's fund our NHS instead.' Just the day before the bus was unveiled, the head of the UK Statistics Authority, Sir Andrew Dilnot, had written to Dominic Cummings, effectively asking Vote Leave to stop using the £350 million figure.

He wrote:

I note the use of the £350 million figure, which appears to be a gross figure which does not take into account the rebate, or other flows from the EU to the UK public sector (or flows to non-public sector bodies), alongside the suggestion that this could be spent elsewhere. Without further explanation I consider these statements to be potentially misleading and it is disappointing that this figure has been used without such explanation. Given the high level of public interest in this debate it is important that official statistics are used accurately, with important limitations or caveats clearly explained.

Dilnot was not the first person to take issue with the number. It had originally been used in the video to mark Vote Leave's launch back in October, with Bernard Jenkin raising concerns at the time. As the campaign progressed, others felt uncomfortable using a figure which at the very least required clarification. Labour Leave's Brendan Chilton said the £350 million was raised as a concern during meetings of David Campbell Bannerman's contact group on numerous occasions. 'Everybody said, "Use the net figure." It was ignored,' said Chilton.

> There were lots of debates about it, we weren't happy about it but they got designation, they could do it, but I have to say we never used that figure, we always used the net as we felt it was more honest. Using that figure, you leave yourself open to criticism – why create an easy target of yourself?

Ruth Lea, the respected economist who had worked as a civil servant for almost sixteen years, ended her official involvement with Vote Leave in February 2016 because of the campaign's use of the figure. 'When I was showed the £350 million, I thought, "I'm going to paddle my own canoe,"' she said. When she saw the figure on the side of a bus three months after quitting Vote Leave, she found herself shaking her head. 'I can make mistakes, I can get things wrong, but at least then it's my fault, I answer for it,' she said.

> I wrote a piece at the beginning of the year on the budget contribution. Very rough-and-ready figures: gross contribution £18–20 billion, you get about a quarter of it back with a rebate and you can spend that how you like – it's in arrears but nevertheless you get that money back and you can spend that exactly how you like. Then of course there's another quarter back in terms of public sector receipts, whether it's farming or regional policy.

The use of the figure was also raised by John Mills with the Vote Leave campaign team when he was chairman. As well as a defence of the claim's validity, he was also offered a more cynical explanation.

'The argument for the £350 million claim was that it was a very, very big number, and that everyone would dispute it but all this would then draw in everybody's attention to the fact that it was a very big number,' said Mills. Even when he pushed for the net figure to be used, he was met with the same argument: 'Their response was that we're better off with a big number because even if it's disputed, just in tactical terms, it keeps the size of the contribution in front of everyone.'

Bernard Jenkin did not know the number was going to be on the side of the bus, and although he was uncomfortable about its use, he saw the benefits of the plan, which had been put in place by Dominic Cummings and the campaign team. Jenkin said:

> Vote Leave deliberately used the £350 million figure out of context in order to provoke a row about it and I remember one six o'clock news with one broadcaster saying: 'But how

do you justify that?' with a picture of the bus with '£350 million for the NHS' on it – you couldn't pay for that publicity!
This was a tension we had to deal with, but I would never
use that figure out of context. Nor would people like Andrea
Leadsom. Whenever any minister or respectable politician
was dealing with this, we would always use the context, but
the Vote Leave propaganda was short of that context, therefore made it very controversial and it cut through.

Jenkin also pointed out that, despite the UK Statistics Authority's
concerns about the figure, it had used the number in its own
publications. 'Why do they approve publication of this figure if
they do not think it should be used? The UKSA chair Sir Andrew
Dilnot told the Select Committee, which I chair: "The £19.1 billion
figure is a legitimate figure for gross contributions,"' said Jenkin.

Iain Duncan Smith also defended the tactic, and said: 'Let's be
honest, it created a row and it alerted the public to the fact we
give money to the European Union.'

He added: 'The figure £350 million was just a kind of characterised figure in a way and it was a catalyst to create the debate,
ironically, about that you give money and that money can be better used here. That was really how it got going.'

While some were opposed to the gross figure entirely or recognised it as a piece of propaganda designed to stoke up a row,
others defended its use. Matthew Elliott, who conceded 'the rows
were good', said: 'When you tell me your salary, you probably tell
me in gross terms what you're paid.' Daniel Hannan used similar
logic to defend the figure, saying:

> If I say to you: 'What's basic rate income tax?', do you say: 'It's
> 20p in the pound', or do you say: 'Well, if you think about
> it it's actually zero because we get it all back in roads and
> schools and hospitals!'? It was a perfectly legitimate thing

to quote the gross figure. What was extraordinary is that the other side walked into the thing of arguing the toss and made that figure a big part of the campaign and all people heard was: 'We're giving a lot of money to the EU. Whether it's £180 million or £350 million, it's a hell of a lot of money.' If they had been clever they'd have said: 'Yeah, it's £350 million a week, but here's what we get...'

It wasn't just the figure on the side of the bus that provoked a row, but also what it was linked to: funding the NHS. The Leave campaign was calling for the UK to quit the EU; it was not a government-in-waiting. Making specific promises on what the money currently spent on EU membership could be used for was out of its jurisdiction. Leave supporters were quick to point out that the text did not say all the £350 million should be spent on the health service, and it was just one of the many things that could benefit from the funds.

That distinction may have been made clear on 11 May when the bus was unveiled in Truro, but Vote Leave's very first billboard poster did promise to give the money to the NHS. Reflecting on the bus slogan, John Whittingdale seemed oblivious to the initial claim: 'I was always happy to defend the £350 million figure. Where it has been wrongly interpreted – I don't think we ever said this, Farage might have done – we never said we will give £350 million a week to the NHS.' When it was pointed out that Vote Leave had made that explicit promise almost as soon as it was awarded designation, Whittingdale said: 'Well, we shouldn't have done.'

Elliott acknowledged that initial claim of giving all the £350 million to the NHS was an error. 'I think we were always very careful but one poster did slip through where it made the full link,' he said.

The row was all too much for Tory MP Dr Sarah Wollaston, who on 8 June announced she was switching from Leave to

Remain because of the campaign's claims over the NHS. She told
the BBC: 'I could not have set foot on a battle bus that has at the
heart of its campaign a figure that I know to be untrue. If you're
in a position where you can't hand out a Vote Leave leaflet, you
can't be campaigning for that organisation.'

Regardless of the merits of its slogan, the bus was performing
its job: getting people talking about the money the UK paid to be
part of the EU. It also successfully carried out its other requirement: getting Vote Leave politicians around the country. Michael
Gove, Priti Patel, Theresa Villiers, Iain Duncan Smith, Douglas
Carswell and other campaigners all clambered aboard the red bus
as they took their message out to the voters. Most of the photo
opportunities involved Boris Johnson, who was snapped playing
cricket, pulling pints, speeding round a race track, clutching a
lobster, kissing a fish and even auctioning off a cow.

Seeing the fun Vote Leave were having, Nigel Farage decided to
get involved with a bus tour of his own. In deliberate contrast
to Vote Leave's executive coach, UKIP hired an old-fashioned
double decker, which was then painted purple. It too had a slogan
on the side, but instead of focusing on a particular issue, UKIP
stuck with a message based on emotion: 'We want our country
back – vote to leave on June 23rd' (Farage and his advisors could
never quite bring themselves to say the phrase 'vote leave' – hence
the word 'to' in the slogan).

By this point, Chris Bruni-Lowe had decided to make UKIP's
campaign 'all about Nigel' and wanted the messaging to appeal
to people's guts, not their brains. His inspiration came from an
unlikely source – a 1993 film about Jamaica's Olympic bobsleigh
team. 'It needed to be like *Cool Runnings*,' said Bruni-Lowe.

> In *Cool Runnings*, the guy says to whatever the character is:
> 'What do you see when you look in the mirror?' and he says:
> 'I see pride, I see passion, I see someone who won't take no

shit from no one and I'm going to stand up for myself.' I said
if we can make the referendum about that, we'll win.

The UKIP bus rolled into towns and cities across the country right
up until referendum day, with the theme from the film *The Great
Escape* blasted out from on-board speakers as a means of firing up
patriotic fervour. After its launch in Dagenham, east London on
23 May, Farage travelled to South Yorkshire, Birmingham, Leeds,
Essex and many other places, where he would address public
meetings and wave his passport in the air, decrying the fact that
it had the words 'European Union' written on the front cover.

Despite the exposure the UKIP bus tour was giving Farage, the
MEP still believed he was being underused in the campaign. On
30 May, he sat down for dinner with Michael Gove at the house of
UKIP donor Christopher Mills, who had issued the invitation to
the pair. Farage had been in contact with both Gove and Johnson
over a number of issues, including the £350 million claim on the
bus ('I begged them to change it. I spoke to Gove. He said: "It's
all a bit late for that,"' remembered Farage), but at the dinner the
UKIP leader had some ideas he wanted to put to the Vote Leave
campaign co-convenor.

One of them was for a campaigning rally at the Royal Albert Hall
with himself, Boris Johnson and Kate Hoey. The plan had originally
been floated at a meeting in the House of Lords with UKIP peer
Lord Pearson, Richard Tice, Hoey and Bruni-Lowe. 'I said, "Why
don't we do the Royal Albert Hall, Nigel and Boris, and why don't
we do five cities in five days, Nigel and Boris touring the country?"
We'll win. We have Hoey, so we'll have Labour. We'll win because
the public will go, "Fucking hell!",' remembered Bruni-Lowe. Farage
brought the plan up with Gove, along with some ideas. According
to a source close to one of the top Vote Leave figures, Farage also
asked to appear on a Vote Leave platform and requested that, for
one day leading up the referendum, UKIP be given free rein in the

campaign – meaning Vote Leave would cease activity for twenty-four hours. Gove listened politely, but turned down all the requests. 'We decided to stick to the strategy, which was Farage was not part of the Vote Leave campaign,' said the source.

Another rebuffed idea of Farage's was to bring together the battle buses of Vote Leave, UKIP and Labour Leave for a symbolic convoy. Farage said, 'It would have been like the Russians and the Americans meeting at the Elbe. It would have been an amazing event.' The UKIP leader put the idea to Johnson in a phone call, but met with a familiar response. 'Boris was really taken with it but he had to consult with his people,' said Farage. 'I put the phone down and thought, "He could be Prime Minister soon and he's got to consult his people."' Bruni-Lowe added: 'That's when Nigel and I realised that Boris would be a shit Prime Minister. He was totally indecisive. He would agree and then say no.'

Vote Leave may have not wanted to work with Farage, but Grassroots Out were still holding rallies where he was always welcome. GO events took place in Herefordshire, Manchester, Portsmouth, Cornwall, Witney, Weston-super-Mare, Bristol and Monmouth, as well as street stalls and leafleting campaigns. While these rallies saw the familiar faces of Peter Bone and Tom Pursglove, there were also figures from Vote Leave at some of the events – including Defence Minister Penny Mordaunt. However, while a degree of rapprochement seemed to be developing between Vote Leave and Grassroots Out, Leave.EU were not happy with the green-tie-wearing campaigners.

On 21 April, it emerged that Peter Bone and Tom Pursglove had been paying themselves money from Grassroots Out. Bone's company PWB received £21,750 in the first four months of 2016 – £20,000 for accountancy services and a £1,750 director's fee. Pursglove invoiced Grassroots Out £19,250 – £17,500 for 450 hours' work as chief executive between 16 December and 31 March, and £1,750 in director's fees.

Banks was furious. He had piled in £5 million into various Leave campaigns by that point, and to see others appearing to earn money from the groups annoyed him immensely. A statement from Leave.EU said: 'We are extremely shocked and disappointed to discover that two elected individuals have treated the GO BREXIT campaign as a business not a cause and would urge them to do the honourable thing and donate the sum directly to a smaller BREXIT group.'

Bone insisted that neither he nor Pursglove benefited financially from the transactions, as they donated the cash back to Grassroots Out. The reason they took the money out of the company in the first place was that they believed if they didn't, their work would have been treated as a benefit in kind by the Electoral Commission, which the pair would have had to pay tax on. The easiest way was to take the money out, pay the tax on it, and then donate the money back.

'To make it absolutely clear,' said Bone, 'we were paid the money, paid the tax and donated the net amount.' Electoral Commission records show that this was the case for Bone, who donated £13,050 to Grassroots Out – reflecting his status as a 40 per cent rate taxpayer. Pursglove, who would be on the same rate thanks to his MP salary of £74,962, paid back £10,300 – slightly less than the £11,550 which would represent the money he received after tax.

Banks's anger about Bone and Pursglove's tax arrangement strategy came a day after he was subjected to the now traditional Treasury Committee grilling. It had started off quite well for Banks, who was given ample time to elaborate on his previous attacks on Vote Leave.

Committee chairman Andrew Tyrie offered up a free hit with the following introduction:

> We need a bit of clarification on a number of the allegations that you in particular, Mr Banks, have made about Vote Leave.

Perhaps I should read a few of those out and then ask you to comment on them. You said that their submission to the Electoral Commission was, I quote, 'full of lies and misrepresentations'. You said Vote Leave are lying and misrepresenting the situation; that 'these people are jokes'; that 'he' in particular – that is, Matthew Elliott – 'wants to be Lord Elliott of Loserville'; and that 'he' – Dominic Cummings – 'has become a liability and a danger to both Leave campaigns'.

Banks replied: 'You saw his evidence last week, didn't you? You do not need to ask that question.'

The session provided fewer fireworks than Cummings's appearance, but did turn slightly surreal when Banks tried to answer a question about President Obama's 'back of the queue' threat by talking about his child's music lessons:

> The only thing I would say on Obama is I took my son to his piano lesson on Monday night and the piano teacher said to me, 'You are someone to do with Brexit, aren't you? I do not like that Mr Obama coming over and telling us what to do.'

Labour MP Helen Goodman replied: 'Mr Banks, I am not asking you about your child's piano lessons. I am asking you about your views on foreign direct investment.'

Banks answered: 'We are allowed a little bit of levity, surely? It is not do or die, surely?'

The only serious news line to come from the grilling was Banks insisting that even if George Osborne's prediction that Brexit would cost UK households £4,300 by 2030 were correct, it was 'a price worth paying to get back our own democracy'. Stronger In were quick to send out a press release flagging up the admission.

With the Treasury Committee grilling over, Banks was able to turn his attention to another project that had been occupying his mind, and that of Andy Wigmore, since the UKIP conference in September. It was while having an evening drink on the veranda of the Earl of Doncaster hotel that the pair came up with the idea of holding a huge rally in aid of Brexit. The original plan was to hire out a football stadium in the Midlands and bus in supporters from around the country. However, Wigmore decided what the campaign really needed was a sprinkle of showbiz, and decided to turn it from a rally to a concert. The NEC Arena in Birmingham, which has a capacity of 16,000, was booked for Sunday 8 May, and 'BPop Live' was launched.

However, Wigmore came up against the same problem many others had experienced when it came to celebrity endorsements: the vast majority don't want to get involved in politics. For every Michael Caine and Ian Botham who was prepared to speak out in favour of Brexit, there were hundreds more who preferred to keep quiet. 'Someone like Michael Caine, their brand's impenetrable and he doesn't give a monkey's. For someone like Ian Botham, he took a huge risk and in hindsight would he do it again? I question that. There were a number of others who wanted to but couldn't or wouldn't,' said Tice, reflecting on his own experience of trying to secure celebrity endorsements for Leave.EU.

Even when Wigmore did manage to get artists to agree to appear, they quickly pulled out once they were made aware it was a Brexit-backing concert. Rumours of bands such as the Stereophonics began to circulate and, at the beginning of March, journalists from the Huffington Post and Buzzfeed were even promised a trip to a recording studio to meet some of the artists lined up. Eventually, drum 'n' bass duo Sigma, singer Ella Eyre and six-piece band the Electric Swing Circus were unveiled as head-liners. However, after Buzzfeed contacted the groups to ask them why they were supporting an anti-EU rally, they all pulled out.

Wigmore was not deterred, and rebooked the concert for Sunday 19 June. It may have been a different date, but the problems remained the same. Alesha Dixon, East 17 and two-fifths of the group 5ive all pulled out when they learned the political nature of the concert. Leave.EU had a third attempt at reviving the show and, in an email sent out on 2 June, unveiled BPop Live's new line-up. 'Journalists wondering how BPop could possibly top East 17 and two-fifths of 5ive need wonder no longer,' it read, as it proudly revealed that Mike, Cheryl, Jay and Bobby – formerly of Bucks Fizz – and Elvis Presley impersonator Gordon Hendricks would be appearing, alongside Nigel Farage, Kate Hoey and Liam Fox – who one assumed would be speaking, not singing.

For some reason, ticket sales were slow – even after the price was dropped from £23 to £5. Alas, on 14 June, the whole event was scrapped entirely. Reflecting on BPop Live, Banks said:

> Originally they had Rudimental, who Andy was friends with. But the press killed it. Every time we put forward a series of artists they got shot down. We actually found it quite funny: 'We've got two-fifths of 5ive and they've just pulled out. Now we've got 3/8ths of Bucks Fizz and one Drifter.

As the days ticked down to 23 June, Labour Leave also stepped up its activity. On 23 April, having helped Vote Leave secure designation, John Mills finally quit the organisation.

In a statement, he said: 'Over the last few weeks within the campaign, I have come to believe that it would be useful and more effective for the Leave campaign if there was a strong and independent Labour voice for the arguments to leave the EU.'

Mills's right-hand man Brendan Chilton, who had switched his support to GO, saw his old friend becoming increasingly distressed at the way Vote Leave were running the campaign:

> The Vote Leave board meetings used to take place on a Tuesday morning and they had the Wednesday committee

meetings. After every Tuesday morning we'd either meet or
I'd go up to his place or we'd speak on the phone and he was
utterly depressed because after every meeting he would say:
'They just don't get it.' All these people sitting on this board,
well-respected people, but they're not campaigners, they are
turning up lording it at the board meeting but not seeing
what's going on on the ground.

Farage, who was becoming good friends with Mills, claimed the
businessman's relief was visible when he left Vote Leave. 'They
abused him, they were horrible to him, they abused his money,
they were disgusting to him,' said Farage. 'I saw John at one
point at a lunch and he looked so ill, I thought, "He isn't going
to make this, he's trying to do the decent thing with these vile
people," and in the end even he cut loose. God, he was so happy
that night.'

With Labour Leave now finally free from Cummings's group,
it was able to focus on getting the left-wing case for quitting the
EU out to its voters. Mills said:

> There was an interesting poll that showed, I think a couple
> of months before the referendum, a very high proportion,
> about 40 per cent or something, of Labour people didn't
> know what the Labour Party's policy was. And I think this
> is partly because the Labour In campaign, to be honest,
> wasn't terribly effective. I think probably the rather half-
> hearted performance by Jeremy Corbyn was a factor in that,
> and I think the fact that Labour Leave gave a sort of home
> for Labour people on the Leave side may have confused
> people to some extent.

It was not just Labour Leave who noticed the apathy from the
party leadership bleeding into its supporters' minds. An internal

memo sent from Stronger In to Labour MPs which was leaked to
The Guardian on 31 May flagged up serious concerns. The paper
reported that:

> Focus groups in London, Brighton and Ipswich over the past
> few weeks showed voters were 'uniformly uncertain' about
> whether Labour was campaigning to stay in the EU. They
> did not know what Labour leader Jeremy Corbyn thought
> or believed he was for remain but 'his heart isn't in it'. In a
> sign that Labour's arguments are not cutting through to the
> mainstream, it revealed that a group of undecided working-
> class women in Liverpool mostly assumed the party was for
> leaving the EU.

The fears Labour Leave had had when Corbyn had announced
he was turning his back on years of Euroscepticism on becoming leader – namely that he would be an enthusiastic campaigner
for Remain – had proved unfounded. He refused to campaign
alongside the Prime Minister, and his speeches were limp,
unenthusiastic and uninspiring. Chilton was delighted with
Corbyn's behaviour, and noted: 'Whenever he made an intervention, it was as if he was willing us on from the background.'

Indeed, during one intervention on 2 June, he spent much
of the speech attacking Downing Street's arguments for staying
in the EU, including George Osborne's claim that the UK would
fall into a year-long recession after Brexit.

'I was at home watching that,' said Chilton. 'I think it was
lunchtime when he made that speech and I always have a glass of
wine with my lunch. I raised my glass to the television.'

As revealed by the Huffington Post after the referendum, the
head of Labour's Remain campaign, Alan Johnson, struggled to
secure meetings with Corbyn to discuss strategy; pro-EU lines
such as 'That's why I am campaigning to remain in the EU' were

deleted from speeches; and the leader even went away on holiday for three nights at the end of May just as the referendum campaign was intensifying.

This lack of enthusiasm from Corbyn and those around him created a space for Labour Leave, or Labour GO, to push forward with its anti-EU message. Whereas Corbyn appeared reluctant to get out on the road, Labour's Eurosceptics were relishing campaigning across the country, and were delighted with the reception they received. Chilton said:

> On more than one occasion we had people coming up to us, some were crying, saying: 'This is what we want Labour to be, we want it to be the party for the working-class people.' It doesn't mean marching off to the left and going mad. It means patriotic centre-left.

While Chilton was delighted to see such support in Labour-voting areas for his Eurosceptic campaign, he knew this could cause problems for the party in the long term. 'We were warning the party, we sent private emails, private memos to Tom Watson, to Jeremy, to the General Secretary, to Alan Johnson, saying: "We obviously disagree on this but you need to be aware that this is what we're finding,"' he said. When asked why he was giving such intelligence to what was at that moment his opposition, Chilton replied defiantly: 'Because we're still Labour.'

Yet, despite all the activity, all the quirky photographs, all the briefings, all the leafleting and all the rallies, the opinion polls were not looking good for the Eurosceptics.

Of the seven surveys carried out from 11 May – the date of the Vote Leave's bus launch – to 19 May, Remain was in the lead in six of them. It seemed that Stronger In's campaign tactic of pointing out the dangers of Brexit, including in Cameron's speech at the beginning of May questioning whether European peace and security would remain if the UK left the EU, was carrying more weight with the public than Vote Leave's messaging.

On Friday 20 May, a frustrated Richard Tice sent an email to a number of Eurosceptic campaigners, including Gisela Stuart, Lord Lawson, Kate Hoey and numerous UKIP and Conservative peers, urging for a change in tactics.

> Dear Gisela, other Vote Leave leaders and key Vote Leave funders,
>
> Halfway through the official designated period, with less than 5 weeks to go, it is increasingly clear that the Vote Leave campaign of Boris and Gove, masterminded by Elliott and Cummings, is failing.
>
> I have not heard anyone on our side say, or write, that it is a well run campaign with a clear strategy. It is turning into a depressing blue on blue male ego battle, between Boris and Dave, with a splash of Michael, which is turning off Tory voters and leaving the rest utterly cold. Most of the campaign appears to be based around £350m / week, to spend on the NHS – the wrong number on the wrong thing.

Tice then set out how he felt the campaign should change:

> 1. VL have given Remain a free run on the economics (despite this being the favoured strategic battleground of Elliott / Cummings):
>   1) The likes of John Longworth, Digby Jones, other business people together with Ruth Lea, and Roger Bootle need to be promoted to address this
>   2) The appalling forecasting track record of the Treasury, IMF, Carney etc needs much greater emphasis
>   3) Greater acceptance that short term uncertainty < 2 years is worth the medium / long term benefits

2. More emphasis on being safer out than in, using our security supporting people like Dearlove
3. Democracy and immigration
   1) Labour people like Kate Hoey and commentators like
      Julia Hartley Brewer need bringing to the fore
   2) Working with not against Nigel
   3) Emphasising that it is about so much more than just the
      economics
   4) More focus that there is no status quo option, Remain
      means more Brussels, more regs, less democracy.

He ended with a final dig at Vote Leave:

An admission needs to be made by the Vote Leave non exec
leaders that Boris and Gove need less exposure, whilst Elliott
and Cummings need to go. The first two have not performed that well on TV where they should be best, and the
latter two's core strategic plan has proven to be utterly wrong
and flawed.
   Such a course of action would actually gain the respect of
the press and the people.
   The country's future is in your hands. There is still time.

Little did Tice realise that Vote Leave were about to go big on
immigration and the idea that 'there is no status quo', and were
preparing to zone in one issue to highlight both of those concerns: Turkey.

CHAPTER 27

'I would say very clearly to people: "If your vote in this referendum is being influenced by considerations about Turkish membership of the EU, don't think about it. It is not remotely on the cards." It is not an issue in this referendum and it shouldn't be,' said David Cameron to Parliament's Liaison Committee on 4 May 2016. Unfortunately for him, his opponents didn't quite agree, and they were determined to make sure Turkey was very much an issue in the referendum.

Turkish accession to the European Union had been part of UKIP's argument for Brexit for years, but usually in the context of evidence of the organisation's expansionist ambitions. Nigel Farage started focusing on it as an issue in its own right in autumn 2015, when the EU began steps to allowing Turkish citizens visa-free access to the Schengen zone in exchange for the country helping to stem the flow of migrants from the Middle East into Europe. Turkey would also take back any refugees who had entered the Continent via its borders.

Another condition of the deal was the reopening of talks regarding Turkey becoming a full member of the EU – a process that had started in 1987 when the country applied for formal membership into the then Economic Community. Progress had been slow, and of the thirty-three chapters of membership Turkey needed to negotiate, only one had been completed by 2015 – science and research, in 2006.

Speaking about the visa-free access deal on LBC Radio on 16 October 2015, Farage said:

> This is all a precursor to Turkey joining the European Union. So listen, folks, if you want Turkey to join the European Union, if you think another 75 million poor people should have access to come to Britain, to use the Health Service, to use our primary schools, to take jobs in whatever sector it may be – if you think it's a good idea for our political borders now to reach Iraq and Syria, then please vote to stay inside the European Union, because that is what is coming down the tracks at you.

Farage's side of the Leave campaign maintained its focus on the issue, and on 4 December 2015 – the week when the EU's deal with Turkey was formally announced – Leave.EU issued a statement titled 'Turkish Delight and EU Security'. It read:

> 'Go sell crazy somewhere else, we're all stocked up here.' So goes Jack Nicholson's line to his neighbour in the film *As Good As It Gets*, and surely the logical response to the EU's latest crazy plan. Clearly, the plan hasn't been thought through. The latest proposal takes craziness to the next level.

It went on:

> Turkey is the main conduit for ISIS's oil for weapons sales. With one hand, Turkey's deeply unpleasant regime bombs our allies, the Kurds; while the other tacitly helps ISIS.
> Furthermore, by the time we have finished the job of destabilising Syria by bombing it to pieces, with no ground

troops, no reconstruction plan, and no replacement for Bashar
Al-Assad, refugees will be flooding into Turkey via its por-
ous border with Syria.

There is a strong possibility Turkey will then issue passports
to these refugees and wave them on their way to Europe. The
PM's position that the EU helps maintain our Security is
clearly wrong. We need to take back control of our borders
as soon as we can.

Realising that linking Turkey, migration and the EU – together
with the €3 billion of financial aid promised by Brussels – ticked
numerous boxes, Farage continued to press on with making Turkish accession a key part of the referendum debate. On
3 February 2016, UKIP produced a three-minute, forty-second
party political broadcast on the subject, which was shown on the
BBC. A Survation poll carried out on behalf of Leave.EU over
10–12 February showed the issue was having some cut-through,
with 38.6 per cent of respondents agreeing that if Turkey was to
join the EU, it would make them more likely to vote out. Armed
with this information, Farage told the European Parliament on
9 March: 'Perhaps this referendum on 23 June will become a referendum on whether we wish to be in a political union with Turkey.
A vote for Remain is a vote for Turkey.'

However, it initially seemed that Vote Leave were not going to
play ball. Boris Johnson appeared to shoot down the notion that
Turkey was on the ballot paper on Tuesday 15 March, during a
phone-in show on LBC Radio. Johnson, whose grandfather was
Turkish, said:

> I think the chances of the Turks readily acceding to the Euro-
> pean Union are between, you know, nil and 20 per cent...
> Well, probably lower than that. I mean, it's not going to
> happen in the foreseeable future. And if it were to happen,

what you wouldn't get is anything to do with free movement. I think that is where people are rightly spooked at the
moment. They think the idea of suddenly 75 million Turks
having the, you know, and all of those coming in to Turkey
notionally having rights of free travel, visa-free travel to the
EU, that's just simply not on the cards.

Johnson's view was not that dissimilar from that of David Cameron,
who told Parliament on 21 March:

Look, I know that in this debate, which I know is going to get
very passionate, people want to raise potential concerns and
worries to support their argument, but I have say that when
it comes to Turkey being a member of the EU, this is not
remotely in prospect. Every country has a veto at every stage.
The French have said that they are going to hold a referendum. So in this debate let us talk about the things that are
going to happen, not the things that are not going to happen.

Yet, as the campaign entered its final few weeks, it seemed that Vote
Leave was starting to reach the same conclusions about the Turkey
issue as Farage and UKIP had reached more than six months before.
In a speech on 14 April, Theresa Villiers said: 'If people believe
there is an immigration crisis today, how much more concerned
will they be after free movement is given to Turkey's 75 million citizens?' This was followed up by Iain Duncan Smith – who had now
stepped down as Work and Pensions Secretary after clashing with
George Osborne over welfare reform – with a speech on 10 May.
Just six days after Cameron had insisted Turkish membership was
not an issue in the referendum, his former Cabinet colleague said:

Turkey is on the ballot paper because the EU is on the ballot paper. As I understand it, the Prime Minister and others

said they wanted a road paved from Brussels to Ankara. The EU has made it very clear that they are going to get visa-free travel and then enter the EU. It is on the ballot paper, everything to do with the EU is on the ballot paper.

On Friday 20 May, the same day that Richard Tice emailed Vote Leave board members and Eurosceptic peers urging the official campaign to talk more about immigration and focus on the fact that there was no 'status quo' option on offer, a new campaign video was released, titled: 'Paving the way to Ankara'.

The 55-second video began with a clip of Cameron's appearance before the Liaison Committee, before cutting to footage of Turkish Members of Parliament brawling at the beginning of May. The video then overlaid Cameron's speech in Turkey in 2011, in which he had indeed vowed to 'pave the road from Ankara to Brussels'. Two days later, Vote Leave claimed in a statement that the birth rate in Turkey would lead to a million people coming to the UK within the next eight years. It was an extraordinary claim, but Vote Leave supporter Penny Mordaunt, who was also a Defence minister, doubled down on the suggestion during an interview on *The Andrew Marr Show* that morning. Marr kicked off the interview by saying: 'You are on the front page of *The Observer* this morning warning that a million people may come here from Turkey in the next eight years, which is strange because very few people expect Turkey to join the EU in the next eight years.'

Mordaunt replied: 'I think it's very likely that they will. In part because of the migrant crisis.'

Later on in the interview, Marr pointed out that the UK had a veto over Turkey joining the EU, to which Mordaunt responded: 'No, it doesn't. We are not going to be able to have a say.'

Cameron was furious and, on the *Peston on Sunday* show on ITV minutes later, he slapped down the junior minister. 'Let me be clear. Britain and every other country in the European Union

has a veto on another country joining. That is a fact,' he said, then
added:

> The fact that the Leave campaign are getting things as straight-
> forward as this wrong, I think should call into question their
> whole judgement in making the bigger argument about
> leaving the EU.
>
> It is very important. They're basically saying vote to get
> out of Europe because of this issue of Turkey that we can't
> stop joining the EU. That is not true, we can stop Turkey
> becoming a member.

The Turkey issue would not go away, and the next day Vote Leave
released a poster with the words: 'Turkey (population 76 million)
is joining the EU.' Alongside the text was a UK passport mocked
up as an open door, with a trail of footprints going through it.

On 6 June, Vote Leave's official referendum mailshot – which
would be distributed to 40 million households – was revealed by
The Spectator. Under the headline 'Countries set to join the EU'
was a map of Europe. There were only three countries directly
labelled: the UK, Syria and Iraq. Five other countries – Albania,
Macedonia, Montenegro, Serbia and Turkey – were coloured red
and marked by numbers, with a key containing their names in the
top-right corner. At a glance, it appeared that Syria and Iraq were
set to join the EU. Matthew Elliott defended this, claiming that
Syria and Iraq were the only ones labelled 'because they were the
biggest'. Elliott said the campaigning on Turkey was instigated by
Dominic Cummings, and it was supported as 'it was a good way
into the migration debate and also one of our key objectives in the
campaign was to basically show the status quo wasn't an option'.

With the campaign shifted to Turkey, and therefore immigration issues, the polls also started to move. Of the fourteen opinion
polls conducted between 20 May and 6 June, Leave was ahead in

six of them, with Remain in the lead in five. The remaining three were dead heats.

The shift of focus on immigration was not lost on those in UKIP, who had been repeatedly told by Vote Leave that immigration would not be the issue that would convince swing voters to back Brexit. 'This is the sheer hypocrisy of these people,' said Farage, while UKIP's head of press Gawain Towler commented: 'That just made us laugh, it made us laugh. We're accused of being bad guys and dreadful and toxic no less – who were the ones who produced the map?!' Tice was equally surprised by the dramatic change in tone: 'They had castigated us for things we had done, it was outrageous, but they realised they were losing,' he said.

Labour Leave's Brendan Chilton admits he 'found some of the stuff on Turkey very unpalatable, I really didn't like it all'. He added: 'It played into the narrative of "the Muslims are coming and Al-Qaeda are coming", and I thought it was just awful. If Farage had done it he would have been a racist and a loony, but because they did it, it's acceptable.'

After the campaign, Elliott admitted that Vote Leave had indeed used some of the same arguments deployed by UKIP. The difference was, he said, they weren't coming out of the mouth of Farage:

> Of course Farage said these things previously. But when a different spokesperson is saying it, it has more resonance with people in a sense that a lot of those swing voters we were keen to attract – a lot of them tuned out Nigel Farage. In a sense they didn't like him, or they didn't trust him, or they thought he was a racist or whatever, and they didn't want to hear from him. The natural upper limit for a UKIP-led referendum campaign would have been at most 40 per cent, and that's being generous, more like 35 per cent. You would have seen basically a two-to-one defeat for the Leave campaign had it been a UKIP-led/Nigel Farage-led effort.

Daniel Hannan and Douglas Carswell also both disputed the
notion that the campaigning on Turkey and immigration was
somehow kowtowing to Farage's tactics. When this point was put
to Carswell, he said: 'No, I really don't think so. EU expansion is a
legitimate point and it's a legitimate concern. It was not the main
thrust of the campaign.' He claimed the most important part of
the campaign was 'take control', whether that be of money going
to Brussels, of UK sovereignty or of border control.

> Yes, in addition to that we also have something to say about
> immigration because it is a concern – not as big a concern
> but it is a concern. We also have something to say about EU
> expansion. If we were running an immigration-based cam-
> paign, why would we use the phrase take control? Why would
> have we emblazoned on the bus what we had emblazoned
> on the bus? You can't sift through everything we said, pick
> out the mention of Turkey and claim that we led on Turkey.

Hannan agreed:

> Immigration was always a valid issue, I don't think it was ever
> going to be our top issue. All of our internal polls showed
> what the published polls showed, which is by far the biggest
> issue was democracy, immigration was quite a distant second
> and even those citing immigration as their top issue, very few
> wanted or expected a very dramatic fall in numbers.

One of the reasons for the shift in focus was that voters were
telling Vote Leave they were worried about the issue. Alexander
Thompson, who joined Vote Leave as its head of film in April
2016, made a telling admission in an interview with *Newsweek*
after the referendum. He said: 'Immigration and Turkey's EU
membership weren't priorities when I started, but when it kept

coming up in focus groups we realised it was a huge issue, and
we changed tack.'

There was, of course, a simple way for Downing Street to neutralise the whole Turkey issue: the Prime Minister could have
vowed to veto the country joining the EU, or even promised a referendum if Turkey ever completed all the chapters for membership
– whether that was in eight years or a thousand years.

Vote Leave's Gisela Stuart believed such an action would have
killed the problem 'stone dead', while Duncan Smith argued that
the more Cameron insisted that the French would veto Turkey's
membership in a referendum, the more it showed how much
power the UK had let ebb away to the Continent. 'Why are we
relying on somebody else?' he asked, before adding: 'It was quite
damaging, the Turkey stuff, for them and I thought they could
have handled that better, but they didn't.'

On Monday 6 June, with Vote Leave's Turkey leaflet about to be
despatched and the polls starting to swing in the right direction,
Brexit backers could allow themselves to feel more optimistic about
the referendum. However, those at Vote Leave weren't letting themselves get carried away, as the following day Nigel Farage was going
to be representing their side in a TV debate with David Cameron.

CHAPTER 28

'**W**hat are my negatives?' said Nigel Farage.

'Well, you're thin-skinned, snarling and aggressive,' replied Gawain Towler.

There was a brief pause as everyone in the room waited to see how the UKIP leader would react. A smile appeared on his face and he started laughing. No one was more relieved than Patrick O'Flynn, who a year earlier had used those exact words when describing Farage. After a period in the party wilderness, O'Flynn was now back at the top table and was one of those helping Farage prepare for his TV performance.

In many ways, O'Flynn was one of the forgotten heroes of the Brexit movement. In 2010, while he was political editor of the *Daily Express*, he convinced the paper to launch a 'crusade' (as the *Express* campaigns were called) to get the UK out of the EU. Half a million readers sent in coupons backing the crusade, which were delivered to Downing Street in 2011. While many sneered at the paper's stance – and its numerous EU-bashing front pages over the years – it provided much-needed coverage for UKIP, which in turn put pressure on David Cameron to promise the referendum in January 2013.

O'Flynn also stuck to his guns when it came to supporting Vote Leave for designation – the only UKIP MEP to do so. His support stayed strong despite Farage repeatedly asking him to change his mind when the pair were in Brussels or Strasbourg on MEP duties.

But the focus was now on the ITV debate, and O'Flynn joined Towler, Chris Bruni-Lowe and Leave.EU's Brian Monteith in the UKIP offices to help brainstorm the kind of topics that might come up.

While the clash would be Farage's first significant TV appearance of the campaign, Cameron had already been subjected to a grilling. On Thursday 2 June, he had appeared on an hour-long programme on Sky News. The first half of the show saw him interviewed by Sky News political editor Faisal Islam, who managed to rile the Prime Minister when he tried to call out Downing Street's 'Project Fear' tactics: 'What comes first? World War Three or the global Brexit recession?' asked Islam.

The audience collapsed in laughter and applause, and Cameron claimed the words 'World War Three' had never left his lips when he gave a speech suggesting the security of Europe could be under threat from Brexit.

The following night, it was the Leave campaign's turn to face a grilling. Surprisingly, Vote Leave did not put up the person many considered to be the de facto leader of the campaign, Boris Johnson, but instead opted for Michael Gove. The decision was taken by Vote Leave after it carried out focus group research. Matthew Elliott said:

> I remember one in particular, basically after all the politicians had come out on each side, and we tested everyone from Boris to Gove to Gisela to other Cabinet ministers, what have you, and one thing that did come up with Michael Gove was 'I may not particularly like him, I don't like what he did with schools, that sort of thing, but he basically let down his best friend, he's followed his conscience, he's friends with the PM yet he's campaigning for Leave and the

PM is annoyed about that and if he's done that, he must be
serious about what he is saying, he must be telling the truth.'

Gove put in a solid performance, but during one speech hitting
back against the avalanche of organisations, foreign leaders and
professional bodies calling for a Remain vote, he delivered a line
that would come to define the Brexit campaign – at least in the
eyes of its opponents.

'I think the people of this country have had enough of experts...'
said Gove, before Islam interrupted with: 'Have had enough experts? People in this country have had enough of experts?'

Gove tried to explain that he meant 'experts from organisations
with acronyms saying that they know what is best and getting it
consistently wrong', but Islam still accused him of Donald Trump-
style politics.

With the opening TV skirmishes delivered, all eyes turned to
Farage to see if he would sink or swim during his questioning
by the studio audience. After arriving at the studio at the Queen
Elizabeth Olympic Park in Stratford, east London on his UKIP
battle bus, Farage and Michael Heaver relaxed by having a quick
cigarette before going into the building. As the pair were smoking, they saw Cameron and his entourage arrive. Never ones to
forgo a spot of mischief, the duo, along with Arron Banks and
Andy Wigmore, rushed back inside to make sure the Prime
Minister would have to walk past them on his way in. 'You could
see the look of shock on Cameron's face and his aides looked like,
"Oh God, we're totally losing our job!",' remembered Heaver. The
Prime Minister said, 'Hello, Nigel.' Farage replied, 'Hello, dear
boy. Good luck.'

With the Vote Leave top brass watching on anxiously, the show
kicked off at 9 p.m. It was an anti-climax in every sense. Farage
was subjected to a light grilling, but there were no real gaffes or
flare-ups – and certainly nothing as controversial as the leaders'

debate in the run-up to the 2015 general election, when he had
talked about migrants with HIV using the UK healthcare system
and accused an entire audience of being biased against him. The
main flash point came when an audience member took Farage to
task for comments he had made in an interview with the *Sunday
Telegraph* the previous weekend. The UKIP leader had claimed
mass sex attacks which took place in Germany on New Year's Eve
– mainly perpetrated by men of north African descent – could
be replicated in the UK if migrants from that part of the world
'get EU passports'. He described the issue as the 'nuclear bomb' in
the referendum debate. In the ITV debate, an audience member
said: 'You have basically suggested that a vote to Remain is a vote
for British women to be subdued to the same horrific assaults.'

Farage: 'Just calm down there a little bit, all right. Sometimes in
life what it says at the top of the newspaper page and what you've
actually said can be slightly different things. I'm used to being
demonised because I've taken on the establishment.'

'Aren't you demonising migrants?' responded the audience
member.

Farage replied:

> What I said about Cologne is it's a huge issue in Germany, it's
> a huge issue in Sweden. I think Angela Merkel has made a
> big mistake by saying 'please everyone come', and what we've
> had is a very large number of young single males have settled
> in Germany and in Sweden who come from cultures where
> attitudes towards women are different. I haven't scaremon-
> gered in any way at all.

It was a tense moment, but as Farage was merely restating views
he had expressed a few days before – and which had been widely
reported – it was by no means disastrous. The UKIP leader
even managed to repeat his campaign trick of brandishing his

passport and decrying the presence of the words 'European Union' on its cover.

Cameron's half-hour slot was mainly focused on migration issues, but he did get in some good digs at the Leave side, including: 'The British thing is to fight for Great Britain in the EU, not Nigel Farage's Little England.'

Although Vote Leave was trying to keep its distance from the debate for fear of being seen to endorse Farage, Gisela Stuart was sent down to the ITV studios to provide commentary after the programme finished. She said later: 'We didn't want to have a story where he split the Leave camp, however, I was prepared that if during that debate he said something which we felt was inflammatory and inappropriate, I was on hand to say it. To be fair, he didn't.'

Even Douglas Carswell, who was still furious that ITV had selected Farage in the first place, did not think his party leader had made any gaffes. 'Fortunately it wasn't too damaging but simply juxtaposing it as a choice between Cameron and Farage was very, very damaging,' he said.

A Stronger In source also agreed that Farage had not delivered the gaffes they were hoping for. 'At the end of the day, Farage is really strong on Europe. Yes, he might turn some people off on immigration, but EU bureaucracy, sovereignty, all that stuff is his strength. It was Cameron who underperformed if anything.'

With the Farage/Cameron programme out of the way, Vote Leave could turn its full attention to another ITV show scheduled for that week – and this time it would be a proper debate. Boris Johnson, Gisela Stuart and Energy Minister Andrea Leadsom would take on Scottish National Party leader Nicola Sturgeon, Labour's shadow Business Secretary Angela Eagle and Energy and Climate Change Secretary Amber Rudd.

To prepare for the clash, Vote Leave hired Brett O'Donnell, the American debating guru who coached George W. Bush in 2004 and John McCain in 2008 for their presidential TV debates.

Recognising that the Remain camp would focus their guns on Johnson, O'Donnell spent more than six hours in the weeks running up to the debate, and an additional three hours on the day itself, coaching the trio in how to behave. Vote Leave's preparation didn't go entirely smoothly, as a water leak in Westminster Tower meant staff had to decamp to Dominic Cummings's house on 2 June while the plumbers were called in. Cummings's wife Mary Wakefield – commissioning editor for *The Spectator*, who was on maternity leave at the time – revealed the carnage caused when Team Brexit pitched up in her living room in an article for the publication:

> Brexit was younger and cheerier than I had imagined: seven twentysomethings sat around the dining table bent over Macbooks; another five sat on the floor. Four men in their thirties treated the kitchen island as if it were a fashionable standing desk. Their cables trailed through the butter. Two Canadian geeks stood by the midget's changing mat, laptops propped on the wetwipe box. In the toilet, a brace of physicists discussed Facebook algorithms.
>
> Around teatime the big beasts appeared: Boris, followed by Gisela Stuart, the Labour MP for Birmingham Edgbaston. They prepped for their TV debate beside a tangle of just-washed sleep suits as the midget and I watched agog. For months now, my life has been dominated almost equally by the baby and the EU referendum. It felt as if fate had fixed it so that reality mirrored my mental state.

Despite the water-related disruption, the preparation was pitch perfect, as on the night itself the Remain trio did indeed zone in on Johnson. Sturgeon claimed he was 'only interested in David Cameron's job', while Rudd said: 'Boris, he's the life and soul of the party, but he's not the man you want to drive you home at the end of the evening.' In a row over the £350 million figure, Eagle pointed at Johnson and told him: 'Get that lie off your bus.'

Yet while the three Remainers focused their anger and attention on Johnson, Leadsom and Stuart were able to concentrate on their campaign message, repeatedly using the phrase 'take back control'.

If anyone was in any doubt that No. 10 had approved the hit on Johnson, Cameron all but confirmed it with a tweet once the show had ended: '.@AmberRudd_MP was a star in the #ITVEUREF debate. She was passionate and clear about why we are #StrongerIn the EU, "leading not leaving."'

The publication of Vote Leave's official leaflet, the Farage/Cameron ITV show and the six-way debate had all taken place in the space of four hectic days. It was a crucial period for the Leave campaigners, and the important question was whether public opinion had moved behind Brexit. Of the five opinion polls carried out between 9 and 14 June, Leave was ahead in four of them. On Tuesday 14 June, the *Times* front page spelt it out: 'Britain on course for Brexit after poll surge: Seven-point lead in record YouGov survey'.

With just over a week to go, Leave looked on course for victory.

CHAPTER 29

A t 10 a.m. on Wednesday 15 June, Gawain Towler sat down outside London's City Hall on the south bank of the Thames and took a sip of his morning coffee. On the table beside of him was a copy of that day's *Times*. The day before, the paper had splashed on Leave being seven points ahead in the latest opinion poll. The front page of the next day's edition seemed to be the Downing Street reaction to the story: 'Osborne to raise taxes if voters go for Brexit – Emergency Budget "would put 2p on basic rate"'. It was the latest scare story from the Remain camp – this time that Brexit would lead to a £30 billion black hole in public finances, spelling tax hikes and spending cuts. Towler, like all the Leave side, dismissed the threat. Besides, the UKIP press chief had his mind on something else that day.

By just before 11 a.m., Towler had walked the short distance from City Hall to Butler's Wharf, where journalists, film crews and photographers were already starting to gather. Moored next to the jetty was a boat decked out in red, white and blue balloons and Union Jack deckchairs. This was the vessel that Towler, Nigel Farage, Arron Banks and a host of media would soon sail up the Thames on. And they wouldn't be alone. Another thirty fishing boats would be joining Farage's ship to form a flotilla on the river. They would then sail en masse down to

Parliament as a demonstration of how the EU controlled the UK's fishing waters.

Although the sky was cloudy and there would be light showers throughout the day, there was no danger of the event being called off, unlike a stunt involving Farage which had been planned for earlier that week. The UKIP leader was offered the chance to take to the sky in a twin-seat Spitfire at Biggin Hill Airport on Monday 13 June. The last time Farage had got in a plane for a political stunt, it had nearly cost him his life. It was on the day of the 2010 general election, and the 'Vote UKIP' banner the plane was dragging across the sky got caught up in the tail fin, sending the aircraft crashing to earth. Farage was left with permanent back problems after the incident. Six years on, and he was seriously contemplating whether to take to the air again in the name of political campaigning. He said: 'I hadn't finally decided if it was yes or no. I think there's only one twin-seater in the country. The chance to do it was there and the weather kiboshed it. Would I have done it? Would I have turned up? Of course I would!'

The Thames adventure would be a much safer way to generate some headlines for the Brexit campaign, and at just after 11.30 a.m. the boat set sail for Parliament. As well as the flotilla on the water, UKIP and Leave activists were also lined up on the bridges that straddle the Thames, all preparing to cheer and applaud the boats as they passed. Douglas Carswell, however, was neither on the water nor on a bridge. 'I got an email from the UKIP London people saying did I want to meet in Parliament Square for something they were planning on doing,' he said,

> and I emailed back and I said: 'Please tell me you don't have some daft scheme' and they said: 'Oh no, no, no, we want to stand on a bridge because a flotilla of boats is going past and we want to make sure other people...' and I just said

> hang on – boats, water, bridges, UKIP activists, counter-
> demonstrators – it didn't feel right to me.

Carswell was certainly right to be worried about counter-demonstrators, but not just on dry land. No sooner had Farage's boat begun making its way up the Thames than a rival ship appeared from the opposite direction, manned by Sir Bob Geldof and a host of activists calling for Remain – including Boris Johnson's sister, Rachel.

Using an extremely loud public address system, Geldof's boat repeatedly blasted out the 1960s soul classic 'In with the In Crowd' as it followed Farage's boat up the river. Geldof even took to a microphone to lambast Farage for only attending one out of forty-two meetings when he was a member of the European Parliament's Fisheries Committee.

'You are a fraud, Nigel. Go back down the river because you are up one without a canoe or a paddle,' he said, before adding: 'You're no fisherman's friend.' Geldof then began sticking two fingers up to Farage and making a wanker gesture at him.

The UKIP leader tried his best to ignore him, and just muttered, 'A load of rich kids,' to himself. Michael Heaver was more forthright in his views: 'What a bunch of cunts.' UKIP MEP David Coburn summed up what many Leave campaigners on the boat were thinking when he branded the rival boat 'millionaires for Remain'.

He added: 'The guy has got a big mouth, he was a crap pop star and he's not even British as far as I understand, he's from the Irish Republic, he hasn't got a say in the matter.'

It wasn't just Farage who was on the receiving end of Geldof's insults. Some of the fishermen who had brought along their own boats to be part of the flotilla were also mocked by the singer. The atmosphere became so uncomfortable than one of the activists on Geldof's boat – Labour supporter Bethany Pickering – actually disembarked from the vessel in protest. She later told LBC Radio: 'We didn't expect it would be a billionaire being condescending to fishermen.'

She added: 'It was very patronising, very much mocking the issue they had, jeering at them, using his ability and his money to drown out what they had to say.

'He definitely swore at the fishing boats – and made gestures at them as well. It just became very negative.'

The Stronger In campaign, which did not organise Geldof's rival boat but were aware of it, initially found the so-called 'Battle of the Thames' amusing. 'Actually, Bob Geldof doesn't poll as badly as you might think,' said a source. However, as the day wore on, the mood in Stronger In changed as they realised Osborne's emergency Budget announcement was losing air time to images of Geldof swearing at Farage and the fishermen.

Speaking afterwards, Farage said:

> The arresting image of the campaign should have been that unwashed yob. That was an amazing moment. Everything you want to know about this campaign was summed up. All you need to do is write about that flotilla and who was on each side and you know why the referendum went the way that it did.

Once Farage was back on dry land, he headed up to Peterborough for a public meeting scheduled for that evening. Appearing alongside Labour's Brendan Chilton, UKIP's Patrick O'Flynn and Tory MP Stewart Jackson, Farage ended his speech by parading round the stage with a UKIP banner repeatedly shouting: 'We want our country back!'

After the meeting, the Brexit campaigners went for a celebratory meal. As far as they were concerned, it had been a fantastic day. But there was another reason the UKIP section of the group were feeling happy. Noticing the smiles on their faces in the restaurant, Chilton asked: 'What're you all laughing at?' A UKIP activist replied: 'Tomorrow we're unleashing our first in a series of posters,' and passed Chilton a phone with a photo of the first image. Chilton took a look at the screen, frowned and handed the phone back.

CHAPTER 30

Douglas Carswell left Vote Leave headquarters after his regular morning briefing in a confident mood. It was the day after the flotilla, and what could have been a credibility-damaging PR stunt by Nigel Farage actually worked in Leave's favour thanks to Sir Bob Geldof's uncouth intervention. The previous week's ITV debate featuring Farage had also passed without any major gaffes, and the focus was increasingly shifting to the Vote Leave top team of Boris Johnson, Michael Gove, Gisela Stuart and Andrea Leadsom. His strategy of keeping Farage away from the Leave campaign was appearing to be broadly successful, and the polls showed Leave were on course for victory – a win that would validate the Tate Plot.

After crossing Albert Embankment, Carswell started walking across Lambeth Bridge to return to Westminster when three poster vans drove past him – each bearing an identical image. Carswell put his head in his hands and uncharacteristically swore to himself as they went past. Perhaps the detoxification strategy wasn't such a success after all.

Minutes after passing Carswell, the three vans pulled up outside Europe House in Smith Square, Westminster. Waiting for them was Nigel Farage and a host of media. The posters were to be the start of a series of images which would be pumped out in the

run-up to referendum day a week later. That day's poster focused
on immigration. Underneath the words 'Breaking point – the EU
has failed us all' was a photograph of a seemingly endless queue
of refugees crossing into Slovenia from Croatia in October 2015.
At the bottom were the words 'We must break free of the EU and
take back control of our borders.'

Introducing the posters, Farage said:

> This is a photograph – an accurate, undoctored photograph
> – taken on 15 October last year following Angela Merkel's
> call in the summer and, frankly, if you believe, as I have
> always believed, that we should open our hearts to genuine
> refugees, that's one thing.
>
> But, frankly, as you can see from this picture, most of the
> people coming are young males and, yes, they may be coming
> from countries that are not in a very happy state, they may be
> coming from places that are poorer than us, but the EU has
> made a fundamental error that risks the security of everybody.

Within minutes of its unveiling, the poster was branded 'disgusting' by SNP leader Nicola Sturgeon, while Labour's Yvette Cooper
said: 'Just when you thought Leave campaigners couldn't stoop
any lower, they are now exploiting the misery of the Syrian refugee crisis in the most dishonest and immoral way.' One Twitter
user even juxtaposed the poster with Nazi propaganda attacking immigration after the First World War. UKIP's head of press
Gawain Towler said:

> There had been a television documentary which had shown
> a Nazi propaganda film in which a column of refugees in
> black and white graininess were there. It will not surprise
> you to know that we had not been watching it. It's inter-
> esting how lefties watch things about Nazis and we don't.

We had no idea of that, of course we didn't, as we don't sit
there watching Nazi propaganda films, it's not what we do.

Carswell was astonished by Farage's tactics, and said:

It's a few days to go before the referendum, you're five to
seven points ahead in the polls, by what conceivable logic do
you publish those Breaking Point refugee posters? Just ask
yourself, is there a single person in the country who would
respond positively to those posters who hasn't already made
up their mind how they are going to vote? So why use those
posters? The only thing those posters are going to do is upset
swing voters and make yourself the centre of attention. Perhaps that is the tactical objective. It hindered us from winning
and it came ruddy close to costing us the referendum.

Daniel Hannan, another key player in the Tate Plot, was also furious and, like Carswell, believed the poster was more about putting
Farage in the public eye than winning the vote:

I think that was ugly campaigning and I think it was objec-
tionable from an ethical point of view but I also think it
was idiotic from a tactical point of view. What swing voter
is going to be sitting at home on the fence about this and is
going to see that poster and think, 'Oh, I had no idea there
was a refugee crisis in Slovenia, I better vote Leave now'?
Again, what was the real motive there? Was it about snatch-
ing the spotlight back or was it about actually trying to
convince anyone?

Vote Leave chairman Gisela Stuart simply thought, 'Oh God!'
when she saw the poster, while Iain Duncan Smith thought it was
not just 'awful' but incoherent.

> It was a bad poster, it tried to mirror the 'Britain Isn't
> Working' poster but it just didn't work. It would have been
> legitimate to say, 'The European Union was at breaking point
> and here is the border of Macedonia' [*sic*], but it was not
> legitimate to indicate that this was the UK, because that was
> not the case. You can't have a false picture, as a number one
> rule. Second, it took it to a level that I thought was unhelp-
> ful because it made a lot of people very uneasy.

The genesis of the poster came in March, when UKIP were
worried Vote Leave was not going to do any campaigning on
immigration. Eurosceptic millionaire Paul Sykes, who had
funded the party's advertising blitz in the run-up to the 2014
European election, was also keen to launch a poster series which
'could be seen from the moon' in the final weeks of the referendum campaign. Working with Chris Bruni-Lowe, the pair
decided to test-run some ideas in May's London mayoral election on the back of UKIP candidate Peter Whittle's campaign.
On 3 May, Farage unveiled a poster of a queue of people with the
strapline 'Open door immigration isn't working – London's population is growing by one million every decade'. The image was
barely commented on at the time, but Bruni-Lowe thought the
theme would work well for the EU referendum, and asked
the Family advertising agency to come up with another queue-
based poster.

Bruni-Lowe said:

> The initial poster that I wanted was a passport picture with a
> load of people in the passport with: unknown image; where
> [are] they from: unknown; where [are] they going: unknown;
> 'The EU has failed us all, let's take back control'. Then we said
> why not use a queue, a legitimate queue of people basically
> trying to get in across the border. The problem we had was at

that time no one was talking about immigration. We needed a hard-hitting campaign.

When the poster came back from the advertising agency, 'Nigel and I agreed it and said that's fine,' remembered Bruni-Lowe, 'there's no issue with that at all because we did something similar in the London election and our view was actually this is quite tame. It doesn't really say anything.'

Farage did not seem to be prepared for the initial outrage it would cause either. He said later:

> The plan was simple, the plan was to do six posters in seven days and this was the first of them. So we didn't have any conventional billboards, we had digi-sites. This was the first of the posters and this was the only one of the posters which was about the EU, not Britain. This was about Merkel's migrant madness, hence the strapline 'the EU is failing us all'.

A few days before the launch, Vote Leave's Matthew Elliott spoke to Sykes over the phone and asked him what advertising he was planning with UKIP.

Elliott said:

> He never told me what was going to be in the ads, he was always very, very cagey. The whole thing was me always saying, 'Come on, share them with us, let us know what's going to be in there.' He always refused to send over any of the artwork or tell us what was going to be in them, other than to do his usual thing of saying it's going to be an ad campaign which you can see from the moon.

With the poster launched, Farage and Bruni-Lowe went for lunch to discuss the next stage in their plan to force immigration to the front and centre of the referendum. The duo had been told that David Cameron was planning to make a speech in which he would warn that a million migrants would rush to the UK immediately after a Brexit vote, before the country had actually quit the EU. It was decided that Farage would pre-empt Cameron's speech by calling for the UK to close its borders to EU migrants as soon as Brexit was voted for.

Bruni-Lowe believed the uneasiness that Leave campaigners such as Carswell and Hannan had over the poster – and the issue of immigration in general – was evidence that they did not understand why people wanted to get out of the European Union.

'The problem with Carswell is he lives in a complete fantasy world,' he said.

> In Clacton when we used to go during the by-election, people would say: 'Douglas, immigration is the biggest issue, I hate all these people coming here.' 'No, you don't understand, it's not immigration, it's health service stuff.' Carswell, like Suzanne Evans, I think, wishes people voted for UKIP for a different reason. So they project 'Ooh, they vote for them for libertarian reasons' – no, they don't – they vote for them because they don't like immigrants in this country; that's pretty much the basic reason. When someone says they want an Australian-points immigration system, they want zero immigration.

While Farage was having fun in London, Boris Johnson was facing a tough time in Norfolk. The Vote Leave battle bus had taken the MP to Lowestoft, where he was due to visit a fish market, but the owners wouldn't let him in. He settled for a fish merchant, and added to his ever-growing series of photo opportunities by filleting a fish for the cameras. The bus reached Norwich at just before 1 p.m., and even though rain was coming down it did not deter a heckler venturing out to shout, 'You're a racist!' at the former London Mayor. The gloomy weather matched the way the day was panning out, and Johnson and his advisors were relieved to get back on the bus and tune in to the Euro 2016 clash between England and Wales.

Johnson's Vote Leave comrade Gisela Stuart was having a much easier morning. Instead of facing hecklers and dealing with the bad weather in Norfolk, Stuart was preparing for an anti-EU rally in Glasgow that night. As Johnson was settling down to watch the football, Stuart was on board a flight to Scotland from Stansted Airport.

Back in London, staff at UKIP's HQ were looking forward to the match. The atmosphere in the party office was 'euphoric', according to Farage, and everyone felt the Leave side had momentum heading into the final week of campaigning. Unable to get into a very packed Barley Mow pub on Horseferry Road, the team decided to watch the game in Bruni-Lowe's flat in nearby Maunsel Street. Farage wasn't actually with his UKIP team, as he was enjoying a glass of champagne in a restaurant, toasting the success of the previous few days.

Someone not campaigning in the EU referendum that day was the Labour MP for Batley and Spen, Jo Cox. Although she was an avowed supporter of Remain, the 41-year-old was instead focusing on constituency matters on Thursday 16 June. Besides, her family had done their bit for the Remain cause the day before, as her husband, Brendan, and two young children had gatecrashed Farage's flotilla on the Thames. However, instead of being on the millionaire's boat with Bob Geldof, Brendan and his children had been zipping along in a motorised dinghy, waving an In flag. The family lived in a barge on the Thames, and so had a greater knowledge of that stretch of water than most involved in the flotilla.

At just before 1 p.m. on the day after the flotilla, Jo parked her car outside the library in the Yorkshire town of Birstall, where she was due to hold a constituency surgery. As she walked across to the library's entrance, she was attacked by a man armed with a knife and a gun. He stabbed her, shot her and then stabbed her again. Bernard Carter-Kenny, a 77-year-old retired rescue miner who was waiting for his wife outside the library, rushed to Jo's aid, but he too was stabbed. Bernard survived. Jo did not.

As the clock ticked down to the 2 p.m. kick-off time of the England *v.* Wales match, news of the attack started to appear on Twitter. At first, it was reported as an attack – albeit a very serious one – but not a murder. The UKIP gang in Bruni-Lowe's flat realised the seriousness of the incident and rushed back to the office, and Michael Heaver immediately contacted Farage.

On the Vote Leave battle bus, not all televisions were showing the football, and as soon as the ones tuned into the news channels flashed up the breaking story, Johnson told journalists on the coach that his day's campaigning was over.

Upon landing at Glasgow Airport, Stuart received two phone calls. The first was from Vote Leave telling her news of the attack and that her event that evening had been cancelled. The second was from Labour Deputy Leader Tom Watson, saying that Jo had not just been injured; she had in fact been murdered.

By the time West Yorkshire Police held a press conference at just after 5 p.m. informing the world that the MP had been killed, all EU referendum campaigning had been called off.

Thomas Mair, a 52-year-old man from Birstall, was arrested on suspicion of Jo's murder, and on Saturday 18 June he appeared in Westminster Magistrates' Court. When asked to confirm his identity, Mair replied: 'My name is death to traitors, freedom for Britain.' His words were a disaster for the Leave campaign. As soon as Farage heard of the killing, he feared it would somehow be linked to the referendum. He remembered thinking:

> Who killed her? Is it an Islamic nutcase, is it somebody reportedly on our side? No one knew. Once I heard I thought: 'God almighty,' and then I suddenly thought: 'Christ, I've just

launched a poster ninety minutes ago with a big strong immigration message.' I knew exactly what they're going to do,
I knew in an instant what they're going to do, and my God,
didn't they.

The juxtaposition of the Breaking Point poster with the murder of
an MP by someone pronouncing 'Freedom for Britain' was stark,
and Farage's campaigning style was once again called into question.
Writing for *The Spectator*'s website, commentator Alex Massie said:

> When you shout BREAKING POINT over and over again,
> you don't get to be surprised when someone breaks. When
> you present politics as a matter of life and death, as a
> question of national survival, don't be surprised if someone
> takes you at your word. You didn't make them do it, no, but
> you didn't do much to stop it either.
>
> Sometimes rhetoric has consequences. If you spend days,
> weeks, months, years telling people they are under threat,
> that their country has been stolen from them, that they have
> been betrayed and sold down the river, that their birthright
> has been pilfered, that their problem is they're too slow to
> realise any of this is happening, that their problem is they're
> not sufficiently mad as hell, then at some point, in some place,
> something or someone is going to snap. And then something
> terrible is going to happen.

As campaigning gently resumed on Sunday 19 June, senior politicians on both sides of the referendum campaign attacked the
Breaking Point poster. George Osborne told ITV's *Peston on
Sunday* the 'disgusting and vile poster' had 'echoes of literature
used in the 1930s', while Michael Gove told the BBC's *Andrew Marr
Show*: 'When I saw that poster I shuddered. I thought it was the
wrong thing to do.'

In an attempt to distance the official Leave campaign from Farage's tactics, Johnson announced at a rally in London on Sunday lunchtime that he supported an amnesty for illegal immigrants.

Appearing alongside Gove and Kate Hoey, Johnson said: 'I am the proud descendant of Turkish immigrants. I am in favour of an amnesty for illegal immigrants who have been here for more than twelve years unable to contribute to this economy, unable to pay taxes, unable to take proper part in society.'

Despite all sides piling in against him, Farage repeatedly defended the image, telling Sky News that morning: 'That poster reflects the truth of what's going on.'

When Farage was asked if he wished he hadn't unveiled the poster, he replied: 'I wish an innocent Member of Parliament hadn't been gunned down on the street. That's the point, and frankly had that not happened, I don't think we would have had the kind of row that we've had over it.'

Farage also claimed on LBC the following day that there was no row about the poster until Jo's death – something which is contradicted by the timing of the comments by Nicola Sturgeon, Yvette Cooper and the Twitter user who juxtaposed it to a screenshot of a Nazi propaganda film.

'When I think back to that Sunday and Monday,' said Farage, 'I've withstood plenty in politics over the years but that was the toughest I've ever faced. It was virtually as if I killed her. It was virtually as if I was responsible myself directly.'

Parliament, which had been suspended while the referendum campaign was taking place, was recalled on Monday 20 June so MPs could pay tribute to their murdered colleague. With Jo's husband Brendan and their two young children looking on, MPs who knew her best gave emotional speeches in praise of their departed friend. Labour MP Stephen Kinnock, who had shared an office with Jo, said:

On Thursday, Jo was assassinated for what she was and what she stood for. I can only imagine what Jo would have thought if she'd seen the poster unveiled before her death. She'd have responded with outrage. Jo understood that rhetoric has consequences. When insecurity, fear and anger are used to light a fuse, the explosion is inevitable. It's the politics of hatred and fear. We must now work to build a more respectful and unified country. Jo Cox, we love you, we salute you.

Later that evening, Farage held his final 'We want our country back' rally in Gateshead, alongside Kate Hoey, John Mills and David Davis. The next morning, he caught the 5.40 a.m. train into London, and arrived at the UKIP office at 9 a.m.

We all sat there, we all looked at each other after what I'd been through in the last forty-eight hours and where the whole thing had been, and we virtually simultaneously said the same thing: 'At least they're speaking about immigration.' And it reminded me of something Bruni-Lowe had said last June. 'If the weekend before the referendum we're talking about the economy and defending 3 million jobs, we will lose.'

Like Farage, Bruni-Lowe had no regrets about the Breaking Point poster:

My view was, and it still is today: it's the best poster we could have possibly run. All throughout the north, everywhere we went, people went: 'Totally agree with that.' It got insane national coverage. If it hadn't have been for that, immigration would not have been on the agenda the final week.

Whether the Breaking Point poster would have dominated the

final weekend of the referendum if the tragic killing of Jo Cox hadn't taken place is impossible to know, but what is certainly true is that, heading into the final week of campaigning, the discussion was over immigration, not the economy.

Yet, despite that, or maybe because of it, the momentum was with Remain. Of the eleven opinion polls conducted from the day after the murder to the end of Wednesday 22 June, Remain were ahead in eight of them. Of the eleven polls carried out before the tragedy, Leave had been ahead in eight.

Even the six-way Wembley Arena debate on Tuesday 21 June failed to noticeably reignite the Leave campaign. The Remain team of Scottish Conservative leader Ruth Davidson, London Mayor Sadiq Khan and TUC chief Frances O'Grady performed better than their three predecessors in the ITV debate, while Vote Leave's unchanged trio of Boris Johnson, Gisela Stuart and Andrea Leadsom stuck to their script and trotted out the line 'take back control' as often as possible.

Stuart later admitted she found it hard to get motivated for the debate preparation after Jo Cox's murder: 'I found it personally really, really hard to come back from the church service on the Monday and then gear yourself up mentally for the Wembley debate the next day.' Preparations up to that point had involved the three Vote Leavers practising against stand-ins for the opposition: Michael Gove's advisor Henry Newman, former Johnson aide Munira Mirza and ex-Labour staffer Andrew Hood played O'Grady, Davidson and Khan respectively.

Stuart said that, coming off the back of the Jo Cox tributes:

> We got together and just talked and just said, 'Look, this is, this is really awful, this is an enormous tragedy. But, folks, pull yourself together.' All of us found it very hard. I think that was one of the moments in the campaign where you really had to fall back to just your sheer stubbornness.

Despite Johnson giving a rousing final speech in which he claimed, 'If we Vote Leave and take back control, I believe that this Thursday can be our country's Independence Day,' the polling still showed Remain were on course for victory. However, just over a year earlier, the polls had spectacularly failed to predict a Conservative victory in the general election. As Thursday 23 June arrived, Leave campaigners were hoping there would be yet another upset.

CHAPTER 31

'I think the Remain side edged it – that's my view.'

Farage was downbeat. The polls had only just closed, and he was predicting defeat. The UKIP leader blamed the defeat on a 48-hour extension to the voter registration deadline earlier in June, which had been implemented by the government after the website for registering crashed. 'They got a huge number of young people. That's going to make a difference. The whole government campaign has been about registering young people and that's made a big, big difference,' Farage told the Huffington Post. He later said he 'shouldn't have answered the phone. I was relatively non-committal but that got turned into a mega story.' Indeed, it was soon being reported that Farage had conceded before the first vote had been counted.

However, his pessimism certainly tied in with an on-the-day YouGov poll, which was published just after 10 p.m. That also predicted a win for Remain, by 52 per cent to 48 per cent. TV cameras at the official Stronger In party beamed live pictures of activists looking relieved. Disaster had been averted. By contrast, the atmosphere in Vote Leave's HQ was described as 'gloomy' by one activist. 'There was a boy who looked like he had been crying,' they added. Dominic Cummings was inside his office, writing projections on a board of what share of the vote Leave needed to get in the different regions in order to get a victory. Bernard Jenkin grabbed a quick word with Cummings, telling him that no matter what differences the pair had had, he really deserved to win the vote. Douglas Carswell was also at Vote Leave HQ, and was preparing to travel to the BBC's studios in Elstree to take part in its referendum results coverage. Before he left, he asked Vote Leave's national organiser Stephen Parkinson to give him some pointers. Parkinson told Carswell where the early results would most likely come in from and what the results would need to be in those seats for it to be a 50/50 split nationally. Carswell wrote the information down on a piece of paper, put it in his pocket and went off to Elstree.

Just across the River Thames, in Millbank Tower, Leave.EU were hosting a referendum party, and the atmosphere was anything but gloomy. The campaign group's own poll, which had surveyed 10,000 people, showed Leave would win by 52 per cent to 48 per cent. To keep the hordes of activists, journalists and photographers entertained, Mike, Cheryl, Jay and Bobby – formerly of Bucks Fizz – were booked to play. The ghost of BPop Live lived on.

However, Leave.EU's poll was hardly mentioned by the media, and at just after 11 p.m., Northern Ireland Secretary Theresa Villiers added her voice to those calling it for Remain.

One person not convinced that Remain were on course for victory was Iain Duncan Smith, who was not happy with Farage's earlier comments: 'He can't resist opening his bloody mouth,' said the former Cabinet minister. Duncan Smith had agreed to appear on the early part of the BBC's coverage and on the way to the Elstree studio from his constituency in Chingford he had a phone call from a local Tory activist with some interesting news. 'We're getting turnouts on these housing estates of 80 per cent, we've got queuing,' Duncan Smith remembers being told.

> He and I both know that housing estates don't vote, well, not much, so if you get turnouts of 30 or 40 per cent that's

quite high. Eighty per cent is unheard of and loads of them
are having to be shown what to do because they have never
voted before. So it was quite interesting actually, that surge
in registration was assumed to be Remainers, I don't think
it was. I think a lot of it was Leavers in housing estates at the
last moment realising they could vote.

Once inside the studio, Duncan Smith told Labour's Deputy
Leader Tom Watson – who was also scheduled for some air time
– what he had heard: 'Tom is an old friend and I said, "What do
you think, Tom?" He said, "I think the establishment is going to
get some big surprises tonight because this turnout is happening
all over the northern seats."'

The first result came in at just after 11.30 p.m., with Gibraltar
unsurprisingly backing Remain by an enormous margin – 19,322
to 823. Minutes later, Farage arrived at the Leave.EU party on
Millbank along with Michael Heaver and Gawain Towler. As
the lift doors opened, a media scrum to end all media scrums
descended on the UKIP leader and his entourage. Towler said:

> Leave.EU in their brilliant media management had allowed
> what was the fucking wall of Jericho. Someone had been an
> incompetent fuck and allowed this madness to set in. We came
> out of the lift and there was this wall. I went out and went,
> 'Right, ladies and gentlemen, we need a space.' It was madness,
> he came in and it was the worst media scrum I'd ever been in.
> He enjoys that sort of thing but basically Arron had invited the
> world's press and so they all turned up. There must have been
> thirty TV crews and snappers and others. I'd already pushed a
> cameraman into a cake. It was absolutely bonkers.

Farage agreed, claiming it was 'insane, dangerous – actually
dangerous'.

Once the media pack had been fought back slightly, Farage gave a speech in which he claimed: 'The Eurosceptic genie is out of the bottle, and it will now not be put back.' As he went off to get a drink in the VIP room, Carswell started talking about the Breaking Point poster on the BBC. 'I think it was fundamentally the wrong thing to do, and let me say why. I think it was morally the wrong thing to do,' he said, then adding: 'Angry nativism doesn't win elections in this country.'

At just after midnight, the Newcastle result was declared. This was predicted as an easy win for Remain. Duncan Smith, who by now was waiting at the back of the Elstree studio to go on Radio 4, barely looked up at the TV screen as the result was announced: 65,405 votes for Remain, 63,598 for Leave.

> I was looking at this and I couldn't quite see the picture and then I suddenly saw the picture and it said 'margin 0.7 per cent'. I went, 'What! 0.7 per cent!' and I whipped the headphones off because I saw Jeremy Vine just walking into a studio to talk about it and I opened the door where they were all discussing stuff and I said: 'I'm going to stop you for a second, have you seen the Newcastle result?' He said: 'Yes.' I said: 'You know what that means, don't you?' He said: 'We were forecasting 10, 15 per cent or even more.' I said: '0.7 per cent means they are going to lose this referendum.' I said: 'Watch Sunderland.'

The Sunderland result was due shortly afterwards, and although this had been factored in as a victory for Leave, the scale of the win would give a serious indication of whether Brexit was truly on the cards. At just after 12.15 a.m., the Sunderland result was announced: 51,930 (39 per cent) for Remain; 82,394 (61 per cent) for Leave. Watching in his home in Essex, John Whittingdale started to believe Brexit was happening. 'Sunderland will go down in the history books,' he said. 'When Sunderland came in, you thought "Christ, it really is true – the Labour areas are turning out for Leave."' Brendan Chilton, who was at the Leave.EU party, was also clocking on to the fact that Labour areas were turning out for Leave:

> Newcastle came through and we were expecting Newcastle, because it's the wealthiest part of the north-east, to be sub-stantially ahead. I looked round and thought, 'We've done it.' Then Sunderland came through and my initial reaction was joy and jubilation, but then I thought, 'Gosh, what does this mean for Labour?'

In Vote Leave HQ, there was an almighty roar when the result came through. 'You could have heard the cheers in Sunderland,' said Daniel Hannan. Cummings poked his head out of his office in disbelief before going back in to double check his numbers were accurate, while, in Elstree, Carswell got his piece of paper out of his pocket to check the results against what was needed for 50/50. 'My piece of paper said for us to win 50/50 nationally we had to be at least 53/54 per cent for Sunderland, and it came in at 61 per cent.'

Carswell turned to Amber Rudd, who was on the panel giving the Remain point of view, and said: 'I think we might just bloody do it.'

As the results flowed in, it seemed Leave was doing better than expected virtually everywhere. Hartlepool, Kettering, Stockton-on-Tees, Merthyr Tydfil, Middlesbrough, Brentwood and Coventry all backed Brexit. At just before 3.30 a.m., it was declared that Sheffield – a city predicted to back Remain, and home to arch-Europhile Nick Clegg – had voted for Brexit. At 4 a.m., with 230 out of 382 declarations in, Leave were ahead by 51.3 per cent to 48.7 per cent. The Leave.EU party, which had moved down to the ground floor of Millbank Tower, was rocking, and Farage – who at the beginning of the evening was convinced his side had lost – decided now was the time to give the speech he had been waiting his whole political life to deliver. After receiving a few hugs and shedding a tear ('It was just so overwhelming,' he said), he addressed the room with TV cameras watching on: 'Ladies and gentleman, dare to dream that the dawn is breaking on an independent United Kingdom.' A huge cheer went up and, standing behind Farage, Michael Heaver punched the air as if his beloved Chelsea had just won the Champions League. Farage went on:

> If the predictions now are right, this will be a victory for real people, a victory for ordinary people, a victory for decent people. We have fought against the multinationals, we have fought against the big merchant banks, we fought against big politics, we fought against lies, corruption and deceit, and today, honesty, decency and belief in nation I think now is going to win. We will have done it without having to fight, without a single bullet being fired. We'd have done it by damn hard work on the ground by people like my friend Mr Banks here.

Farage went on, but almost immediately one phrase in his speech was picked up by those watching: 'without a single bullet being fired'. It was just over a week since Jo Cox had been shot and stabbed to death.

'I realised as soon as I said it,' remembers Farage.

> If you speak without notes and on an impromptu basis you will sometimes say things in a way you didn't mean, as I found many times over the years. What I should have said was 'without donning khaki'. *Channel 4 News* picked me up on it and I said: 'Right, I apologise.' I was thinking about Ireland and the Royal Navy shelling Dublin.

Farage, Towler, Banks, Heaver and a few others left Millbank Tower to carry on drinking at Chris Bruni-Lowe's flat, some having to settle for drinking wine out of milk jugs as there weren't enough glasses to go round.

Over at Vote Leave, the big roar was saved for the Birmingham result. At just after 4.30 a.m., it was announced that the UK's second city had voted Leave by 50.5 per cent to 49.5 per cent. A jubilant Daniel Hannan jumped onto a table and began reciting the speech from Shakespeare's *Henry V* which the title character delivers before the Battle of Agincourt. 'Old men forget: yet all shall be forgot / But he'll remember with advantages / What feats he did that day: then shall our names / Familiar in his mouth as household words…' Hannan swapped out the names of Harry the King, Bedford and Exeter, Warwick and Talbot, Salisbury and Gloucester, and replaced them with Vote Leave activists before concluding, '… Be in their flowing cups freshly remember'd. This story shall the good man teach his son.' Dominic Cummings also jumped up on a table, but instead of reciting Shakespeare he proclaimed: 'We did it! We fucking did it!' before punching the ceiling and causing plaster to fall down on the happy people below.

At 4.40 a.m., the BBC referendum coverage host David Dimbleby stared down the camera and made it almost official: 'The decision taken in 1975 by this country to join the Common Market has been reversed by this referendum to leave the EU,' he said. Bernard Jenkin, who had gone back home but returned to Vote Leave HQ to watch the final results come in, found himself being hugged by Iain Duncan Smith. 'Do you realise it's been twenty-five years, Bernard?' said one Maastricht rebel to the other. 'It's over! It's over now!' replied Jenkin.

Michael Gove, who had gone to bed at 10.30 p.m., was woken by a phone call from a close aide at 4.45 a.m. 'I don't know if you've seen the news, but it's good news – we've won,' Gove was told. 'Really?' he replied. 'I suppose I had better get up.'

Also getting a phone call at the same time was Kate Hoey. The Labour MP had nipped back to a hotel room near Leave.EU's party to get some rest when the result came through. Amid his celebrations at the bottom of Millbank Tower, Brendan Chilton realised his friend was nowhere to be seen. Chilton called her and said: 'I hope you're sitting down, love, because Britain's just voted to leave the European Union.'

While the other Vote Leave supporters were celebrating in London, Gisela Stuart and Matthew Elliott were in Manchester. The Electoral Commission had chosen the city as the place where they would make the official announcement, and the pair had been despatched to represent Vote Leave. The Electoral Commission were not going to announce the final result until every vote had been counted, but the Vote Leave duo had a 7 a.m. train to catch back down to London. It was decided to give the victory speech at 5.35 a.m., and Stuart stepped up to the podium. After describing the result as 'democracy at work' and calling for a cross-party approach to negotiating Brexit, she slipped into her mother tongue of German to proclaim Britain an open and welcoming society 'which will continue to be cooperating with European countries on an international level'.

By 7 a.m., all 382 counts had declared. Leave had secured 17,410,742 votes to Remain's 16,141,241. On a 72.2 per cent turnout, 51.9 per cent of those who voted had gone for Leave; 48.1 per cent had backed Remain.

As the dawn broke on 24 June 2016, the world's media descended on College Green opposite the Houses of Parliament. News crews from across the globe were present, and milling around were numerous politicians and activists. David Davis, Iain Duncan Smith, Hilary Benn, Peter Mandelson, Douglas Carswell and many more were all drawn to the patch of grass to give their views on the historic vote. The author also travelled down and, squatting on the floor at the front of a media scrum at about 7.15 a.m., watched as Farage delivered another victory speech. The UKIP leader was flanked by Arron Banks, Andy Wigmore, Richard Tice, Michael Heaver and many more as he called for a 'Brexit government' to implement the decision. Farage and his cohort then made their way to Bruni-Lowe's flat and turned on the television to see what would happen next.

Over at Vote Leave, Gove was also watching the television. At 8.18 a.m., he saw David Cameron walk out of the famous black door of 10 Downing Street, holding the hand of his wife Samantha, and approach a podium. 'Good morning, everyone,' said the Prime Minister. After acknowledging the referendum result, Cameron turned to his own future:

> I will do everything I can as Prime Minister to steady the ship over the coming weeks and months, but I do not think it would be right for me to try to be the captain that steers our country to its next destination. This is not a decision I've taken lightly, but I do believe it's in the national interest to have a period of stability and then the new leadership required. There is no need for a precise timetable today, but in my view we should aim to have a new Prime Minister in place by the start of the Conservative Party conference in October.

With his voice cracking, Cameron ended by saying: 'I love this country and I feel honoured to have served it and I will do everything I can in future to help this great country succeed. Thank you very much.'

Gasps went up in the Vote Leave office, and the atmosphere was one of shock. Many in the room were Conservative activists who had fought hard just a year before to make sure Cameron stayed in Downing Street. Now, they had helped bring about his departure.

Over at Bruni-Lowe's house, the UKIP gang also watched in
silence. As Cameron walked back into Downing Street, Farage
said: 'Well, I do feel for him a bit, I know what it feels like.' Banks
remembers there was a few seconds more of silence, and then:
'Everyone just threw stuff at the TV and shouted: "Fuck off!"'

CHAPTER 32

With David Cameron on his way out, it was assumed that Boris Johnson would be his successor in Downing Street. Alas for him, he was unable to convince Michael Gove that he was up to the job and, just hours before Johnson's campaign launch, the Justice Secretary withdrew his support and announced that he would be standing for the leadership himself. However, many of the Leave-backing MPs in the Conservative Party preferred to support Andrea Leadsom, and it was she who was put forward to challenge Theresa May for the leadership. The Tory Party membership would have the final say on who would be the new Prime Minister, but before campaigning had even begun, Leadsom pulled out following a disastrous interview with *The Times* in which she claimed that her position as a mother gave her 'a real stake in the country's future' compared to her childless opponent. An unopposed May became Prime Minister on 13 July 2016. In her first Cabinet, Boris Johnson was made Foreign Secretary, David Davis was Secretary of State for Exiting the European Union and Liam Fox was International Trade Secretary. The three high-profile Leave campaigners were jointly tasked with carrying out Brexit. Michael Gove was dismissed to the back benches.

Nigel Farage announced he was standing down as UKIP leader on 4 July, claiming that after twenty-two years in politics: 'I want my life back.' He spent much of the summer in the United States and even addressed a Donald Trump rally as part of the business mogul's campaign to be President.

The Labour Party underwent a collective breakdown, with shadow Cabinet members resigning en masse – partly in protest at Jeremy Corbyn's lacklustre leadership during the referendum, but also as the culmination of a year of unhappiness at the way he was running the party. Corbyn, who refused to stand down, was described by more than one Leave campaigner interviewed for this book as 'the quiet hero of Brexit'.

As for what Brexit itself actually looks like, at the time of writing, it is not clear. In the two and a half months since the referendum, Theresa May has offered little more than the words she said when she first entered Downing Street as Prime Minister: 'Brexit means Brexit – and we're going to make a success of it.'

It will be for future authors to make that judgement.

ACKNOWLEDGEMENTS

The EU referendum was the most significant political event in UK political history for more than forty years. Even before the first vote was cast on 23 June 2016, it was clear the country was deeply divided along economic, cultural and class grounds. As this book shows, the various Brexit camps mirrored this division, with some campaigners determined to focus on existential ideas of sovereignty and democracy, while others believed the only way to win was by highlighting the practical effects of being in the EU: uncontrolled immigration.

I would like to thank all of those from the Brexit campaigns for sharing their reflections with me, especially at a time when many were still trying to digest the result and its implications.

I would also like to thank my colleagues at the Huffington Post – Stephen Hull, Paul Waugh, Ned Simons, Graeme Demianyk and Martha Gill – for their invaluable support.

I am very grateful to my family, in particular Deborah and Michael Horlock, Jennifer and Steve Murphy, Nigel Bennett, Heather Bennett, Mark Berry and Alice, for stepping in and providing some much-needed babysitting as the deadline got nearer. Special thanks to Chloe Bennett and Grace Marshall for helping with research, and Sandra and Manuel Pino for boosting the international sales.

Finally, and absolutely crucially, I would never have even started – let alone finished – this project without the love, help and support of Alessandra Pino. She is the most selfless person I have ever met, and I will now stop talking about Brexit – I promise.

And as for Lucia, this book was the reason your dad looked at you over the top of a laptop screen for the first few months of your life. I hope one day you read it and forgive me for that.